Socia¹ The   ¹€

Social Theory and the Environment

David Goldblatt

Polity Press

First published in 1996 by Polity Press
in association with Blackwell Publishers Ltd.

Editorial office:
Polity Press
65 Bridge Street
Cambridge CB2 1UR, UK

Marketing and production:
Blackwell Publishers Ltd
108 Cowley Road
Oxford OX4 1JF, UK

ISBN 0–7456–1326–8
ISBN 0–7456–1328–4 (pbk)

A CIP catalogue record for this book is available from the British Library.

Typeset in 9½ on 11pt Palatino
by Wearset, Boldon, Tyne and Wear
Printed in Great Britain by Hartnolls Ltd, Bodmin, Cornwall

This book is printed on acid-free paper.

Everybody talking bout protecting de planet
As if we jus cum on it
It hard fe understan it.
Everybody taking bout de green revolution
Protecting de children and fighting pollution
But check – capitalism an greed as caused us to need
Clean air to breathe, Yes
. . .

From Benjamin Zephaniah, 'Me green poem'

Contents

Preface

....

It has become a truism to say that in the final decades of the twentieth century we stand on the verge of all-consuming environmental disaster. Nevertheless, there are voices on either side of this position. In the doubters' corner the argument runs that this claim is a massive overestimation of the likely course of events; that the scientific evidence on which such judgements are based is of such doubtful accuracy that all announcements of apocalyptic change should be rejected. In the doomsayers' corner the argument runs that we have already passed the point of no return. The cumulative consequences of a century and a half of economic expansion have already sealed the fate of the global environment, though its sharpest consequences have yet to appear. This book is written from the middling position. On the one hand, I accept with some reservations and a healthy scepticism the mainstream scientific and ecological arguments about contemporary environmental change: that it is widespread, worsening and likely to be extremely serious locally and globally. On the other hand, I don't accept – and this is I suppose an article of faith – that we have crossed over into an unstoppable cycle of environmental decline and social dislocation. But we are probably closer than we think. It is with the mixture of hope and urgency generated by this position that I have tried to write this book.

It stands as an interrogation of the study of environmental degradation and environmental politics in four of the most significant contemporary European social theorists: Anthony Giddens, André Gorz, Jürgen Habermas and Ulrich Beck. Very simply, I have tried to ask and answer the following questions. What are the social and structural origins of environmental degradation in modern societies? What are the structural origins of environmental movements? What role can an environmentally orientated politics play in curbing and curtailing environmental degradation? I have also tried to think about some of the parameters of a successful environmental politics and its relationship to the traditions of socialist political theory. Anyone wanting an introduction to the engagement of social theory with environmental issues or a more detailed interpretation of the writings of Giddens, Gorz, Habermas or Beck can profitably use all of, some of, or just one of the central five chapters. Although the arguments of one chapter are often carried across into other chapters, I believe that these studies can stand by themselves. In addition, I hope that beneath the studiousness of the text there is a core series of overlapping arguments that run from the introduction to the conclusion – arguments that are not merely scholastic but political and moral.

Social theory in its most illuminating moments has sought to span the difficult divide between the mere description and explanation of modernity, and an assessment of the moral dilemmas that face us and the political resources available to us to tackle them. Contemporary forms of environmental degradation present one of the most, if not the most, complex and catastrophic dilemmas of modernity. If social theory can make a small contribution to illuminating those dilemmas and sketching the contours of a moral and political response then it will have served us well.

Acknowledgements

....

This book has been a rather long time in the making and I have incurred some very substantial debts of thanks in writing it. John Thompson, who has read it in draft forms more times than he could possibly bear, has been an endless source of encouragement, advice and constructive criticisms. He has kept things on the rails when they were in mortal danger of running off them and deployed a ruthless eye for the weak argument or unsubstantiated assertion. His role cannot be overestimated. Thanks also to Sarah Bond who has alternately endured, cajoled and encouraged me, as well as doing some fantastic proofreading. David Held and Tom Shakespeare have been attentive and helpful readers and their criticisms and advice have been gratefully received. Thanks are also due to the Polity people who made this happen, especially Julia Harsant and Gill Motley, and Ann Bone, whose grasp of grammar and sentence construction has been a real lesson. Finally, this book would not have been possible without the dedication and support of Ivor, Roberta and James Goldblatt. It seems scant reward for a lifetime's love, but then there is more to life than books. The usual disclaimers apply: all the limits and weaknesses of the argument are mine, all mine.

The epigraph to the book is taken from *City Psalms* by Benjamin Zephaniah (Bloodaxe Books, 1992), by kind permission. Figures 1, 2 and 3 are reproduced and adapted from figures in Jürgen Habermas, *The Theory of Communicative Action*, vols 1 and 2, © 1984 and 1987 by Beacon Press, by permission of Beacon Press.

Introduction:
Social Theory, Environmental Degradation and Environmental Politics

This book explores the contribution of some contemporary social theorists to two issues: the origins and consequences of environmental degradation in modern societies, and the conditions under which political forces can be successfully mobilized against environmental degradation. With regard to the first issue it is hardly contentious to argue that economic and demographic change are significant causes of environmental degradation. However, it is worth exploring the precise mechanisms set in motion by these forces in more detail than is often attempted. In addition to considering these well-worn paths of explanation, I shall also examine the dual role of political and cultural power in fostering environmental degradation and, on rare occasions, in curtailing it. The emergence of political movements that seek to curtail environmental damage is one of the most significant consequences of modern environmental degradation. Whether such movements can fulfil their political vocation is another question. I plan to consider these questions through an examination of the work of four contemporary social theorists: Anthony Giddens, André Gorz, Jürgen Habermas and Ulrich Beck.

There are good reasons for being wary of this approach. First, the theoretical legacy left to us by classical social theory has some substantial limitations both for examining the relationships between societies and their environments, and for exploring the origins of a politics of the environment. Second, the study of the relationship between the environment and human societies is necessarily an interdisciplinary affair; to rely on a single discipline, however rich or diverse, would be profoundly limiting. Third, the four writers on whom I have focused are not the only contemporary theorists who have turned their attention to the relationship between the social and the natural, or to the rise and prospects of environmental social movements. In defence of this approach, I accept that the nineteenth-century foundations of contemporary social theory offer rather limited help in answering my questions, and that in any case we shall have to draw on other disciplines. None the less, in this introduction I intend to examine, albeit briefly, the legacy of classical social theory and in particular the work of Karl Marx, Max Weber and Émile Durkheim. In doing so, I want to suggest that, despite substantial problems, contemporary social theory retains some purchase on my concerns.

Marx, Weber and Durkheim on Environments and Societies

The idea of social theory is not a simple one. There are those more empirically inclined sociologists who see it as the abstract musings of theorists disengaged from the sobering consequences of detailed empirical research and low-level theory building. Social theory has aimed higher, but only because it has cast off the necessary ballast of carefully framed and testable hypotheses and the detailed collection of epistemologically sound data. I share some of those doubts about social theory as an enterprise. However, I do believe that it occupies a distinct, important and valid space in the spectrum of sociological methods and conjectures. At the very broadest level, the investigation of the historical origins, institutional structures and dominant trajectories of change of modern societies have given social theory its disciplinary *raison d'être* and separated it by theme, if not always by method, from other sociological enterprises. For this reason, if no other, the vocabulary of nineteenth-century social theory will shape any inquiry into contemporary environmental degradation. The strengths of that vocabulary are diminished by the limited interest social theory displayed in the relationship between human societies and their natural environments and its antiquated understanding of it.[1] That misunderstanding is not contingent but in many ways inscribed within the conceptual structure of the discipline. Ted Benton has argued (of sociology in general, rather than just social theory) that the way in 'which sociology came to define itself, especially in relation to potentially competing disciplines such as biology and psychology, effectively excluded or forced to the margins of the discipline . . . questions about the relations between society and its ''natural'' or ''material'' substrate'.[2]

However, this is only true of the second wave of classical social theory. In the first half of the nineteenth century both Auguste Comte and Herbert Spencer considered sociology to be epistemologically and ontologically dependent on, or subordinate to, biology. Comte drew on biological analogies and metaphors of form and function and the relationship between organism and organs to explore the interrelationship of individuals and institutions in modern societies, while Spencer's work was the first of many attempts to marry Darwinian models of evolution, selection and change to social development.[3] More concretely the work of the classical political economists returned again and again to the relationship between the natural environment and the human economic prospect. Malthus, most obviously, inquired into the social consequences of rapid population growth in the context of limited environmental resources with which to feed that population. Both David Ricardo and John Stuart Mill explored the potential limits to growth in an expanding but essentially agrarian economy; and they both concluded, though by different argumentative roots, that the explosive growth of the early nineteenth century would eventually reach both natural and economic limits of exhausted soil and declining rates of return.[4]

By the third quarter of the nineteenth century the explosive pace of Western industrialization had rendered the gloomy prognosis of both Malthusian demographics and Ricardian agrarian economics redundant; population growth continued unabated at historically high rates, while agrarian productivity continued to rise and formed a diminishing role in a much broader process of economic growth. It is therefore no surprise that those early attempts to engage with the social and economic origins and consequences of environmental change were bypassed. In Marx's work, where one might have expected such an engagement, the dynamic of capitalist industrialization shifted agricultural economics to the margins. In any case, a more pressing issue for sociology was always going to be its supposed dependence on or subordination to the natural sciences in general and biology in particular. If sociology was to emerge as a distinctive body of knowledge, then its subject matter – society – would have to be cordoned off from the realm of biology and nature. This was precisely the thrust of both Durkheim's and Weber's methodological arguments, which rejected all forms of biological determinism.

Of the classical trinity, Weber's work conducts the most limited engagement with the natural world. There are some reflections on the environmental origins and implications of nomadism in his study of Judaism. Yet his historical investigations of antiquity, despite the centrality of agrarian production in his work, yielded little direct study of the historical impact and social implications of differing natural environments.[5] A brief note on the importance of rivers and water transport is overshadowed by detailed discussion of patterns of land ownership and the dynamics of the slave mode of production.[6] His studies of China and India are no more environmentally informed.[7] Weber's theoretical reflections on the matter are equally cursory. Indeed the only relevant discussion appears in a few brief paragraphs in the opening chapter of *Economy and Society*. Weber's main concern is to deny the relevance of psychological and physiological explanations in sociology. None the less, he does argue that 'in all the sciences of human action, account must be taken of processes and phenomena which are devoid of subjective meaning . . . favouring or hindering circumstances.'[8] In other words, non-human, unintended processes, such as climate, are of significance if they affect human action. This is, however, hardly saying much.

Given that economics and demographics are obvious points of interaction between societies and their environment, the reasons for the greater environmental sensibilities of Marx's and Durkheim's work should be clear. Durkheim, in taking population density and its relationship with

material resources to be the driving force behind the evolutionary stratification of human societies, made the natural world a decisive causal factor
in human history.[9] Marx had acquired a persistent concern with the
notion of the natural from his study of Hegel. However, it is not his discussions of human nature and species being, but his material understanding of human labour that concerns us.[10] Like Durkheim, Marx placed the
economic interface of human societies and the natural world at the centre
of historical change. By contrast, Weber never gave demographics a central causal role in history, while his theory of economic action significantly differs from Marx. Weber defined action by reference to the ideal type
of purposive rational action. Therefore the relationship between means
and ends was more significant than the ontological relation between
human subject and natural object. In any case, whereas Marx defined economics in terms of production and the transformation of the natural
world, Weber understood it primarily in terms of peaceful exchange.[11]

Even so, the work of Marx and Durkheim is, at best, of limited use to
us. First, because their theoretical framework for examining the relationship between societies and environments is too unspecific for our purposes. Their understanding of the natural environment was always
constrained by their limited knowledge of biology. Or rather, their work
was constrained by the limited knowledge and scope of biology itself.
This is not of course to suggest that their work was ignorant of contemporary biology; in fact, their work is rich in biological metaphors. Rather it is
to suggest that the internal dynamics of the natural world and the precise
impacts of different economic and demographic processes on human
physiology and ecosystems alike had yet to be registered. Ecology, toxicology, climatology and epidemiology remained in their infancy and were
overshadowed by the contemporary intellectual dominance of evolutionary theory. Second, the primary ecological issue for classical social theory
was not the origins of contemporary environmental degradation, but how
premodern societies had been held in check by their natural environments, and how it was that modern societies had come to transcend those
limits or had separated themselves in some sense from their 'natural' origins. It is that dynamic in the modernization process that Ferdinand
Tönnies captured in his description of the transition between *gemeinschaft*
and *gesellschaft*.[12]

In retrospect the mid-nineteenth to early twentieth centuries appear as
an ambiguous moment in the ecological history of modern societies.
Durkheim explained the emergence of modernity and its unique economic and social capacities in terms of a progressive division of labour and
political stratification, in which individuals and societies could find their
competitive niche; population and resource pressures spurred the technological innovation and social differentiation on which modern industrial
society was built. Once stratified it was the abnormal forms of the division
of labour that upset the balance of modern societies rather than natural
resource constraints.[13] Marx never allotted such a prominent causal role to

demographics. However, as we know, he did focus on the sociology of production. Human beings, in pursuing their needs through collective labour, transformed both their environment and their forms of social organization. It was this, and the successive modes of production generated, that led to an irrepressible dynamic of economic development and the transformation of the material world. With the advent of capitalism and industrial technology, that dynamic would prove capable of generating the material abundance on which an advanced form of social organization could be based. Modern societies were indeed unconstrained by natural limits. Nor did it seem at the time that the economic capacity of capitalism would prove to be environmentally problematic in any fundamental way.

That said, it was becoming clear to some observers that the socialized nature created by modernity was beginning to reimpose itself on human societies. Engels, as early as the 1840s, found the urban environment to be aesthetically repugnant and an active contributor to the misery of the poor. Marx himself was aware of the capacity of capitalism to undermine soil fertility and abuse natural resources.[14] But these reflections have only derived significance in retrospect. They are at best illuminating asides rather than core areas of concern or investigation to Marx and Engels. Thus the classical social theorists were historically late enough to witness not simply the escape of modern societies from their organic constraints, but also their dynamic capacity to transform the natural world as well. Yet they were too early to register fully the implications of those transformations; far from transcending ecological constraints, modern societies were rapidly acquiring new ones of their own making.

This rather limited legacy in terms of focus and theoretical argument is responsible, at least in part, for the equally thin record of environmental concerns in the mainstream sociological theory of the early and mid-twentieth centuries. Among the many traditions of interpretive sociology, the absence of environmental concerns is hardly surprising. Such resolutely idealist models of social relations and social action were unlikely to engage with the underlying material substrate of modern societies. More surprising is the absence of any sustained engagement of either Marxism or functionalism with the natural environment. For all Marx's historical limitations he clearly laid down a possible theoretical agenda and a set of conceptual tools for interrogating the society–environment relationship. Of course, the notion of nature recurs throughout the writings of both classical and Western Marxists but it is invariably a purely philosophical construct. On the theoretical side only Jean-Paul Sartre makes passing reference to the environmental transformations through his painful neologism – the practico-inert.[15] On the historical side the lone figure of Karl Wittfogel stands out, arguing that Marx's model of the static Asiatic mode of production could be explained in terms of the centralized control of water resources by oriental states in areas of hydrological scarcity.[16] The work of Talcott Parsons – the epitome of twentieth-century functionalism – displays a similar gap between potential and performance. At the very core of Parsons's work is a conception of human beings and human societies bounded by an external natural environment. Alongside this static model of human societies, Parsons proposed a model of social evolution in which societies continually responded to the limits set by their natural environment, evolving in complexity and capacity so as to transcend those limits. Yet such was the abstraction of the Parsonian model that his conception of the natural environment remained as empty as the diagrammatic boxes he deployed to describe it.[17]

Contemporary Social Theory, Environmental Degradation and the Work of Giddens and Gorz

The limitations of classical social theory for our purposes are, first, that it does not possess an adequate conceptual framework with which to understand the complex interactions between societies and environments, and second, that where it has addressed such issues it has focused on the ways in which human societies have transformed their environment without attending to the negative consequences of those transformations in any sustained fashion.

In dealing with the first of those limitations, it is to the methods and perspectives of environmental history that I shall initially turn.[18] In its broadest sense, the discipline of environmental history has set out to investigate the ways in which the natural environment has constituted a causally significant factor in the shaping of the historical process. It is this focus that makes it a more suitable resource for my purposes than social theory, which has tended to explore the interaction of the social and the natural in terms of gender, the body, sexuality, etc.[19] Environmental history has been supplemented by other disciplines: anthropology, demography and geography, and not least by advances within the discipline of ecology itself.[20] Most importantly, the static concept of an unchanging, if internally organized, natural world in nineteenth-century biology was successively transformed by the concept of the dynamic ecosystem.[21] As a consequence, historians have learnt to view the natural world as a complex system of interactions between communities of flora and fauna, micro-organisms, soil, water and climate, and to trace each of these variables across entire ecosystems and societies.[22] As a discipline, environmental history has, perhaps paradoxically, yet to tackle its most pressing contemporary concern: the origins and consequences of environmental degradation in the modern world. Perhaps the focus of environmental history on agricultural societies, where the level of environmental degradation is more muted, may explain this. But it must be, at least in part, the very enormity and complexity of such a historical process that has discouraged the painstaking task of empirical reconstruction. It is because of that enormity and complexity that social theory comes into its own. We may have abandoned classical social theory's understanding of society and environments, but we cannot abandon its unique capacity for making explicable the complex, large-scale processes that have produced and organized modern societies.[23]

Among contemporary social theorists and historical sociologists the constraints which the natural world applies to human societies have been reinvestigated with a new vigour and a more sensitive ecological eye.[24] However, less attention has been paid to the origins and consequences of environmental degradation in modern societies. It is for this reason, first and foremost, that I have chosen to interrogate the works of Giddens and Gorz. Both writers have attempted to integrate an explanation of the origins and consequences of environmental degradation into a broader understanding of the development and dynamics of modern societies.[25]

There are, however, additional reasons for analysing the work of these two theorists. In Giddens's case the first reason is that his explanation of environmental degradation focuses on the interaction between capitalism and industrialism. I shall argue in chapter 1 that this provides a powerful, if incomplete, starting point from which to explain the origins of environmental degradation. Second, Giddens's social theory has paid particular attention to the spatial dimension of social processes and the methods of geography. This has allowed him to investigate the sociological nature of urbanism and globalization and their contribution to environmental problems. In chapter 2, I shall argue that this enables us to extend considerably the scope of our understanding of environmental degradation. Third, Giddens's interpretative approach to social theory and the multicausal models of social processes he has developed have allowed me to incorporate in my study the contribution made by political power and cultural attitudes to the generation of environmental degradation. I shall therefore supplement and extend Giddens's work in both chapters. Finally, Giddens incorporates an explanation of the origins of environmental social movements into his broader social theory. Thus his work allows us to consider the dual qualities of cultural and political power: that they may both facilitate and control the process of environmental degradation.

The relevance of Gorz's work to our concerns is fourfold. First, his studies draw on the work of environmental economists, and show a sensitivity to the detailed dynamics of contemporary capitalist economies that Giddens's work does not display. Second, he explores mechanisms of environmental degradation that Giddens does not: the impact of modern consumption and the environmental impact of technologies. Third, he pays much closer attention than Giddens to the socioeconomic consequences of environmental degradation. This emphasis on Gorz's work will allow us to explore the ways in which the political and economic institutions of modern societies recognize and respond to the environmental degradation they have created. The most interesting aspect of Gorz's work is his reflections on socialism and the means by which cultural preferences and the demand for environmental sustainability can triumph over the dynamic of economic and political interests. I shall return to this below. Before doing so I want briefly to explore the contribution of classical social theory to the explanation of political mobilization, the theory of socialism and the legacy that this has left for exploring the mobilization of environmental politics.

Classical Social Theory: Politics, Culture and Socialism

If classical social theory as we understand it is a limited tradition with which to understand environmental degradation, does it fare any better in explaining environmental politics? Marx, Weber and Durkheim lived just long enough to witness the negative impact of modern societies on their environments. However, they died too early to register the emergence of a politically significant environmental movement. Marx died just as environmental organizations were forming in Britain and the United States, for example the Sierra Club, the Royal Society for the Protection of Birds and the National Trust. In early twentieth-century France and Germany, other political conflicts dominated the landscape surveyed by Durkheim and Weber. None the less, these writers have left a substantial theoretical legacy on political mobilization. In their political sociology the classical social theorists all derive two basic mechanisms of political mobilization from their accounts of the institutional structures of modernity. First, they describe how the social structure of modern societies determines the economic and political interests of major social groups. Second, they all offer an account of the cultural development of modernity in which new types of knowledge and moral ideals are generated. These may well stand opposed to the structure of interests and the current dynamics of modern societies. Thus, in addition, they all reflected on the most significant oppositional politics in modern societies: the socialist movements of the West. These reflections provide a special connection to our concerns. I shall argue that, despite its obvious differences and distance, their debate over socialism remains significant for exploring the environmental movement and the transformations proposed by it. Before examining those connections I shall sketch the relevant outlines of the work of Marx, Weber and Durkheim.

Durkheim, viewing the long gestation of industrial society, found himself within a modernity as yet incomplete. An expanding and increasingly complicated division of labour characterized modern societies. In breaking with the segmental stratification of premodern societies, functional specialization yielded mixed political and cultural consequences. Extensive stratification should have generated a structure of interdependent interests in an increasingly complex world. Indeed, the need for solidarity was inscribed in the complex differentiation of modern societies, as specialization and diminishing economic and political self-sufficiency demanded increasing levels of co-operation. However, structurally generated interests were insufficient to maintain social solidarity. In opposition to the political economists, Durkheim maintained that modern societies could not be reproduced simply by the exercise of self-interest in market exchange. Social solidarity required the rational intervention of collective agencies in societies and the moral regulation of a shared normative framework.

Thus Durkheim perceived two dimensions to the development of cultural modernity: the emergence of rational knowledge about the workings of the social world, and the creation of secular notions of justice and equality. Together, these cultural transformations would secure rational control over the world and underwrite the normative solidarity of modernity without stifling the creative dynamism and moral responsibility of individuals. This benign balance lay some way in the future. In the meantime, the abnormal forms of the division of labour generated structural differences in economic and political interests, producing political conflict rather than making the need for interdependent co-operation transparent. Moreover, modern societies had yet to establish a sufficiently sophisticated secular morality or the institutional mechanisms through which this could be actualized. Liberated from the oppressive uniformity of mechanical solidarity, the needs and desires of the modern individual had been set free without being bound to collective identities or systems of moral regulation; anomie and egoism followed. Despite the possibility, indeed necessity, of moral control over politics, opposing interests prevailed in political mobilization, and social dislocation followed. Durkheim understood socialism as an attempt to regulate the intrinsic inequalities and irregularities of an advanced economy. Socialism did not address, however, the question of moral regulation. Indeed it assumed that moral regulation was identical with economic equalization. Durkheim, by contrast, argued that occupational groupings were the most effective mechanisms for the representation of functionally differentiated interest groups to a benign state, and that secular education was the key to maintaining a morally informed social solidarity.

Marx, like Durkheim, recognized the dual role of interests and ideals in the mobilization of modern politics. However, the structural generation of opposing interests was not an abnormal form of the division of labour but inscribed in the basic economic structures of capitalist societies: the inequitable ownership of the means of production and the nature of the wage–labour contract. The moral regulation of an inherently unjust economic and political system was not countenanced. Moral arguments appeared as the ideological reflex and legitimation of structurally established interests. The significance of cultural change lay in that fact that the relentless transformation of the world by the dynamic of capital accumulation dispelled the rural idiocy and isolation of premodern, peasant life. It forcibly brought the industrial working classes face to face with the harsh realities of that dynamic, unfettered by the metaphysical illusions and religious ideologies that had bound their peasant ancestors to the dominant order. The significance then of Marx's theory of socialism is that the dynamic of a politics driven by interest and ruthlessly disclosed by the pattern of cultural change would herald the creation of a society in which significant differences of interest would be dissolved: it would see the abolition of private property and the division of labour, and the dissolution of the state. Marx was able to achieve this sociological conjuring trick by making the interests of the working class coincide with the interests of humanity as a whole, and by assuming that the economic changes he foresaw were compatible with the maintenance of an abundantly productive modern industrial order. Thus sectional interests were transformed into the common good. Justice would be secured by the inevitable direction of history rather than by the cogency of its case or its capacity to mobilize political action.

Weber found the elision between working-class interests and the common good, as well as the economic implications of socialism, to be rather more problematic. According to Weber, politics was mobilized by structurally generated economic and political interests. However, where Marx saw only economic interests and ideological justifications of political positions, Weber asserted the centrality of cultural nationalism and value choice in mobilizing modern politics. Weber, like Durkheim, argued that cultural change could mobilize political action. However, the cultural resources of modernity could not underwrite the sort of objective normative framework that Durkheim proposed. Irretrievably fragmented by specialization and robbed of the universalizing powers of religious worldviews, modern culture could not rationally underwrite the common good, and thus people could not rationally choose between different moral positions. Only the unique and particular shared bonds of language and ethnicity that motivated modern nationalisms could approximate to this. The Durkheimian solution to the pathologies of modernity was therefore blocked. Against Marx, Weber remained sceptical as to whether the exercise of working-class self-interest could generate a society in which conflicts of interest were dissolved. In the first place he put national interests above class interests. But more significantly he argued that the mobilization of class-based interests in modern nation-states inevitably resulted in the bureaucratization of politics and political parties themselves. Bureaucracies, like economic systems, did not respond to the calls of solidarity or justice but to the demands of interests, of power and of money. In the context of an increasingly complex society and the establishment of mass democracy, the bureaucratization of social institutions and political organization were almost inevitable. The best resource that modern culture could make available to actors was the hope that a rational calculation of political circumstances might make moral choices and their implementation rather clearer, while nationalism might provide a mechanism for the enlightened redefinition of class interests.

What is the significance of these discussions? First, environmental politics is mobilized by both interests and ideals. The former might include the threat of environmental damage and the threat of reduced profitability or employment. Moral claims and ideals might include the rights of future over current generations or the irreducible value of all life-forms. Second, the interconnections drawn between interests and ideals, social structure and culture are important in explaining the trajectory of environmental politics, the fact that interests can ideologically shape moral claims, while the growth of knowledge and moral argument can lead to an enlightened redefinition of interests. Third, the discussions of socialism in classical social theory all share a similar problem: how can the dynamics of economic and political life, shaped and propelled by the exercise of power and the influence of interests, be brought into line with the moral perspectives of modern culture? To put it another way, how can culture and morality regulate or control economic and political systems? How can solidarity and justice prevail over power and money in the motivation of action? These problems also lie at the heart of environmental politics. If I am right in arguing in this book that economics, demographics and politics are the central causes of environmental degradation, then an environmentally orientated politics is necessarily concerned with their control or regulation. Rather than responding solely to the dictates of economic and political interests, the moral case for the preservation of the natural world and the enlightened self-interest of environmental sustainability must decisively figure in the exercise of economic and political power. Marx relied on the coincidence of interests and morality to solve the problem, Durkheim promised an evolutionary shift to a state-organized secular morality, and Weber gave up the chase altogether. He pleaded for the preservation of social practices as yet unengulfed by bureaucratic organization but could only find the demagogic force and moral will of plebiscitary leaders. In the late twentieth century, in the face of globally devastating environmental degradation, the first two solutions have been rendered unlikely, the third most unpalatable.

The Mobilization of Environmental Politics and the Work of Jürgen Habermas

For our purposes, there are two great strengths of classical social theory: its capacity to situate political mobilization in the context of the broader shifts and structures of modern societies, and its continuing attempt to understand the interplay of interest, ideals and cognitive understandings of the world in the mobilization of politics. However, an important argument, and one I shall return to on a number of occasions in this book, is that we shall not be able to grasp the dynamics of environmental politics until we have understood the causes and consequences of environmental degradation. Given the rather limited record of classical social theory in this area, and despite all the strengths I have outlined, its usefulness in examining environmental politics is necessarily restricted. In chapters 1 and 2, I shall begin to sketch the role of politics in facilitating and controlling environmental degradation. In chapter 3, I shall develop a much fuller model of the interrelationship between economics and politics in the causes and consequences of environmental degradation. It is only on this basis that I shall begin to explore in detail the conditions under which an environmentally orientated politics is mobilized.

Thus, in chapter 4, in connection with the work of Habermas, I shall be ready to address the mobilization of environmental politics head on. Clearly, Habermas is not the only social theorist to consider this issue.[26] However, there are a number of significant reasons for focusing on Habermas's work. First, his recent work has provided one of the most thoroughgoing reassessments of classical social theory, and in so doing he has generated the most comprehensive reinterpretation of both the institutional organization of modernity and its cultural development. Second, he has used this framework to investigate the emergence of new social movements and to gauge their potential political significance. Third, he allows us to examine the ways in which changing social structures have produced a new organization of economic and political interests, and how these in turn shape the mobilization of contemporary environmental politics. Fourth, he allows us to examine the ways in which cultural change and modern moral knowledge about the environment have emerged, redefined interests and contributed to the emergence of environmentally orientated political movements. Fifth, in keeping with the interdisciplinary approach which I have advocated, Habermas's work draws on and attempts to incorporate some of the most significant insights of political scientists who have investigated the structural origins of environmental politics.

Ulrich Beck, Environmental Politics and the Risk Society

Finally we come to the work of Ulrich Beck. What really distinguishes Beck's work is that for him alone among contemporary social theorists the catastrophic potential of global environmental degradation occupies centre stage. Indeed Beck goes so far as to argue that the modernity described in the works of the classical social theorists is being transformed into a fundamentally different type of society – a *risk society*. That transformation is driven, in part, by the emergence of pervasive and historically unique levels of environmental danger and risk of such a magnitude and form that conventional models of modern society cannot capture their origins or consequences. In addition, the work of Ulrich Beck reconnects with issues raised in all the other chapters of this book, as well as posing questions and investigating issues that none of those touch on. In chapter 5, I will review Beck's model of the risk society and explore its explicitly environmental dimension. His claims regarding the transformation of classical modernity into a risk society are closely paralleled by Giddens's model of a radicalized late modernity in which environmental social movements respond to newly perceived environmental risks and dangers. Beck also investigates the ways in which contemporary political and cultural power relations serve to obscure the origins of environmental degradation and protect the perpetrators of that degradation. His work, therefore, provides a useful supplement to the model of environmental politics and policy-making in Gorz's work. Finally, Beck like Habermas argues that democracy and democratization of both the conventional political process and the previously depoliticized areas of economic decision-making provide an essential element of an environmentally sustainable politics.

Socialism and Social Theory

I wrote above that I was concerned not only with the reasons for environmental degradation but with what, politically, we might do about it. The first five chapters of this book address some of the issues that this problem raises. We are unlikely to stem environmental degradation until we have a relatively accurate understanding of how and why it occurs. Similarly, once we have grasped this, we are unlikely to be able to intervene politically unless we understand the conditions under which environmental politics has been successfully mobilized and the constraints under which that mobilization operates. One constraint under which any politics operates is the requirement that the economic and political alternatives it offers have some plausibility and attractiveness. Thus I shall address the issue of socialism and environmental politics in the conclusion. All four of the theorists that I am analysing have built on the collective insight of the classical social theorists – that socialism entails the regulation of economic and political power in accordance with cultural and moral ideals. Moreover, each has done so from a perspective that acknowledges the limitations and failures of socialism as a political force and as a form of economic organization in the twentieth century. Their work therefore retains a significance for the dilemmas that face both a socialist and an environmental politics. In the conclusion I shall assess their proposals and draw up a balance sheet of the contributions of these contemporary social theorists to the questions I have asked, questions that classical social theory, for all its strengths, left unanswered.

1
Capitalism, Industrialism and the Transformation of Nature: Anthony Giddens

Two of the key concepts social theory has developed to define and describe modern societies lie at the heart of contemporary environmental debate: is capitalism or industrialism responsible for the devastating environmental record of the modern world? The resonance of that debate is not simply of historical interest, for the policies we propose in order to forestall the current ecological crisis will depend on how we diagnose its origins. The green parties of Western Europe have tended to argue that industrialism is the key to explaining environmental degradation under both capitalist economies and the state socialism of the former Soviet Union and postwar Eastern Europe. They have, therefore, called for programmes of voluntary deindustrialization. Marxists, by contrast, have sought the structural roots of environmental degradation in the dynamics of the capitalist mode of production, for which the usual recipe of socialist economics has been offered as the solution – although they have invariably failed to account adequately for the capacity of state socialism to achieve equal levels of environmental damage at lower levels of overall production. Environmental economists of both a social democratic and liberal orientation have argued that an unregulated or incorrectly regulated capitalism is the problem rather than anything intrinsic to the operation of markets and the private ownership of capital. Giddens's work provides our starting point for examining these controversies.

Giddens's Social Theory: an Outline

The difficult task of assessing Giddens's prolific output has already been performed with a greater sweep than I can attempt here.[1] A summary will therefore serve my purposes. Three overlapping chronological phases can be identified in Giddens's writings. In the early 1970s his work was characterized by a settling of accounts with the key figures of nineteenth-century social theory, primarily in *Capitalism and Modern Social Theory* with a comparative analysis of Marx, Weber and Durkheim.[2] Here, Giddens acknowledged capitalism as the central object of study for social theory, but never sought a simple reinvigoration of historical materialism. On the contrary, Giddens argued that much of that legacy, as well as those of Durkheim and functionalism, would have to be shed if the historical development of Western capitalism was to be grasped and its immense internal variation illuminated.[3] Just such an intention informed *The Class Structure of the Advanced Societies*. Assessing the validity of both Marxist and Weberian models of class, Giddens powerfully reinterpreted the different forms of class structure, consciousness and struggle in different capitalist and state-socialist societies.[4] For my purposes, however, the most important argument of the book concerns historical changes in class structures. All social formations prior to capitalism had been either tribal societies, in which class analysis was inappropriate, or class-divided societies; only capitalism could be accorded the status of class society proper, and it was that status that marked out its unique dynamics and organization.[5]

The second phase of work began with the 1976 publication of *New Rules of Sociological Method*, in which Giddens focused on a series of recurrent problems in social theory: epistemology, methodology and the relationship between structure and agency.[6] He critically examined the various traditions of interpretive sociology, as well as the functionalist legacy in social theory.[7] Both positivistic and naive interpretive epistemological projects in the social sciences were rejected and the Parsonian resolution to the problem of order was readdressed. Despite the demands of *Capitalism and Modern Social Theory*, this has been the keystone in Giddens's developing research project: an attempt to redress the balance between the individual and society or between agency and structure in the analysis of social action. He sought to transcend deterministic formulations, which effectively write the conscious human agent out of social theory. Yet he has also sought to recapture the bounded and determined nature of social action.[8] The outcome of this inquiry has been Giddens's theory of structuration.[9] Having laid the ontological and epistemological foundations of a substantive social theory, in the 1980s Giddens returned to the concrete ground of actual historical societies. Here he deployed the newly honed theory of structuration in a continuing critical encounter with historical materialism. Central to the third phase of his work has been the displacement of a historically unique capitalism as the prime subject of contemporary social theory; the focus has become modernity, its institutional orders and the transformation of both social structures and everyday life under the impact of heightened risk and reflexivity.

Giddens's critique of Marx is primarily contained in his two-volume *Contemporary Critique of Historical Materialism*.[10] Here he has not only challenged the most basic tenets of historical materialism, but developed an alternative and comprehensive social theory on the same ground. It would be misleading to limit the scope of these rich works to a few substantive themes, but three stand out. First, Giddens rejected all evolutionary models of societal development or historical explanation. This position is underwritten by his discontinuity thesis and the demonstration of the many different trajectories of social development.[11] Second, he has rejected any purely endogenous theory of social development; rather, Giddens emphasizes the importance of the relationship between different social formations along time-space edges.[12] Third, his earlier work on concrete social formations has been enriched by a consideration of space and time in the constitution of social structures; the nature of cities; the importance of the absolutist state and nation-state in the formation of Western capitalism and the modern global state system; the associated industrialization and centralization by nation-states of the means of violence and information gathering and use.[13]

The upshot of such a complex and differentiated analysis is a firm rejection of both economic and technological determinism in explaining either the origins and structure of capitalism or – in a striking shift of theoretical focus – *of modernity*. The latter, for Giddens, is characterized by the distinctive combination of four institutional orders. The exact classification of the orders has shifted in his work, but in the most recent formulation they are capitalism, industrialism, surveillance and military power. These institutional orders emerged together in the West and have become effectively globalized. In *The Consequences of Modernity* this analysis has been developed in confrontation with theories of postmodernity, arguing that its themes of epistemological, personal and aesthetic fragmentation and uncertainty are best accounted for in terms of the radicalization of modernity's core institutions. The psychological, political and phenomenological dimensions have been explored in, first, *Modernity and Self-Identity* and more explicitly in connection with issues of gender, sexuality and family life in *The Transformation of Intimacy*. Most recently Giddens has sought to reconnect this new model of modernity with an explicitly political agenda in which the limits to both contemporary socialism and neoliberalism are tested against a modernity they can no longer comprehend.[14]

How has this theoretical trajectory brought Giddens to consider the historical and structural origins of environmental degradation in modern societies? Externally, the rise in environmental concern of the 1980s has had its effects on Giddens's work and the political and existential implications of global environmental change have formed an important component of his emerging political agenda. But the developing theoretical logic of his work has allowed him to make two significant and interconnected arguments. First, he has argued that the conjunction of capitalism and industrialism is responsible for modern environmental degradation. He has, in shifting his focus from capitalism to modernity, subsequently reassessed the causal origins of environmental degradation. Second, recalling the discontinuity thesis, he has argued that whatever the precise causal origins of environmental degradation, the modern world heralds a more wholesale transformation of nature than human societies have ever been capable of before.[15]

Giddens on Capitalism, Industrialism and Modernity

Giddens's most extended discussion of capitalism and industrialism is initially analytical, delineating the unique features of these forms of social organization.[16] The uniqueness is the whole point of the argument. They are separate and irreducible, empirical historical phenomena; there have been capitalist societies that have not been industrial and industrialized societies that are not capitalist. Giddens also considers the historical relationship between capitalism and industrialism by reflecting on the two dominant approaches to this problem in social theory. The first approach argues that industrialism can be understood as the outcome of a developing capitalist society that both temporally predates it and is a condition of its emergence. For Giddens this is the essence of the Marxist theory of capitalist development.[17] The second approach, exemplified by the work of Durkheim and Raymond Aron, argues that capitalism is a temporary phase in the longer development of industrial societies or a specific variant of a causally prior industrialism.[18] The resolution to this debate is necessarily twofold. As Giddens writes: 'I do not wish to pretend that these matters can be settled on the level of conceptual cogency alone. They depend also upon a definite empirical assessment of the trends of development of modern societies . . .'[19]

Analytically Giddens's tactic is to review Weber's account of capitalism, using it as an antidote to the shortcomings of Marx's analysis, and as a prelude to developing his own analytical and historical positions. Giddens places particular importance on Weber's organizational account of capitalism. However, given the thrust of his own discontinuity thesis, he finds Weber's distinction between capitalism as a form of historically unspecific economic action and capitalism as the structural organization of a mode of production unsatisfactory. Giddens thus sides with Marx in establishing the distinct and generic qualities of modern capitalist societies and turns to his theory of commodification, particularly that of labour power.[20]

Giddens acknowledges the existence of commodities and commodification in other social formations, but argues that their nature in capitalist societies is radically discontinuous with that of their predecessors.[21] First, the commodity form, as the principal system of exchange, extends at a greater level of intensity, over a greater geographical range, and covers more goods and services. Second, and this is really the crux of the matter, labour itself is commodified as labour power on a massive scale. The implications of this are enormous and provide the point of departure for Giddens's fivefold classification of capitalist society. First, he classifies it as an economic order serving as 'the primary basis of the production of goods and services upon which the population of that society as a whole depends.'[22] When this feature of capitalism is conjoined with the structural economic imperatives of the investment-profit-investment cycle, economic decisions and actors clearly achieve an importance in capitalist societies that cannot be accorded to them in precapitalist societies. Second, underlying that importance, the cycle is conjoined with commodified labour and product markets to form an economic sphere distinct from the vertically hierarchical and horizontally parcelized economy and polity of feudal Europe. Third, that separation or insulation is predicated on the existence of private property in the means of production; it is therefore part of the wider process of commodification which creates both private property and the propertyless, who are required to sell their labour as labour power. This fundamental transformation provides the primary axis of modern class differentiation and results in the creation of endemic class struggle. Giddens is careful to clarify that not all social divisions and struggles can be reduced to or explained in terms of class structure, despite the centrality of class conflict.[23] Fourth, the separation of polity and economy at the level of institutional orders is marked in capitalist societies by complex institutional alignments between the activities of the state and those of private property.[24] Fifth, the 'capitalist state' can be used synonymously with 'capitalist society', because the nation-state and its boundary-defining mechanisms are intrinsic, rather than incidental, to the nature of capitalism.[25]

How then does Giddens conceptualize industrialism? He has, since his earliest writings, been a stringent critic of the concept of industrial society.[26] None the less, he does not wish to reduce industrialism to a historical epiphenomenon of capitalism, and nor does he wish to accept the standard analytical formulation of industrialism as factory production plus technology.[27] He rejects the latter on the grounds that the impact of new technologies cannot be focused on the system of mechanized production alone, and points to the impact of transport and communications technologies on a range of social activities.[28] Similarly the location of industrialism in the factory is considered too narrow to capture the specific organizational changes that occur with the advent of industrialism. Giddens thus identifies four defining characteristics of industrialism. The first two are essentially technological features. Industrialism entails the mobilization of inanimate sources of power in the production and circulation of commodities and the mechanization of those processes.[29] The conjunction of these two developments in the routinized flow of goods and production come to constitute an industrial economy. All three features must be located (with some significant exceptions) in centralized workplaces, wholly devoted to productive activity and quite separate from the domestic locale, to form a 'homogeneous productive order'.[30]

The analytical separation complete, Giddens then turns to the substantive historical questions. He does so by considering the historical validity and explanatory power of the terms 'capitalist society' and 'industrial society'. Giddens finds the latter to be wanting on two counts. First, it cannot explain the dynamic quality of modernity, its inherent and incessant transformatory powers and the acceleration of the scale and speed of social change. None of the usual accounts of industrial society, nor Giddens's own account of industrialism, can provide an explanation of this.[31] Second, the notion of an industrial society would suggest that industrialism as a productive order has a substantial effect on the constitution and organization of other social structures. Again Giddens argues that the term simply cannot carry the explanatory weight placed on it.[32] However, his own definition of capitalism, given the investment profit cycle and the chronic impetus it imparts to technological development and economic expansion, does account for the transformatory qualities of modernity. Similarly, given the inherent relationship between polity (capitalist nation-state) and insulated economy, the term capitalist society is preferable to that of industrial society. The rejection of the Durkheimian tradition does not entail a whole-hearted acceptance of the classical Marxist position on the relationship of capitalism to industrialism. In contrast Giddens argues that capitalism, industrialism and the emergence of the nation-state should be seen as 'three distinct *"organizational clusters"*, associated in a direct way with one another in their original European context, but which should be kept analytically distinct and which can have separate substantive consequences when instituted in other societal orders'.[33]

Even if the effects of industrialism require that it be viewed separately from capitalism, Giddens argues that their original historical relationship is somewhat closer. There are 'elective affinities' between the two which allow him to talk of a generic capitalist-industrialism.[34] These affinities are threefold: first, that the inherent dynamism of capitalism is associated with a propensity towards technical innovation in the manufacture of commodities; second, the commodification of labour power, generic to capitalist societies, is a basic condition of the suitability of the work-force for regularized, mechanized production processes, characteristic of industrialism; third, the expropriation of peasants to create wage-labourers is a precondition of the mobility of the work-force required for the centralized working practices of the industrialized economy. It would therefore appear that Giddens is suggesting that capitalism, although not the only economic order capable of combining with industrialism, is historically unique in its ability to create the preconditions for the emergence of industrialism.

However, in the argument of *The Nation-State and Violence*, a degree of confusion exists. On the one hand Giddens wishes to retain a relative autonomy for the impact and consequences of industrialism. Although there are elective affinities between capitalism and industrialism, this 'does not mean that industrialism is confined in its influence, or potential influence, to capitalist societies alone'.[35] On the other hand Giddens argues that, in a world-historical perspective, the environmental implications of industrialism have been actualized in the form of Western capitalist-industrialism, which produces 'the initiation of a massively important series of alterations in the relation between human beings and the natural world'.[36]

Giddens resolves this dilemma through the central theoretical construction of his recent work: the four institutional orders of modernity. In *The Nation-State and Violence* the orders comprise: private property, surveillance, the means of violence, and the transformation of nature and the production of the created environment.[37] In describing this formulation Giddens had argued initially that although analytically, and to an extent empirically, the impact of industrialism has been separable from capitalism, its major environmental impact in the last two hundred years has been in combination with capitalism. Giddens then appears to withdraw from this position, arguing for the primacy of industrialism rather than capitalism or industrial-capitalism in the production of the created environment and the transformation of nature: 'The technological changes stimulated by the energetic dynamism of capitalist development involve processes of the transformation of the natural world quite distinct from anything occurring before. Such processes are, however, *intrinsically linked to industrialism rather than to capitalism as such.*'[38] The idea that industrialism has independent causal consequences for a society appears to be repeated in one of Giddens's few references to the state-socialist societies of postwar Europe. He suggests that similar problems of governability existed in both East and West, prior to 1989, by virtue of their shared industrial base and irrespective of their fundamental differences of economic ownership and organization.[39] The shift in Giddens's work towards industrialism as a central component of modernity, quite separate from capitalism, is completed in *The Consequences of Modernity*. A remodelled version of the four institutional dimensions dispenses with the rather cumbersome 'transformation of nature/created environment' formulation and erects industrialism as a distinct order in its own right.[40] Giddens therefore appears to have attributed contemporary environmental problems to the institutions of industrialism.

We should note that Giddens has attributed two distinct but related environmental consequences to the impact of industrialization. On the one hand he has been concerned with processes of material-physical environmental change, which he has referred to as the transformation of nature. Writing in *The Consequences of Modernity* he specifies those transformations as 'ecological threats . . . the outcome of socially organised knowledge, mediated by the impact of *industrialism* upon the material environment'.[41] On the other hand he has described a more diffuse set of cultural changes. With reference to what he calls the 'created environment', he writes: 'Modern urbanism, so different in most respects from cities in earlier societies, is the most tangible and consequential expression of this phenomenon . . . it involves transformations in the relations between the habits of day-to-day social life and the *milieux* in and through which they are ordered.'[42] I will return to this cultural dimension in chapter 2 and focus now on 'ecological threats'.

In explaining the origins of environmental degradation Giddens's shift from capitalism-industrialism to industrialism alone initially appears convincing. I suspect, as Giddens appears to be suggesting, that much of current environmental degradation can be traced back to the operations of modern industrialized economies and the industrializing sectors of developing countries. I shall argue, however, that these societies do not cause that degradation primarily by virtue of being industrialized.

Giddens, in his earlier work, was convincingly sceptical about the notion of an Industrial Society. Not surprisingly, he suggested that the conjunction of capitalism and industrialism was responsible for environmental transformation. However, he offered no detailed explanation of this position, and neither specified the precise agencies of environmental change, nor established a chain of social causation from economics and technology to environmental damage. I intend to argue that Giddens therefore failed to exploit an important theoretical opportunity. For while the conjunction of capitalism and industrialism might have proved a convincing framework for exploring contemporary environmental degradation, and one which I shall pursue, his shift to industrialism as the central cause of those problems is ultimately not plausible. Its implausibility rests first at an analytical level. Giddens fails to distinguish between, and work through the implications of, (1) the agencies of environmental transformation that are the actual points of physical contact between a society and its environment; (2) the pattern of causation that lies behind the origin, distribution, deployment and mobilization of those agencies; (3) the precise nature of their ecological and social consequences. I intend to argue that industrialism is primarily, though not exclusively, an agency of environmental change. To explain the causes of the latter we shall have to reconnect industrialism with capitalism, state socialism, politics and culture. It is surprising that Giddens abandoned the theoretical path I am recommending. Having initially claimed in *The Nation-State and Violence* that industrialism lacked the explanatory power possessed by the notion of a capitalist society, Giddens left us wondering precisely why he believes that industrialism alone is responsible for environmental threats.

Analytical weakness is matched by the absence of detailed causal explanation. In *The Consequences of Modernity* Giddens has not supplied us with any arguments of this type, beyond the vaguest of references to the powers of technology, nor has he converted his analysis of industrialism into a specification of its precise environmental implications. Moreover, while the conceptualization of industrialism, as one of the interconnected institutional orders of modernity, has reopened the possibility that its conjunction with other orders is responsible for these problems, Giddens has not pursued such a strategy. He appears, in the interests of theoretical symmetry, to have placed the origins of ecological threats squarely at the door of industrialism. It is surprising that a writer who has sternly warned against technological determinism and displayed a deep aversion to monocausal arguments should take such a stand. It is not inconceivable that capitalism and state socialism have generated the same environmental consequences for different reasons that are due to the peculiar natures of their economic and political organization, rather than by virtue of the industrial technology they share. Nor is it inconceivable that while this technology presents similar problems and potentials for ecological damage, both types of society have failed to deal with or respond to them adequately, but for different reasons. Moreover, those reasons may not be simply economic or technological, where the emphasis of Giddens's argument lies, but political and cultural as well.

Giddens's historical arguments are equally imprecise. This is an indication of a more general failing to attend sufficiently to historical questions. For while Giddens quite rightly argued that his analytical position could not be seen in isolation from historical investigation, he has not followed that argument through. Theoretical weakness has been compounded with a lack of empirical support for his argument. Giddens has failed to capture the differences in environmental impact between different historical societies. Thus, while he has suggested that modern societies mark a fundamental dividing line in the nature of environmental degradation, he has yet to specify why. As we shall see, in failing to attend to the particular nature of this turning point, he has missed the most important environmental consequence of industrialism: the unleashing of capitalism.

Giddens's analytical separation of these distinctive modern institutions may allow us to pursue the questions he has raised in more depth, but it will, as I have suggested, first require a clarification of the interaction between societies and environments. On the basis of this model and a reformulated description of industrialism, I intend to demonstrate the implausibility of ascribing environmental damage to industrialism alone; to specify the peculiar contribution of industrialism to environmental damage, particularly its historical unleashing of otherwise constrained capitalist economies; to provide a causal explanation of how capitalism and state socialism are equally environmentally culpable, but through different mechanisms; and begin to trace the role of political and cultural forces in aiding, abetting and occasionally stemming the process of environmental degradation. These are forces that Giddens has hardly attended to at all.

Reconceiving Societies and Environments

The analytical weakness of Giddens's work on environmental change is not dissimilar to that of the classical social theorists: a conceptual vocabulary unable to grasp the complexity of the relationships between societies and environments. In his most recent work he is aware that the dividing line between societies and an unmediated nature is not clear.[43] There have rarely been any parts of the world that can be considered untouched wilderness. Even if human beings have not settled a region, their impact may be felt at a distance. Once they have entered a region and begun to hunt or farm or build, is it clear whether the dividing line between the social and the natural has been irrevocably lost? Do a hunter's footprints on a forest floor make a mediated nature?[44]

Despite these inevitable ambiguities it is important to view the social and the natural separately so as to indicate different causal forces at work in historical processes. Giddens leans this way in stressing both the 'transformation of nature' (societies transforming environments) and 'ecological threats' (environments affecting societies). However, if sociology is to illuminate these aspects of environmental change, we must depart from the former and refine the latter. Both 'transformation' and 'nature' are insufficiently precise terms. If we are interested in an empirically testable analysis of the causally significant types of environmental change, then we need to know which bits of nature have been transformed and in what way. The clearance of forests, polluting of rivers and the extinction of animals cannot be understood in terms of the 'transformation of nature' alone. It is helpful to reconceptualize the notion of nature in terms of the biological concept of ecosystems. We are concerned with the constitution, internal rhythms and operations, not of an undifferentiated nature, but of specific natural ecosystems and the biological cycles in which they are implicated. We must identify what human beings require of their environments. This will allow us to understand why societies transform the natural world, what features of the environment they transform and in what way. The transformation of ecosystems can then be reconceived in terms of four interrelated concepts: direct causes of change, indirect causes, material ecological impacts, and social consequences. The analysis of consequences must define the concept of an ecological threat with greater clarity; when do those consequences become a threat, and when is environmental change environmental degradation? Finally, understanding the consequences of environmental change requires a cultural or interpretive dimension: how do different societies understand their environment and the processes of change for which they are responsible?

Nature as Ecosystems

An ecosystem consists of living and inorganic components: populations of different flora, fauna and micro-organisms, soil, geological forms, water and the atmosphere. But what makes them a system rather than a collection of dead and living objects is that they exist in a dynamic interrelation with each other. They are linked by food webs, mineral and hydrological cycles and the circulation of energy. They are invariably in a state of flux: population levels rise and fall, predators move with their prey, parasites' numbers increase and decrease with their hosts'. Ecosystems may, through a variety of homeostatic mechanisms, change around a point of dynamic equilibrium. Others may undergo quite profound shifts over time: scrubland may develop on a fire-cleared heath, be converted through colonization by plant and animal species to woodland. The capacity of different ecosystems to survive shocks and changes will also vary.

The demands societies place on their environment include the provision of non-renewable and renewable energy resources and raw materials: fossil fuels and solar energy, iron and wood respectively. The environment also supplies certain vital life support systems: the provision of a breathable atmosphere, the homeostatic control of certain pests and diseases, a certain stability of climate, the hydrological cycle. Finally, in anthropomorphic terms, the environment provides certain economic services to societies: absorbing pollution, washing waste away, soil fertility, etc.

Only on the basis of this kind of understanding of ecosystems can we accurately trace the consequences of human action. Consider the example of seventeenth-century New England colonists who denuded hillsides of forest cover for timber, firewood and agricultural acreage. The consequences of that process were many. In terms of environmental services, soil fertility was lost. Soil erosion resulted from the absence of tree roots holding the hillside top soil together. This was compounded by a decrease in local transpiration rates, leading to decreased precipitation and a further hardening of the remaining soil due to the increase in sunshine. In terms of resources, the decline in forest cover limited the amount of land available for shifting Indian agriculture and diminished the habitats for economically important fur-bearing mammals. It also led to local timber shortages, since the wood resource was used at a rate greatly exceeding its renewable capacity.[45] To describe all of this as the 'transformation of nature' is not very revealing.

Rethinking the 'Transformation of Nature': Direct and Structural Causes

Having established a sharper conceptual vocabulary with which to describe environmental change, we need to attend to the details of the transformation process itself. We can begin with what I shall refer to as *direct causes* and *structural causes*. The distinction is useful, and one which Giddens fails, in this context, to make. Peasant slash-and-burn agriculture is, in the conventional sense of the term, a cause of deforestation in Brazil. However, identifying this cause hardly helps us to understand why peasants have moved to the Amazon basin in such large numbers, and why, once there, they practise a peculiarly devastating form of agriculture. Throughout this book, I wish to distinguish between these two levels of causality. On the one hand there are the *direct and immediate interactions of human behaviour with the ecosystem* (such as agricultural practices). On the other, there are the *structural and historical pressures, constraints and opportunities that lead groups and individuals to conduct their economic or demographic behaviour in an environmentally problematic way* (such as urban underemployment, lack of capital for peasant farmers, etc.). I describe the former as direct causes of environmental degradation and the latter as structural causes. Let us consider a further example of this distinction. Cars are a direct cause of urban air pollution, releasing large volumes of toxins into the atmosphere: a direct form of interaction between human behaviour and the urban atmosphere. However, the important questions go beyond this. Why are there so many cars? Why, given the dangers of their emissions, are there such lax controls on car use? Why are alternative forms of transport so poor? Motor transport is clearly a *direct cause* of environmental degradation, but it is only by understanding the nature of contemporary political and economic decision-making that we can trace the *structural causes* of this.

Demographics is the clearest direct cause of environmental change. All other things being equal, an increase in population will increase demands on an ecosystem. However, changes in population geography, density and absolute numbers must in themselves be causally explained. Why is there a rise or fall in numbers and densities? What economic or cultural pressures lead to changes in the geographical distribution or density of a given population? Moreover, the environmental impact of these demographic shifts must be considered with reference to the types of production that a given population deploys. Thus, in an economy predominantly based on hunting, population growth may lead to a greater number of animals being killed in a given area, or to the spread of hunting to a larger area, or to an increasing range of different species being hunted. By contrast, in an agricultural economy, population increase will lead to more land being cultivated, or to land in use being cultivated more often, and thus to natural ecosystems being disrupted more extensively, or more often.[46] Thus we cannot grasp the impact of population change without reference to the basic techniques of production: hunting, agriculture and industrialism. These economic practices are therefore direct causes of environmental change: the human practices which have specific, direct, material impacts on the environment. However, unlike demographics, they qualitatively shape a society's potential forms of environmental interaction. Each type of production is characterized by the different ways it uses renewable and non-renewable resources, and environmental services. This has important implications for what counts as environmental degradation in a given society. I shall return to this issue below. Before doing so we must investigate the reasons why these different forms of environmental interaction become forms of environmental degradation. We therefore need to turn to the question of structural causation.

If the argument above is correct then we should track the structural causes of environmental degradation to the constraints on and opportunities for economic and demographic behaviour. This does not mean that all economic and demographic change has environmental consequences. Nor does it mean that economic and demographic change is caused by economic and demographic factors alone. It is of course affected by the exercise of political, military and cultural power.[47] Economic and demographic behaviour may in turn be shaped by the results of environmental degradation. The diminishing supply of firewood forces societies to find alternative energy supplies like coal, which then create new environmental problems. In addition, environmental degradation may result from internal changes in the natural cycles of the environment, such as the little ice age of the Middle Ages.[48] Degradation may also result from changes internal to that society; the dynamics of markets and the formation of private property alter the ways in which an economy interacts with an environment. An effective sociology of environmental degradation requires us to analytically separate these forces. Giddens, by contrast, pays no attention to the environmental implications of demographic change and discusses only one type of production: industrialism. Moreover, he does not examine the ways in which environmental degradation and change can affect the economic and demographic causes of the problem. Above all, I shall argue that he predominantly and incorrectly characterizes industrialism as a *structural* rather than a direct cause of environmental degradation and fails to specify why industrialism generates a peculiar potential for environmental degradation.

A Typology of Material Environmental Impacts

Before we can proceed to the issue of environmental degradation we require an outline of the types of actual material interaction that occur between societies and environments. I suggest the following four-point typology as a useful but not exhaustive guide.

1 Change in population levels and geographical distribution of plants/animals/micro-organisms.
2 Alteration of soil and geological forms.
3 Alteration of chemical composition: atmosphere, water systems and life-forms.
4 Alteration of biological systems: meteorological, carbon, nitrogen, hydrological, food webs, ecosystems.

Where (1) is concerned, human beings have consciously and unconsciously intervened in their ecosystems to increase, decrease, extinguish and geographically transform species populations. They have also altered the genetic composition and behaviour of species. Population shifts can be the result of natural changes such as long-term shifts in climate, but it is human agencies and their unintended consequences that concern us. For example, large populations can be rapidly diminished if the process of hunting is not controlled to match the reproductive rate of the prey. In reducing the population of one species, those that feed on them will unintentionally be diminished, while those it feeds on will be increased. Agriculture is, in essence, the simplification of ecosystems to increase their food output. Such impacts do not stop at changes in species distribution but have important effects on soil, geomorphic forms and ultimately all the nutrient cycles of an ecosystem (processes 3 and 4). Geographical distribution has also been altered by conscious intent. The physical transportation of species from one habitat and ecosystem to another is the most important. This can have dramatic social effects, as the Arabic importation of horses into Western Africa and the subsequent transformation of warfare and social structure suggests.[49]

With regard to geological forms, in (2), the most powerful instrument of change for most of human history has been the impact of natural forces: wind, rivers, tides, rain, etc. It is only in the modern era that the technological capability has existed for major human changes of this sort – for example, the construction of the Panama and Suez Canals in the nineteenth century or the vast hydrological and dam projects of the twentieth century. The consequences of change may be both economic and, more recently, aesthetic. The transformation of soil is, given its intimate connection with agricultural performance, of even greater import. Again, vegetation changes due to the introduction of new plants or the removal of herbivores by hunting can lead to changes in soil cover and structure. Changes in the courses of rivers and types of agricultural practices can alter the physical structure of the soil. Chemical changes can result from the same processes, but are also linked to shifts in climate and the use of fire in agriculture.[50]

Both (3), the alteration of chemical composition, and (4), the alteration of biological systems, can be affected by any of the foregoing processes and are themselves interconnected. I separate them only for analytical clarity. The addition of mercury to a river (process 3) can result in the killing or poisoning of fish (process 1), and the mercury can enter human bodies through an altered food chain (process 4). Or similarly the greenhouse effect is caused by the addition of carbon dioxide, methane and CFCs to the atmosphere (process 3), leading to changes in the meteorological system (process 4), leading to changes in habitats and species distribution (process 1).[51]

This ecological description of environmental change should make clear the need for an interpretive approach to these processes.[52] The perception of environmental impacts and their consequences ranges between conscious intent and unacknowledged or unintended consequences. The history of the pesticide DDT is instructive. This highly toxic, inorganic compound was used extensively in postwar agriculture. In the middle decades of the twentieth century, DDT accumulated in plants unable to excrete it and then in the animals and human beings that consumed the plants. DDT affected the population levels of plants and animals, as well as human health, without anyone being consciously aware of its biological consequences. These effects would have continued in the absence of knowledge of its pathological effects.[53] We should note that the knowledge actors possess is not necessarily accurate. We can and do hold false beliefs about environmental consequences. Nor have actors necessarily changed their behaviour on the basis of the knowledge they have possessed. But then we must investigate the origins and consequences of imperfect knowledge and shifts in cultural understandings of the environment. Giddens's failure to emphasize sufficiently the interpretive dimension of environmental change has led him to underplay the role of politics and culture in the actual processes of environmental degradation. Once such a dimension is acknowledged, politics and disputes over meanings become directly enmeshed in the environmental implications of economic action and technological deployment.

The Social Consequences of Environmental Impacts: Defining Environmental Degradation

A question remains about the social consequences of ecological change. When does human-generated environmental change become environmental degradation?[54] These are not synonymous. Some environmental change may well be considered benign. I wish to consider three analytically separate forms of environmental degradation: economic-demographic constraints and opportunities; direct impacts on human health; and aesthetic-moral implications. I think that Giddens's notion of an ecological hazard, as a threat to physical, human well-being, encompasses just the first and second. But all three constitute environmental degradation when measured against the goals and aspirations of the human beings they affect. For ecological threats alone, this is so whether humans know that these consequences can be traced to their own economic and demographic behaviour or not. Aesthetic-moral concerns by contrast cannot operate behind our backs. Going beyond Giddens, the distinction is worth making and the precise nature of those constraints and concerns worth pursuing.

Economic-demographic consequences of environmental degradation produce an alteration in conditions of and constraints on economic action and demographic behaviour. They will vary historically according to the dominant type of production in a given historical situation, for, as I have argued, the demands that an economy makes on an ecosystem are variable. Particular types of production will generate particular patterns of degradation. In hunter-gatherer societies, economic-demographic constraints produced by environmental degradation include an altered distribution and volume of game and edible plants. In agricultural societies, changes in the patterns of seasons and climate and the fertility of soils constitute environmental degradation. In industrial societies, shortages of non-renewable resources are a distinctive form of environmental degradation. One constraint resulting from these changes would be shifts in the availability of food and raw materials, affecting the population level that can be supported. These changes will also have a major impact on human health. A diminishing supply of food, or an increased frequency of natural disasters, not only limits future economic performance and demographic change, but also affects human well-being. Similarly a rise in pathogenic micro-organisms or widespread mercury poisoning, which we would initially characterize as a health effect, would have major consequences for the productivity and death-rate of a work-force. Thus the dividing line between economic-demographic and human health consequences is somewhat blurred. None the less, the distinction is worth making. I would argue that those forms of degradation which directly impinge on individual bodies with pathological consequences constitute health threats.

Aesthetic-moral questions are of a different order altogether. Examples are protests over ancient hedgerow destruction, on account of their symbolic importance and their function as a habitat for otherwise extinct butterfly species, and the campaigns to save the whale and protect ancient woodlands. In these cases we are not considering a response to threats to human survival or economic prosperity (as conventionally understood), but a response rooted in a different register of values. This again points to the importance of the cultural dimension in any environmental history. For why should some individuals in certain historical circumstances make that type of valuation, and how is that valuation measured against the more immediate interests of either survival or prosperity?

In summary, an abstract model of the relationship between societies and environment would differentiate between direct causes of environmental degradation and its structural causes. It would differentiate between the capacities and potentialities of different systems of production as agencies of environmental change, and combine this with a sensitive appreciation of the impact of demographic change. It would trace the causes of social actions that affect ecosystems, particularly economic and demographic behaviour, though it would not restrict the causes of that change to economics and demographics alone. It would specify the type of material impacts produced, known and unknown, and their multiple ecological and social consequences. It would be sensitive to the range of cultural perceptions, knowledge and valuations of the environment. It would trace the implications of ecological changes, distinguishing between those perceived by participants and those operating behind their backs, between those affecting economics, demographics and health and those contravening moral-aesthetic standards. It would do so with reference to the sorts of demands and requirements that different systems of production place on the environment. Having constructed this model, we must see if we can improve on Giddens's account of environmental degradation.

Capitalism and Environmental Degradation

In defining modernity in terms of the four institutional clusters and thus drawing the line between the premodern (non-industrial, non-capitalist) world and the modern (industrial and capitalist) world, Giddens has obscured an important case study of environmental degradation: the capitalist agricultural societies of early modern Europe, particularly England and the Dutch Republic. The latter were responsible, as we shall see, for extensive environmental change and were experiencing environmental threats of their own making. Therefore they provide an illuminating case study for examining the causal importance of capitalism alone in generating environmental change. Given Giddens's shifting account of the causal origins of modern environmental degradation, from capitalist industrialism to industrialism alone, this case study is of particular value in assessing the validity of his changing theoretical position. Moreover, it will also allow us to examine more closely the historical relationship between capitalism and industrialism. For while Giddens has argued that capitalism created some of the preconditions of industrialism, he did not examine the impact of industrialism on capitalism. Rethinking the environmental consequences of capitalist agriculture will help us to specify the environmental consequences of the industrialism it helped generate. I shall argue that the institutions of capitalism are the main structural causes producing modern environmental degradation, and that industrialism, as Giddens conceives it, is primarily a direct cause of degradation. However, I believe that in the historical transition from capitalist-agriculture to capitalist-industrialism it is fair to talk of industrialism as a structural cause of environmental degradation rather than simply as a direct cause.

A useful approach to the environmental consequences of a capitalist agricultural society is the work of the historian E. A. Wrigley.[55] Wrigley characterizes the economy of seventeenth- and eighteenth-century England as an 'advanced organic economy'. The term describes an economy that was not simply agricultural but sustained an expanding urban population employed in manufacturing and services.[56] It was an economy in which the rate of output growth allowed it to support an expanding population. Intensive (rather than extensive) growth came from capital investment in land, rationalization and concentration of land holdings, expanding markets and a range of technological and stockbreeding improvements. In short, it was an economy characterized by the emergence of capitalism.[57] However, there remained perpetual bottlenecks in this upward spiral of economic growth. These bottlenecks were the consequence of environmental change induced by the same processes of economic growth. For although it was an advanced economy, it was fundamentally reliant at every level on the products of the land, for food, energy, transport and raw materials for industry. Wood was the dominant domestic and industrial fuel. Metal smelting, glass, pottery and brewing were all reliant on wood. Wind and water both made a contribution to energy production via wind and water mills, and were irreplaceable as means of efficient transport, but their usage remained limited to the few sites available for efficient mills, while their economic role was diminished by the growing demands for energy in sectors for which they were technologically unsuitable.[58] Given these limitations, industry and transport had to make use of animal and human muscle, the volume of which remained tied to the productivity of the land. Finally every industry remained dependent on organic raw materials: furs, cotton, leather and wool for all the textile trades; charcoal for every metal trade; wood for construction and shipbuilding materials and for fuel in glass and pottery manufacture; seaweed or potash in the fledgling chemical industry.[59]

In terms of our model of environmental change, the *direct causes* of transformation in this period were agriculture (for food, fuel and raw materials), non-industrial manufacturing, hunting and demographic expansion. The *impacts* were fundamental changes in the distribution and numbers of plant and animal species, and in some cases their eradication, the disruption of ecosystems, as well as a serious depletion of soil fertility. The *consequences* were serious economic and demographic constraints, above all a shortage of renewable raw materials leading to spiralling prices, with telling effects on human health and demographic expansion. Those economic constraints were not simply applied to the advanced organic economy. The societies of the Americas, swept into the emerging world economy, experienced environmental change that led to such fundamental economic constraints and shortages that traditional economic and social practices became untenable. What remains unclear, so far, are the *structural causes* of these changes and their ultimate historical consequences.

The pattern of structural causation is, perhaps, most clearly visible in the impact of the advanced organic economy outside its heartlands: in the hunting of seals, whales and fur-bearing animals, and forestry and ranching. All these activities relied on organic raw materials and were conducted until the twentieth century with predominantly preindustrial technology: harpoons, clubs, snares, sailing ships, fire and axes, although at a later stage the railways proved an important factor in expanding the spatial scope and total scale of environmentally problematic activities.[60] In each of the hunting cases, species were driven to the point of extinction, while forestry and ranching transformed huge landscapes, undermined their fertility and induced local climatic change. Within fifty years of the seventeenth-century Russian expansion into Siberia, 75 per cent of the main fur-bearing animals had been lost to organized hunting.[61] This pattern of destruction followed Russian hunting expeditions from the Urals, to the Pacific and ultimately to parts of the American mainland. In New England, the combined efforts of colonists and Indians denuded the area of beaver, wolf and bear in the course of barely a century of intensive hunting.[62] Fur seals, elephant seals and whales, hunted for their oil, skins and blubber, fared no better in the late eighteenth and nineteenth centuries. Across the islands of the South Atlantic and the Pacific and Indian oceans, and on the coasts of Alaska and Newfoundland, seals were extinguished at rates far exceeding any conceivable replacement level.[63] On the American plains west of the Rockies, the buffalo was almost completely extinguished for hides and meat, to be replaced by overstocked cattle ranches, reducing the fragile vegetable cover to almost nothing and the already fragile top soil to hard-baked earth and dust.[64]

If we recall Giddens's analytical definition of capitalism, there are clues as to the structural causes of these phenomena: the commodification of more objects; the existence of private property; the creation and extensive connection of competitive product and labour markets; the centrality of money to the economy. However, Giddens's list is not complete, and nor does he draw out the environmental consequences of those economic mechanisms. Here I want to outline those mechanisms briefly under three headings: (1) a sustained demand for products from large and extensive markets, maintained by both economic success and demographic expansion; (2) an inaccurate pricing system fuelled and exploited by the peculiar vices and virtues of private property and unregulated common property in a capitalist economy, combined with a cultural and economic perception of the natural world as commodified and limitless; (3) shifts in the nature of consumption.

Structural cause 1: expanded and sustained demand The economic success of capitalism is important in explaining its capacity for environmental transformation. In the absence of industrial development, a rise in population and per capita consumption, and therefore greater pressure on environmental resources, depends on the sustained production of an agricultural surplus. Such a surplus in the pockets of entrepreneurial farmers, as well as the fortunes accumulated in trade and commerce, created the expanding demand for products such as ermine, sable, whale oil, etc. These markets were, moreover, of a size and resilience that could support the cost of distant environmental exploitation and the long and complex trade routes through which its products had to flow. The expansion of both the money economy and systems of credit, analytically central to capitalism, provided the means for systems of exchange which would otherwise have entailed prohibitively high transaction costs.[65] When that economic success could both raise the purchasing power of elites, who had been importing furs and so on for many centuries, and support a growing population, the size of markets would grow even faster, raising demand, maintaining prices and encouraging more intensive and more extensive use of natural resources.

Structural cause 2: market pricing and private property The nature of the pricing and property system of the advanced organic economy was equally important in these distant processes of overexploitation, and both pricing and property were shaped and supported by the cultural perspective of its economic agents: the assumptions of abundance and commodification. Simply put, prices in a market economy notionally reflect contemporary levels of supply and demand. Moreover, they are extended to a great many more objects and resources. In so doing they take the place of customary practices and systems of judicial or traditional regulation in determining economic action. In effect this is not only an economic change, but a cultural one, albeit with major economic consequences. Capitalism gave rise to a cultural perception of the natural world as yielding commodities or potential commodities, with no sense of limits or restraint.[66] Therefore, prices do not take account, all other things being equal, of the interests of future generations, or of those not directly engaged in an exchange, or of other economic actors who are using the same resource, or even of the medium-term interest of those involved in the exchange themselves. As a consequence resources will be used as long as there is a demand for them. In the case of finite resources, like the numbers of fur-bearing animals in a forest, the price mechanism may reflect scarcity: prices will increase as numbers diminish. However, this makes it economically rational, in the short term, to exploit a dwindling resource. Whether these resources are held as private property or unregulated common property, the absence of any countervailing force to the price mechanism will ensure that economically rational agents will exploit resources, to the point of extinction in the case of hunters, or to the point of diminished and unprofitable returns in the case of agriculturists. Given that there is competition between economic actors in an unregulated market over a fixed quantity of common resources, there is a further incentive to make the most of resources while they last. Restraint shown on the part of any individual actor will result in diminished economic returns to themselves, with no benefit to the common interest, because other economic actors will take up the slack that they have left.[67]

Structural cause 3: shifts in the culture of consumption A further cultural factor, overlooked in Giddens's analysis, is changes in attitudes to consumption. While consumption is limited by the overall success of an economy's performance and the distribution of its surplus, it can also be a factor in the stimulation of markets. Addiction to novelty, a wider social spread of the consumption of status items, and the creation of fashions all helped to expand the range and demand for goods – furs and hides in particular – above a level at which they could be environmentally sustained.[68]

The self-same processes were at work in the English and Dutch heartlands of the advanced organic economy: forest clearance, soil exhaustion, raw material shortage, rising prices and the ever present threat of demographic expansion outpacing agricultural output. In contrast to the experience of the Americas and Siberia, these economies held their resources as private property. However, it proved no better than unregulated common property in keeping the advanced organic economy from pressing on its environmentally determined limits: forests were cut down, landscape rationalized, marginal land squeezed and with it a range of plant and animal species extinguished. Shortages and overpopulation loomed on the horizon and the economic growth of the previous century appeared to be under threat. The capacity of capitalism for environmental destruction at home and overseas would in the end, it seemed, be tempered by the ecological limits which it could temporarily exceed, but from which it could not ultimately escape.

It is worth comparing the economic experience of the Dutch Republic with England in this respect. The Dutch Republic, which only falteringly experienced industrialization in the late eighteenth and early nineteenth centuries, saw its advanced organic economy fall into decline. Troubled by spiralling energy and material prices and diminishing returns on an overworked agriculture, population growth slowed, cities stagnated and trade diminished.[69] As a consequence its capacity for environmental degradation was stopped in its tracks. At the same time the English economy roared ahead. How was it then that the English economy avoided the fate of the Dutch economy? We are interested, ultimately, in modern society's environmental record. What made eighteenth-century England and the Netherlands modern was the confluence of capitalism with industrialism. Giddens has argued for the importance of capitalism in the emergence of industrialism and he is right to do so. I intend, however, in part following Wrigley, to examine the way in which industrialism, once it began to emerge, transformed the organic capitalist economies and how, in so doing, the English organic economy avoided the fate of its Dutch counterpart. To investigate these issues, I want to return to Giddens's analytical conception of industrialism as a means for examining both its historic structural role in environmental change and its predominant contemporary role as a direct cause of environmental change.

Before doing so I want to review my analysis of Giddens's position and look forward to some of the issues I will develop in later sections of this chapter. It is my intention in these sections both to demonstrate the limits of Giddens's arguments, and where appropriate to develop new and stronger arguments. So far I have argued that Giddens's definition of modernity as both capitalist and industrialist has led him to ignore the important case studies of advanced organic, capitalist economies in England and the Dutch Republic. Their experience shows that capitalism alone can and does have significant consequences for the natural environment. Although Giddens hints at the reasons for this, he does not elaborate the actual mechanisms of environmental degradation under capitalist economies. My critique of Giddens has highlighted these limitations and has attempted to flesh out those *structural causes*. Perhaps, most significantly, I have argued that these economies faced considerable internally generated environmental limits to their economic expansion. It is only by understanding those limits that we can accurately estimate the enormous impact of industrialism. Because he does not examine those limits, Giddens does not register the most important environmental consequence of industrialism: *the unleashing of capitalism*. I shall explore that aspect of industrialism in the next section. In the following section I shall explore the mechanisms of modern environmental degradation. I intend to demonstrate the relative roles of capitalism and industrialism in those processes. I shall demonstrate the strength of Giddens's initial position – that capitalist-industrialism is responsible for environmental degradation – and the weakness of his later position – that industrialism alone generates modern environmental degradation. I shall then examine the role of political power in generating environmental degradation. This is an issue that Giddens's focus on capitalism and industrialism has left somewhat unexplored and its absence from his discussion of environmental degradation constitutes an important limitation of his work. My discussion is intended to show why one cannot ignore the exercise of political power. In the final section I shall consider an important challenge to the arguments that I have developed in earlier sections. If industrialism alone cannot account for the nature of environmental degradation, and we must therefore take capitalism and political power into account, how are we to account for the appalling environmental record of industrialized but non-capitalist societies: the state socialism of the Soviet Union and Eastern Europe?

Industrialism: an Analytical and Historical Assessment

Giddens outlines four defining characteristics of industrialism: mobilization of inanimate power; mechanization; factory-based production; economic centrality. To these I would add: the importance of new raw material sources in general and fossil fuels in particular; the importance of theoretical science; the necessity of a complex division of labour, high levels of capital formation and structural change within the economy. I would suggest that any discussion of industrialism should be sensitive to the question of historical periodization. I also place a greater emphasis than Giddens on the implications of high energy use.

The preceding section should have made clear the importance of a switch in raw material resources. Industrialism is not characterized by the mobilization of inanimate power in general. Wind and water were already in extensive use under the advanced organic economy, but both remained limited in supply.[70] Rather, it was the switch to inorganic energy supplies, and inorganic raw materials in general, that stemmed its peculiar pattern of environmental degradation and lifted the ecologically imposed limits of the advanced organic economy.[71] The switch entailed a shift from charcoal to coke in metal-smelting industries, allowing for the cheaper production of a wide range of metals, all of which replaced the use of organic raw materials in tools and buildings. In construction, bricks and concrete replaced wood, while in textile production cotton gave way to synthetic materials.

The significance of a relatively advanced theoretical and practical science is more complex. Of course, science and industrialism, as with capitalism and industrialism, are causally and analytically separable. Certain civilizations have deployed machinery and used inanimate power in the absence of science: the spinning wheel in India, gunpowder in China.[72] Conversely, Galileo, Copernicus and Newton made significant scientific advances prior to the industrialization of Europe. None the less, there would seem to be, to use Weber's term, 'elective affinities' between the two. We can concede that the earliest stages of the industrial revolution in England were accomplished without any widespread application of science to economic activity. The key forms of mechanization in the cotton industry, the production of coke for adequate metal smelting and the earliest steam engines were as much the outcome of gifted amateur tinkering, beneficial economic conditions for innovation and the redeployment of already existing technologies as they were the outcome of concerted scientific reflection and discoveries.[73] However, the historical origins and subsequent development of the same process can be affected differently by different forces. In the case of advanced industrialism, a very much wider range of raw materials – for example, uranium, aluminium, rare heavy metals – has been mobilized, requiring complex extractive processes that must be both technically and economically feasible. It has also produced a wide range of usable materials that do not exist in the environment, or exist in such small quantities as to make their use economically prohibitive: organic chemicals such as benzene, halide hydrocarbons, phenols, etc. Advanced industrialism has also developed increasingly sophisticated techniques for working these materials and produced machines that can do things human beings cannot do, or do only very slowly and inaccurately. A theoretical science would appear to be a precondition of the sort of sophisticated control these processes require: extremes of pressure and temperature, controlled and precise mechanical force, chemical manipulation.[74] Indeed, directed scientific research has been instrumental in the emergence of all the most significant industrial innovations of the late nineteenth and early twentieth centuries, for example, the internal combustion engine and electricity production.

I would suggest that the activities Giddens includes under the heading of industrialism necessarily entail a fairly high and complex division of labour. It is inconceivable that widespread mechanization and the array of technological development implied by industrialism could have been achieved without a significant level of differentiation in terms of employment, training and knowledge.[75] Moreover, the division of labour not only occurs within the productive process itself but engenders structural differentiation across the whole economy. The process of industrialization entails not simply the rise of industry but a massive decline in the numbers of people required in agriculture and an equally rapid expansion of the service sector in all its different forms. It also requires a level of capital formation and deployment qualitatively different from that in preindustrial societies. In this respect a further elective affinity between capitalism and industrialism is that the former is capable of a level of capital formation and concentration without which the productive infrastructure of industrialism would be rendered impossible.[76]

In assessing the environmental consequences of industrialism, there is a need for some sort of periodization – a point somewhat lost in Giddens's analysis. Acknowledging differential rates and trajectories of industrialization, certain key technologies have transformed the productive forms and environmental impacts of industrial societies. I will not attempt to chart such a comprehensive technological history, but shifts in the dominant forms of energy production (from coal to oil and nuclear-based electricity), transportation (from horse to rail to car) and other raw material use (the rise of organic chemical use, the importance of new metals technologies) would be most important. In the context of this and the following chapters, I shall not confine myself to the environmental consequences of any one period of industrialization, although I am sensitive to the criticism that only by attending to such a periodization can the history of environmental degradation be adequately explained.

How does this characterization of industrialism support the idea that it unleashed capitalism? To put it another way, how was it that at the moment of industrialism's historical emergence it acted as a structural cause of environmental change rather than simply as a direct cause of environmental degradation driven by the structural pressures of dynamic capitalist institutions? As I suggested, the answer lies in the economic implications of high energy use and the ability to mobilize it in a form suitable for powering machinery. For if, as Giddens argued, capitalism furnished the appropriate economic and cultural context for the development of industrialism, then industrialism not only lifted the advanced organic economy out of its raw material limits but multiplied the inherent growth potential of an already dynamic economic system. The progressive mechanization of agriculture not only allowed a massive increase in productivity but released huge amounts of land previously reserved for maintaining horses and oxen. Similarly, the application of new chemical fertilisers and scientific stock-breeding boosted production with a declining work-force. Railways expanded markets, cut the perennially prohibitive costs of land transport that had bedevilled preindustrial economies and, although initially encouraging the expansion of the horse population for deliveries, contributed with the internal combustion engine to their demise as a form of transport. This further reduced pressure on the land. Within manufacturing itself, the combination of an absence of raw material constraints, high energy availability and its appropriate mobilization through machinery made possible an enormous rise in the productivity of manufacturing.[77] Most important of all, it did so at a rate that outstripped a rapidly increasing population, leading to a massive and sustained growth in the real incomes and levels of consumption of not just economic and political elites but eventually the entire population.[78] So it was that the English organic economy did not suffer the same fate as its Dutch counterpart; not only did it maintain a high rate of agricultural and manufacturing growth, but these were massively increased. Capitalism had, indeed, been unleashed and thus we may conclude that industrialism has acted as a structural precondition of the future environmental degradation attributable to a much enlarged capitalist economy.

Capitalist-Industrialism and Environmental Degradation

How then did this combination of a nascent industrialism and the capitalism it had set free from its organic limits transform the environment? Further, how did their combined effects differ from the impacts of the advanced organic economy? In short, this combination retained all the destructive characteristics of the advanced organic economy, magnified them and added a number of its own peculiar vices. Industrialism had unleashed capitalism, alleviating the economic and demographic consequences of its earlier forms of environmental degradation. Now the institutional dynamics of capitalism would shape the direct impact of industrialism on the environment. We should note that Giddens argues that the phenomena of urbanism and globalization are causally tied to the development of industrialism and capitalism. I shall deal with their environmental impacts in the next chapter. Here I shall concentrate on the *direct causal* impacts on the environment of demographic change and industrialized economic growth driven by the *structural* dynamism of a capitalist economy. In particular I shall look at the environmental problems of economic growth; of the transformatory power of technology; of agricultural change and population growth in modern societies; of pollution as an externality; of finite fossil fuels and raw materials and the consequent 'limits to growth'. Drawing on my causal account of capitalism's capacity for environmental destructiveness and my analytical account of industrialism, I shall substantiate my claim, against Giddens, that industrialism alone is not the cause of modern environmental change. Rather, it is predominantly a *direct cause* of environmental degradation and must be conceptualized in relation to other aspects of the social order. While Giddens's discussion of the interrelationships between the different institutional orders of modernity is consistent with such an approach, he has not attempted to explain quite how capitalism and industrialism combine to produce characteristically modern forms of environmental degradation. Indeed, as I argued earlier, his insistence in *The Consequences of*

Modernity that industrialism is the central cause of contemporary ecological threats has obscured the possibility of developing such an argument in his own work.

Economic Growth

At the causal core of contemporary environmental degradation is the problem of economic growth, in terms of overall gross domestic product (GDP) and in terms of rising per capita income. We should be clear, in contrast to a number of environmentalist and green positions, that the modern world's proclivity, if not capacity, for growth is a consequence of the dynamics of capitalism and not industrialism. We can confidently argue that industrialism may have released capitalism from its organic ecological constraints, massively boosted its *potential* for growth and fundamentally altered the possible types of interaction human societies could have with their ecosystems. However, as Giddens rightly argued in his analytical assessment of capitalism, it is the investment-profit cycle in the context of competitive markets that is the institutional mainspring of the individual and corporate drive for expanded production and profit – in a word, for growth. That is not to say that other institutional frameworks cannot also unleash industrialism, although as state socialism has demonstrated with such clarity, none has yet managed to do so with the same degree of efficiency and effectiveness.

The causal element of the green argument may be wrong, but that need not contradict its conclusions. The argument runs that unlimited growth will necessarily exhaust finite natural resources, inorganic raw materials, land and the capacity of the environment to absorb pollution.[79] Therefore it may be that economic growth not only creates environmental threats, but – rather than being equated with increasing prosperity – simply reflects the increasing costs of environmental damage, such as higher health expenditures.[80] Economic growth, in fact, stands as a cipher for a complex of economic processes whose combined impact generates unsustainable levels of environmental degradation and whose dominant mode of accounting has ceased to register anything but its own bizarre logic.

However, a number of qualifications need to be made to this argument. Economic growth is measured in terms of GDP, which is a monetary aggregate of the goods and services exchanged within an economy. As such it is not necessarily a very reliable guide to levels of resource consumption, pollution emissions, etc. The experience of the Western economies since the oil shocks of the early 1970s has shown that increasing GDP can be associated with static or declining levels of energy and resource use.[81] Furthermore, an increase in GDP might reflect substantial growth in the performance of live music concerts, recycling businesses and the sale of pollution abatement equipment, whose environmental impacts are quite minimal and may be beneficial.[82] However, *in historical terms the structural causal connections between economic growth, increases in personal consumption and increasing environmental damage have remained steady in industrial economies for the last two centuries.* That causal relationship can be traced to the capitalist organization of markets, property and the economic culture it has generated, combined with the novel capacity industrialism provides for environmental degradation.[83]

The Transformatory Power of Technology

The mobilization of energy and the mechanization of production help create one of the distinctive ecological impacts of an industrial economy: the wherewithal to transform landscapes and geomorphic forms on a scale and at a speed and level of change otherwise inconceivable. There is a certain paradox in the capacity of industrialism to release the advanced organic economy from its self-imposed environmental threats only to allow an even more intensive assault on the surface of the earth. Capitalism, unleashed, could outstrip the ecological barriers that once held it in check. That assault has been both intensive and extensive.

Agriculture and demographic pressures have been the main direct causes of extensive transformation. I shall return to them below. Intensively, it is major productive and infrastructural projects as well as urban growth that have transformed geomorphic forms so massively: river diversion, reservoir construction, artificial harbours, open cast mining, urban sprawl, large-scale waste disposal sites.[84] Clearly, it is the advent of industrial technology and energy use that makes possible something like the damming of the Colorado River, but we would be hard pressed to explain its actualization in terms of technological potentialities alone.

Agriculture and Demographic Impacts

Extensive transformation has been conducted primarily by the agricultural sector seeking to feed an increasingly large, and in the West increasingly wealthy, market. The volume of farmland opened up by industrialized economies has been immense.[85] Rivers can be diverted, huge marshes drained, entire forests cleared, and all supplied with transport links to markets that ensure the profitability of the process and thus maintain the momentum of expansion.[86] In this respect the capacity of capitalist societies to diminish the direct transaction costs of economic exchange has facilitated its environmentally destructive capacities. The fertility of the land has been artificially maintained by the external inputs of synthetic fertiliser and pesticide, although substantial improvements in technique cannot be discounted. The environmental impacts of this within industrialized nations have been profound. A wide range of species, habitats and entire ecosystems have been eradicated or changed beyond recognition: the American Prairies, Southern Siberia, nearly all European forests, as well as a huge number of rich and varied small ecosystems left in the niches of an undercapitalized, preindustrial agriculture.[87]

However, it is not simply the operations of a corporate, market-orientated agriculture based in the West which have caused extensive environmental transformation. Equally adept at environmental degradation have been modes of subsistence and export-based agriculture in the South.[88] The structural pressures that have shaped these direct causes of environmental degradation are complex and there is hardly space here to consider them in the detail they deserve. What we can say, first of all, is that the development of environmentally problematic export crops in the South cannot be separated from the structural demands of debt financing and import costs that the current system of international trade and finance imposes on the South. Second, the expansion of such agriculture has pushed subsistence agriculture further onto the ecologically precarious margins of southern ecosystems. Brazilian peasants have practised unsustainable agriculture in the rain forests because they cannot find work in the cities and the more suitable land has already been claimed by the export-orientated beef and wheat sectors.[89] This is a complex matter, but the point here is that the operations of international markets, the inequitable ownership of private property and the unequal terms of trades within markets are, alongside other purely domestic pressures, at the root of these environmental problems. Industrialism, where it has been applied, has acted only to speed and facilitate an environmentally damaging economic dynamic already in motion.

A further factor in explaining the environmental impact of the agriculture of both developed and developing nations must be their massively expanded populations. They have yet to encounter the demographic checks of poverty, disease and rising food prices on a scale encountered by the advanced organic economy or indeed any agricultural society. The profundity of that change may be measured by the fact that it took approximately ten thousand years for the global population to reach five billion in the late twentieth century. It will probably double again by the late twenty-first century.[90] As with agricultural productivity, industrialism broke the initial constraints that held populations in check. Industrialism opened the door to agricultural and demographic expansion, lifting some basic limits on food production, energy supplies and potential land use. But it has been capital, quite literally, which has mobilized that technology, has set ploughs (or rather tractors) to work, and paid the increasingly high incomes of the increasing numbers of Western consumers who have bought its products. Where capitalism has not done so, this agricultural and demographic explosion has not been accomplished by industrialism alone.

Externalities

The role of pesticides and fertilizers points to another specific ecological impact of industrialism: its incredible expansion of the numbers, volume and toxicity of externalities. Externalities are the costs of an economic transaction or productive process which are neither paid for in monetary terms nor experienced in environmental terms by those involved in the exchange.[91] They are passed on outside of the exchange to innocent third parties who must unwittingly and unwillingly bear the cost.[92] The vastly increased varieties of materials and production processes that have been made available by access to usable high-energy sources and the deployment of mechanization and theoretical science have brought with them a range of old by-products produced at new levels that induce environmental change and constitute environmental threats (carbon dioxide), as well as completely novel by-products that do so, often at quite infinitesimal concentrations: arsenic, mercury, radioactive compounds, nitrates, PCBs, phenols. The question remains: why has the release of dangerous chemicals into the environment been allowed? Moreover, we need to ask why those benefiting from these productive processes have not borne the cost of their release or the control of their emission. I would argue that there are cultural, economic and political forces at work.

If we recall the cultural and interpretive emphasis of the section on reconceiving societies and environments above, one reason for this absence of control is clear: it has not always been apparent that these by-products are being released at all. Even if it is known, then the consequences may not be clear. In contrast to the biological reach of preindustrial by-products, these new chemicals enter into the more inaccessible parts of ecosystems and ultimately into humans, with serious consequences for their health. They are lodged in animals, accumulate in water courses, are held within the soil or float out of sight in the atmosphere. However, if the consequences are known it does not necessarily follow that anything will be done about it. In any case, Western societies have put a great deal more technical effort and resources into developing the sophistication of production processes than in tracking their by-products.[93]

The origins of ignorance and inaction bring us to the political and economic elements of these processes: the same issues that we encountered in the abuse of unregulated common property in colonial New England or the sealing islands of the South Atlantic. The crucial point is not so much what gets commodified but, paradoxically, what does not. For in capitalist economies, as Giddens argues, the process of commodification and the establishment of markets become near universal for goods and services for most of the population. As such, those things that are not actually commodified, like the atmosphere, or rivers, or soil systems beneath the top soil, or the oceans, are in economic terms free goods with a zero price. *In the absence of any political or legal intervention* they will therefore be used as much as any economic actor wishes, because it does not, in any obvious economic way, cost actors anything to put sewage in the sea or CFCs in the atmosphere. Economic actors, in technical terms, externalize some of the costs of production. But while the consequence of commodification in New England was a failure to price the interests of future generations, in this more contemporary case there has also been a failure to price the current costs which are paid in a myriad of different ways by different people according to the environmental damage caused.

Finite Resources and Limits to Growth

None of this should suggest that industrial economies have permanently transcended the organic limits to growth of their predecessors. Rather, the final distinctive feature of capitalist-industrialism is the introduction of new limits and constraints to economic growth. Historically these have so far only been encountered as health hazards and localized if profound soil degradation, debilitating populations or making economically viable agriculture impossible. What awaits on the horizon are limits and constraints never before encountered, from a dizzying height of economic prosperity never before attained. The first limit is the finite quantity of inorganic energy supplies and raw materials on which industrialization relies. This alone is the distinctive and singular structural problem bequeathed to us by industrialization rather than any accompanying economic organization. Second, there is the release of toxins and the eradication of vegetation and fauna to the point where human health is deeply imperilled and the crucial biological cycles of ecosystems are fundamentally dislocated. Industrialism does not simply disrupt the functioning of ecological systems but can shift them so far from the point of dynamic, controlled equilibrium that their very capacity to continue is irretrievably destroyed. The advanced organic economy overstepped the limits of ecological equilibrium and on occasion completely transformed localized ecosystems. Industrialism appears to have the capacity to destroy the very possibility of a stable and sustainable equilibrium. These two problems are linked, for the burning of fossil fuels is the most important contributor to the most fundamental of environmental problems: global warming and climatic change. The point about capitalism, in this respect, is that it is hurtling towards those limits at a staggeringly fast pace. Moreover it is doing so under the aegis of a political economy that imposes profound structural limits on the capacity of modern societies to slow the pace of advance, let alone alter its direction. How these constraints and consequences might realize themselves are questions for chapter 5 and chapter 3 respectively. Here, though, I want to examine the contribution of political power to these processes in general and then look at the culpability of state socialism in particular.

Politics and Environmental Degradation in Capitalist Societies

So far, I have only hinted at the place of politics in the history of environmental degradation. We must now consider it more closely. On the one hand, Giddens has not made the role of political power in the causal origins of environmental degradation explicit. On the other hand, his model of capitalism developed in *The Nation-State and Violence* does make explicit the connections between economic structures and political power. He argues, for example, that the mutual dependency of antagonistic social classes locked within the same mode of production creates one of the major fault lines of political conflict in capitalist societies; and that there is an institutional bias of the state towards capital's interests on account of the state's structural dependence on revenues generated by the capitalist economy. Giddens's work is, therefore, not necessarily incompatible with pursuing the role of political power in the generation of environmental degradation. However, Giddens has not laid out in any systematic fashion the connections between politics under capitalism (or any other mode of production) and the trajectory of environmental degradation. This must be considered a serious limitation to his work. Finally, there are two further political issues that Giddens has not pursued and which I believe to be particularly important: the relationship between capitalism and democratic polities; and the implications of electoral and representative politics for the process of environmental degradation.[94] Thus a more systematic account of how politics in capitalist societies is implicated in the process of environmental degradation includes: (1) control over territory; (2) the regulation or not of property and markets; (3) the political control of externalities; (4) the political direction of economic policy, particularly the management of economic growth. I shall consider each in turn.

Political control over territory With regard to control over territory, capitalism has a geographical and historical tendency to outpace the reach of political control. New England Indians had been swept into the emerging networks of the international economy before they were made subject to colonial political and legal jurisdiction. However, the consolidation of the colonial economy ultimately required political and legal victory as well. Military coercion, when and where required, ensured that a capitalist system of property and exchange was built and maintained. The same is ultimately required in all capitalist economies. If private property is conceived as a bundle of rights held by an individual or organization over objects or pieces of territory, then those rights can only be maintained through political and legal control, especially if in economic terms others choose not to view or treat them as private property.[95] In this respect, the environmental impact of capitalism and industrialism stands on the politico-legal maintenance of private property and the associated rights of owners to transform that land in any way they please or find economically advantageous. Ultimately politics, not economics, determines what is a commodity, what is not a commodity and what rules of exchange apply.[96]

The political regulation of common resources and markets With respect to common resources, such as the available fur-bearing animals in Siberia or New England, the absence of direct political control, combined with the economic rationality of markets and profitability, are the causal mechanisms at work in environmental degradation. In a situation where there is no private property we have already argued that the rationality of competitive markets is such that each economic actor must use those resources to their greatest individual advantage as quickly as possible. The market is, in itself, blind to the problems of unsustainable extraction and the finitude of resources. The pricing mechanism only takes into account current levels of supply and demand. Futures markets introduce a certain temporal extension, in response to relatively short-term fluctuations, but are quite incapable of responding to long-term questions of absolute depletion.[97] In the absence of politico-legal intervention markets will not take account of that problem, until actual scarcity begins to bite. The fact that this will make more inaccessible reserves profitable to extract does not circumvent the problem of finitude itself. However, the absence of intervention does not mean that there is an absence of political activity. Rather, the continued exclusion of political control from the market and the economy often requires the utmost political exertion.[98]

The political regulation of externalities The problem of political non-intervention (and the political activity required to maintain it) also applies to the control of externalities. The political intervention required to detect the environmental implications of current economic action, to price them as externalized costs and to make polluters, taxpayers and/or consumers pay for them (or to introduce the appropriate regulatory regimes) is necessarily limited by the institutional alignments of the capitalist state. Giddens's arguments prove fruitful, if not surprising. For so long as polities rely on capitalist economies for their fiscal income, there are significant, if not insurmountable, pressures to limit the imposition of environmental costs on business.[99] Moreover, this structural constraint on the politics of prevention is enhanced by the occupation of key posts in the political and administrative elites of capitalist societies by those ideologically sympathetic to business interests.[100] We will return in more detail to the power of capital to shape political responses to environmental degradation in chapter 3.

The politics of growth and environmental degradation However, business interests are not the be all and end all of the problem. The political commitment to growth and the prioritization of economic interests over long-term economic effects and shorter-term health and aesthetic concerns have not been confined to capital and right-wing politics alone. Perhaps more importantly, the other dominant political forces within capitalist societies have for the most part been equally committed to economic growth. Social democracy embraced economic growth as a way out of its electoral dilemmas. For if redistribution of wealth and the funding of welfare services were to be achieved in societies where their imposition entailed direct and substantial confrontation with the economic interests of business, finance and large sections of the middle-class electorate, then economic growth allowed for a politically less painful division of the spoils.[101] The commitment to full employment in the postwar West by social democrats has made the pursuit of growth even more important. Combined with what Giddens calls 'the mutual dependence of capital and labour on the same system of production' and the existence of domestic and international competitive markets, the pursuit of growth has become even more environmentally problematic. For to penalize a business on environmental grounds is, in the context of the private ownership of capital and plant, to penalize the work-force as well. If a government penalizes one firm, it may become uncompetitive relative to other firms in the economy. If it penalizes all businesses equally, they may become uncompetitive relative to unregulated firms in the international economy. Capital may well move or shed jobs. Either way the short-term interests of social democracy's natural constituency are poorly served, both through reduced employment and diminished fiscal income. Thus the institutional alignment of the state in relation to economic growth and the direction of state policy face not only the interests of capital but have increasingly had to face the constraints of electoral politics. Not all capitalist societies have been democratic throughout their history, but it is somewhat surprising that Giddens has paid so little attention to this central element of their historical experience.[102]

Non-democratic capitalist polities have not had to address the peculiar demands of electoral politics. None the less, they have been forced to maintain political loyalties just the same. On occasion fierce nationalism and aggressive military expansion have served this end. Military expansion requires enormous economic development and offers an effective legitimation for unfortunate but necessary pollution. Where such an outward-orientated militaristic policy has been impossible or rejected, it seems clear that rising standards of living for a sizable part of the population combined with a good dose of domestic political repression are equally effective. This has hardly made these polities fertile ground for environmentally sustainable economics. Given then that growth, historically if not logically, has entailed increasing environmental degradation, an almost universal political commitment to it has been instrumental in nurturing capitalism's environmental destructiveness, limiting the interest of electorates in curtailing it, and stunting the capacity of governments to intervene environmentally in the production process.

The difficulty of environmentally regulating capitalist economies is in many ways rather unremarkable, and the constraints of electoral politics are well known. What is remarkable and of unique historical significance, is, first, that stiff environmental regulations have been enacted under capitalist democracies, and second, that mass political mobilization against the consequences of environmental degradation has occurred. Explaining political action and inaction in terms of environmentally problematic interests is theoretically fairly simple. What is substantially more complex is the explanation of political action in terms of ideals, and how, if at all, it has been possible to force environmental costs back on to business or to gain electoral support for policies that actively limit the environmental consequences of their actions. How and why industrial-capitalist societies have generated such a politics, somewhat against the odds, is of central importance in sociologically examining the history of environmental degradation, for it is with the emergence of new cultural values and moral perspectives that politics ceases to be simply an enabling condition of environmental degradation. Rather, politics may become an active brake on the process of environmental degradation. I shall take up those values and politics in the following chapter, where I shall consider Giddens's account of environmental movements, as well as in chapter 4, with Habermas's account of the structural origins of environmental politics.

Conclusion: State Socialism, Industrialism and Environmental Degradation

Where do these arguments leave Giddens's own account of environmental degradation? In *The Consequences of Modernity* he argued that industrialism was the central cause of contemporary environmental degradation. I believe that we can now conclude that industrialism, with the exception of problems related to unrestrained fossil fuel use, is not responsible *per se* for the contemporary world's environmental record. In attributing that record to industrialism, Giddens has mistaken structural and direct causality and underplayed the role of capitalism, demographics and politics. Industrialism has made qualitative and quantitative increases in environmental degradation possible for a number of reasons: its mobilization of enormous sources of manageable energy; the sophistication and transformatory power of the types of mechanized production it has made possible; the generation of potent new externalities. Thus it has transformed the ways in which modern societies directly interact with their environment. However, the actualization of these phenomena has been contingent rather than intrinsic. Just because one has the technological capacity to tear up large tracts of forest or destroy the fertility of soil does not mean that one automatically does it. Industrialism may well provide the potential for such transformations, but as one commentator has said of technology, it only 'opens doors'.[103] As Giddens himself persuasively argued (prior to *The Consequences of Modernity*), industrialism does not provide an explanation for the dynamic potential of modernity. It may causally determine some characteristics of the society within which it is deployed (division of labour, secular science, etc.), and even the characteristics of environmental degradation, but not their existence or levels. In this regard his more recent work is a step back from his earlier analysis in *The Nation-State and Violence*, where he argued that the conjunction of industrialism and capitalism was responsible for environmental degradation.

However, if the actualization of industrialism's potential for environmental degradation is contingent *in theoretical terms*, it is far less contingent *in historical terms*. Giddens was correct to argue for elective affinities between the development of capitalism and the emergence of industrialism. It is unlikely that industrialism would have emerged without the sorts of changes capitalism had generated in English society: resource shortages, mobile labour, an increasingly scientific culture, etc.[104] But more importantly from an environmental perspective, industrialism, as a *structural cause*, unleashed English capitalism from the organic limitations to which its own environmental destructiveness had brought it. Then, paradoxically, its technologies of production breathed new life into capitalism's voracious economic appetite and demographic and urban growth potential. In doing so, industrialism magnified the capacity of capitalism to discount the long term, produce externalities and overstep ecosystem fragility and resource finitude. Once the peculiarities of English capitalism had helped to generate industrialism, it was almost inevitable that industrialism itself would be caught in the maelstrom of accumulation.

The questions of science and state socialism remain. My own analysis suggested that industrialism requires the development of a theoretical science.[105] Moreover, I have argued for the importance of the way in which the environment is perceived as a contributory factor to the scale and scope of a society's environmental impacts. As such, we might still claim that industrialism is a structural cause rather than simply a direct cause of environmental degradation. It has been argued that there is an inevitable cultural correlation between science and highly instrumental attitudes to the natural and social worlds, and that the latter are a precondition of the acceptance of and enthusiasm for environmental degradation that industrial societies have shown.[106] However, instrumental attitudes to nature are not possessed exclusively by industrial societies. Indeed they are the historical rule rather than the exception. Few societies can have been as rapacious in their regard of the natural world as preindustrial Europe; what else would make cultural sense in agricultural societies so close to the edge of subsistence, so dependent on the vagaries of soil and climate?[107]

As with my remarks on politics, what is surprising is not that capitalist societies erect structural impediments to the cessation of environmental damage, or that industrial societies are dominated by instrumental attitudes to the natural world, but that despite this an environmental politics has been mobilized and that industrial societies and scientific cultures have developed, albeit falteringly, an account of the moral worth and aesthetic beauty of nature.[108] In fact, scientists have formed the intellectual avant-garde of that cultural shift every bit as much as those writing from a perspective deeply critical of science.[109]

A tougher test case remains for my arguments concerning industrialism. If capitalism, both economically and politically, is the main structural causal force actualizing the potentially environmentally destructive aspects of industrialism, and a scientific culture is at best an ambiguous cultural factor in encouraging it, how does such an analysis illuminate the appalling environmental record of the state-socialist economies from the late 1940s to the late 1980s?[110] What in those societies was responsible for driving economic and demographic growth in an ecologically unsustainable direction? State socialism both imported industrialism and drove it in a particular direction.[111] Although private property and profit did not exist in the same sense as in capitalist economies, there was certainly an equally obsessive concern with increasing levels of material production. Here, the spur was not of individual profit or the particular dynamics of the profit-investment cycle, but the politically orchestrated drive to industrialize backward economies. For the elemental facts about preindustrialized societies are their comparative political and military weakness and persistent, miserable poverty, both absolute and relative, for the vast majority of the population. Growth, therefore, was the key to two pressing political problems: satisfying public demand for comparable standards of living to the West; and achieving security by matching Western levels of military deployment.[112]

Despite their immense inefficiency, these economic regimes did achieve substantial rises in levels of industrial output and, grain imports into the Soviet Union notwithstanding, raised or maintained agricultural production to a level that supported substantially increased urban populations.[113] Industrialism had made those changes possible, but it was always mobilized and driven by the command economy that introduced it. The question is why did an economy unencumbered by the problems of capitalism so manifestly fail to curb the consequences of the industrialism it had nurtured? As with capitalism, the answers are both economic and political.

Given our emphasis on the importance of the absence of political control over economic decision-making, one might expect a society that has placed the latter so squarely beneath the former to have had the capacity to 'order' economic policy away from environmentally threatening behaviour. However, it would appear, despite political control over the pricing mechanism and investment decisions, and the state ownership of industrial infrastructure, that the demands of economic growth and military security overrode the need to price and take account of environmental costs, current and future.

Given their drive for growth, the planning systems of the socialist economies always made production the key criterion of success. As such, those positive economic incentives which existed were orientated to raising production. This is how the largest bonuses and incentives were made available to workers and management.[114] Given the inefficiencies of the system in matching supply and demand, in encouraging innovation, in using labour productively and ensuring quality, those few positive incentives to raise production assumed even greater importance than they might otherwise have done. Against that, demands that environmental impacts be minimized in the production process or accounted for in capital investment plans were minimal. Politics was no more influential in curtailing the environmental consequences of military activity. The size of the Soviet military, its enormous industrial base and its proclivity for environmental damage made its control almost as pressing an issue as control of the civilian economy.

The state ownership of common resources, rather than making possible the inclusion of common and future interests, has actively encouraged their overintensive usage. This was made particularly problematic by the absence of proper rental charges on land used by mining enterprises and an inability of enterprises to increase charges for products as the cost of extraction increased. There was, therefore, a tendency for those enterprises to extract resources until the cost of doing so matched the selling cost. As the latter could not be increased by the enterprise, it became economically logical to move on from one partially utilized mining strip to the next. So a great deal more land was damaged than was otherwise necessary.[115] Thus it is clear that the pricing system of a command economy is not necessarily more amenable to environmentally benign outcomes than that of market economies. Indeed, in their very disengagement from the realities of supply and demand in the real economy, bureaucratically determined prices may be even more environmentally problematic. Massive energy subsidies in Eastern Europe produced phenomenally inefficient levels of resource use. The failure to price raw materials accurately led the lumber industry of the Soviet Union into enormously wasteful harvesting methods because it did not pay the costs of the wood products wasted.[116]

The political and legal systems of state-socialist societies have been equally culpable. Where they have existed (and there was in fact a very large body of Soviet legislation on conservation and pollution), laws have never been enforced with the same vigour as production targets.[117] Disincentives were weak and fines for polluters substantially less than the bonuses for increased production; it therefore proved economically rational to pay the fines out of increased production rewards.[118] In any case, environmental regulations were only weakly enforced by the agencies responsible. The weakness of that response leads us to the central political causes of the problem.

Clearly, it was not in the interests of the political elites of these societies to 'burden' the industries they relied on with the control of externalities and the interests of future generations. And it was elites that were making these decisions. Studies of Soviet environmental policy suggest that, irrespective of environmental law and the creation of environmental agencies, it was the decisions made by party bodies rather than environmental bureaucrats that were most important. Given the already precarious financial state of many enterprises, demands that pollution abatement equipment be fitted and/or substantial fines with real economic bite be levied would only have hastened their decline.[119] The management of those industries and the environmental enforcement agencies had little interest in opposing those decisions and non-decisions. Where the latter attempted to regulate, they were often overridden by more senior bureaucracies closer to the heart of the economic planning system and the drive for growth.[120] In these respects they are little different from business interests in the West. However, what they did not have to contend with, and which perhaps explains in part their even more atrocious environmental performance, was a politically organized and electorally threatening opposition and an independent civil society. For if economic elites cannot be counted on to detect, monitor and oppose externalities, depletion and degradation, and if state regulatory agencies cannot be relied on to be impartial, then only the threat of electoral defeat and organized social protest can force their hand.

If the threat of the former and the strength of the latter are limited in capitalist societies, they were either absent in state-socialist societies after the Second World War, or orientated to other more basic issues, such as those of civil rights and economic well-being.[121] The control of environmental information, the repression of dissident political activity, the absence of any enforceable checks on the productive process, and, quite understandably, the centrality of other issues to the political movements that did emerge, have meant that the imbalance in capitalist societies between the contribution of politics to environmental degradation and its more limited capacity to halt it was replicated in state-socialist societies to an even greater degree. Capitalism and state socialism have been the *structural causes* at work in actualizing the worst environmental implications of industrialism and demographic expansion. They have, however, undoubtedly been facilitated by two shared characteristics: their inequitable distribution of political power, and an economic logic of unrestrained demand for public and private consumption.

2
Urbanism, Globalization and Environmental Politics: Anthony Giddens

Having argued that, alongside economic and demographic change, the struggle for and execution of political power may both facilitate and retard environmental degradation, I want to extend that analysis in two ways: by considering the spatial as well as the temporal dimension of environmental degradation; and by beginning to ask under what conditions political movements that limit environmental degradation are mobilized. I shall do so by examining Giddens's analyses of urbanism and globalization, which in turn have each generated differing explanations of environmental politics.

There are some points of clarification to be made. I noted that Giddens had distinguished between two types of environmental change: the material impact of 'the transformation of nature', and the cultural impact of living in a 'created environment'. While he had initially ascribed the transformation of nature to the conjunction of capitalist-industrialism, he then shifted his position; industrialism alone is now the key culprit. This shift has also been applied to the experience of the created environment and has underwritten Giddens's changing interpretations of urbanism, globalization and environmental politics. I shall argue that the cultural emphasis in his discussion of the created environment led Giddens to underplay the specific material environmental consequences of modern urbanism, while the shift in causal argument has left him with an implausible explanation of the cultural changes registered. Further, I shall argue that his analysis of urbanism leads him to abandon a spatial understanding of environmental degradation, and this is only partially redeemed by his discussion of globalization.

Space, the City and the Created Environment

The study of urbanism, geography and the created environment are not of incidental importance to Giddens.[1] Over the last decade he has argued that the spatial organization of social processes must be incorporated into social theory and that urban sociólogy, with its emphasis on spatial organization, is therefore of pivotal importance to the discipline.[2] Giddens has explored the spatial dimension of social processes in connection with two issues: the cultural and spatial consequences of the shift from social to system integration; and the sociological discontinuity between the premodern and the modern city. Thus the geographical elements of Giddens's work are intimately linked to his discussion of the cultural experience of the city.

From the Premodern to the Modern City

Giddens is concerned with the way in which agents reproduce social structures in time-space. Social integration refers to the reproduction of social systems through face-to-face interaction and is characteristic of premodern societies.[3] System integration describes the reproduction of structures by actors greatly separated in time and space. In premodern societies system integration is of secondary importance because social structures and practices are not stretched to any great extent across time-space. They are characterized by high levels of time-space routinization; people repeatedly do specific things, in specific places, at specific times. Time and place are therefore essential features of the social meaning of action, their regularity providing the material grounding of the recursiveness of social life.[4] Thus time-space routinization is a central element in the maintenance of the structures of tradition. For Giddens, the ontological security of tradition, a sense of an undisturbed and legitimate order to social life, is normatively grounded in the repetitive time-space paths of day-to-day life. This feature of the premodern world is destroyed by the advent of modern urbanism and the created environment.[5]

In *The Contemporary Critique of Historical Materialism* Giddens argues that the city in capitalist and class-divided societies possesses fundamentally different characteristics.[6] In class-divided societies the city acts as generator of 'effective space'. The conjunction and concentration of religious, administrative and military activities in cities made them containers of power. However, the associated rise of capitalism and the nation-state changes the city in three ways.[7] First, the main crucible of power, the specific geographical locale within which authoritative resources are generated, shifted from the city to the nation-state.[8] Second, the relationship between the country and the city, which formed the main axis of class and political organization in precapitalist societies, was effectively dissolved. The city's concentration of power was diffused across an entire nation-state encompassing both city and countryside, while simultaneously being centralized within the nation-state apparatus.[9] Thus: 'The development of capitalism has not led to the consolidation of the institutions of the city, but rather to its eradication as a distinct social form.'[10]

Third, the factors affecting the organization of urban space were fundamentally changed by the emergence of housing, product and labour markets. It is here that we return to the interaction of the natural and social worlds. For in class-divided societies, according to Giddens, 'The city sustained a close ecological integration with nature that almost completely disappears in much capitalist urbanism . . .'[11] The principal reason for the suppression of the natural features of modern cities is the commodification of space and time.

Here, Giddens picks up two separate, but interconnected, strands of social theory: the Weberian concern with the dissolution of tradition, and an account of the normative emptiness of modern life that characterizes theories of mass society.[12] In so doing he draws together his discussion of social integration and tradition with that of the changing nature of the city and the new relationships created between societies and the natural environment. Giddens argues that 'the transformations of labour and property that assume concrete form in the emergence of capitalist urbanism are the chief origin of a radical weakening of tradition . . .'[13] These commodifications resulted in human beings experiencing the natural world in fundamentally different ways. As Giddens points out, Marx's account of commodification not only describes a loss of control by workers over their labour, but also the way the intimate and meaningful relationships of human beings with the natural world achieved through their labour are destroyed. The meaning of natural forms of time, such as the seasons, is overturned by the imposition of commodified clock-time. The natural contours of the spatial environment are dissolved in the wholly manufactured 'created space' of modern cities. Thus large areas of the time-space organization of everyday life in modern societies are purely habitual, lacking any normative component. In Giddens's terms, ontological security is relatively fragile.

Giddens began by arguing that capitalist commodification produced the alienated created environment and that the rise of the capitalist nation-state eradicated the city as a distinct social form. His later work, however, shifts position. In the concluding remarks on capitalism and industrialism in *The Nation-State and Violence*, Giddens argues, somewhat cryptically: 'When connected to the pressures of generalised commodification, industrialism provides the means of radically altering the connections between social life and the material world. *The main mediator of this process is urbanism* . . .'[14] The created environment of modern urbanism would therefore appear to be the outcome of capitalism and industrialism. However, in *The Consequences of Modernity* and *Modernity and Self-Identity* the concept of urbanism hardly appears. What was once claimed to be an essential component of social theory no longer appears to be so central. The one concept that Giddens does continue to use is that of the created environment. In *The Consequences of Modernity* he argues that:

Industrialism becomes the main axis of the interaction of human beings with nature in conditions of modernity . . . In the industrialised sectors of the globe – and, increasingly, elsewhere – human beings live in a *created environment* . . . Not just the built environment of urban areas but most other landscapes as well become subject to human coordination and control.[15]

Capitalism, Industrialism and Urbanism

Thus, while this final argument is hardly fleshed out, it does suggest some shifts in Giddens's thinking. First, he appears to be ascribing the production of the created environment to industrialism, for it is industrialism that is transforming the natural world and thus producing the created environment. Second, within the category of the created environment he appears to be introducing a conceptual subdivision between the urban built environment and the non-urban created environment. Two questions arise from these arguments: (1) whether industrialism, capitalism or their combined impact is responsible for the production of the modern created environment and the dissolution of tradition; and (2) in what sense, if any, does urbanism act as the *mediator* of that process. At the same time we must assess the fruitfulness of these arguments in explaining the origins and geography of environmental degradation and environmental movements.

(1) In contrast to his later argument that industrialism, perhaps alone, or an urban mediated capitalist-industrialism, produces the created environment, Giddens initially and most persuasively argued otherwise: that the rise of the nation-state was responsible for the dissolution of the cities of class-divided societies as power containers, and, despite caveats, that capitalism's distinctive processes of commodification were the agents responsible for the alienated landscape of a created countryside and city alike. No argument of similar weight was offered in *The Consequences of Modernity* for industrialism as the responsible agent. This is not to suggest that Giddens's initial argument is correct. Rather, it is to say that he has yet to offer an alternative plausible account of the origins of the created environment, the transformation of the relationship between societies and their natural environments and the dissolution of tradition.[16] Moreover, he has yet to demonstrate what, if anything, distinguishes the created environment of modern cities from any other spatial location inside modern nation-states. If the city has been dissolved as a power container, subsumed within the created environment of the modern world, and made indistinguishable from the countryside, what is left of a distinctively urban milieu? As I noted above, he has introduced the notion of the urban built environment as a separate element of the created environment, but it has hardly been pursued in a systematic or satisfactory way. What after

all does *built* refer to in this context? Is he referring to the presence of humanly created structures? A ploughed and fenced field is as much a human-created structure as a shopping mall. This collapse of the urban in class-divided socieities into the created environment of modern societies may well be an accurate analysis of the geographical constitution of the latter. But if it is, it is so at the price of robbing Giddens's claims regarding the 'urban', and the importance of urban sociology, of any critical lever-age.[17] Urban sociology has thus been reduced to the study of the relation-ship of human beings with an all-pervading created environment in which spatial differences have become irrelevant.

(2) This problem could perhaps be remedied by an answer to our second, question, as to the sense in which the urban might be a mediator of the impact of capitalist-industrialism. This answer suggests that there are characteristics distinctive to urban locations. Demonstrating this requires a close investigation of the meanings of urbanism and mediation. We can suggest three possible meanings: (a) geographical, (b) cultural, and (c) causal. In terms of (a), Giddens could be arguing that the city or modern urban areas are the geographical locale in which the created environment is produced and within which the actual material operations of capital-ism, capitalist-industrialism, or industrialism alone, are conducted. In terms of (b), mediation could refer to the cultural experience of the creat-ed environment. The created environment is not simply experienced at a purely physical, material level but, as his discussion of the dissolution of tradition suggests, at a cultural and psychological level as well. Thus modern urbanism is the point at which the culturally transformed experi-ence of the natural world is most acutely felt. In terms of (c), Giddens could be suggesting that there are specific urban social relations which are causally important. The urban is not a passive container but actively inter-acts with, or mediates between, capitalism and/or industrialism in some way so as to produce an outcome that a non-urban capitalist-industrial-ism would not.

It would seem that (a), the urban as the geographical locale of the trans-formation of the natural world, is what Giddens has in mind. Giddens has argued that capitalist urbanism is the physical site of the wholesale trans-formation of the natural into wholly manufactured created space. But if we also accept his argument that the created environment so produced is everywhere, then this amounts to arguing that, whatever social processes are at work, they have wrought their effects all across the globe. In a broad and rather abstract sense Giddens seems to be correct. After all, none of the landscapes of modern societies are untouched by human action; the farmed countryside is every bit as transformed as the land on which cities stand. Yet there must be a nagging doubt here. Of what valid-ity is a theoretical concept that subsumes the West Midlands conurbation under the same heading as the Scottish Highlands?[18] In that perspective there is perhaps room for specifying a peculiar quality to the urban alone.

Giddens's notion of the built environment suggests that he has recognized this but has yet to deliver a convincing exposition of the essential qualities of the urban. I shall return to this below.

The meaning (b) of urban mediation, as a point of normatively denuded cultural experience rather than geographical location, also seems to hold. The ontological fragility and normative vacuum of modern life are not only experienced in the urban milieu but are closely related to the particular nature of capitalist urbanism: the transformation of time-space paths and the commodification of urban land. But, once again, we must ask where, geographically, is this occurring? If these features are synonymous with the created environment then it exists everywhere. In defining the created environment primarily in experiential or cultural terms, the environmental and material specificity of cities has been lost and significant spatial differences eradicated.

If two of the possible meanings amount to rather less than we might have expected, what of the possible meaning (c): that there are distinctive urban forms and social relationships that are analytically distinct from those of capitalist-industrialism, and that those urban relationships are responsible for the transformation of the environment? It would seem from Giddens's repeated emphases on the centrality of a distinctive urban sociology that such relations and causal impacts exist; why else should there be a separate urban sociology? Yet the advent of modernity has resulted in the eradication of the city as a distinct social form. What therefore remains is the created environment of urbanism, common to what were once the distinctive locales of city and country. Giddens does not wish to argue that such a situation is solely the result of the emergence of capitalism, and the conjunction of capitalism with a separable industrialism is pointed to as an additional causal factor. But, *the urban itself is put forward as a consequence of the process of modernization, and not in any active sense as a determinant of that process.* We must therefore conclude that Giddens, whatever his intentions, is unable to make mediation carry meaning (c). Thus the promise of a social theory that placed urban sociology at its centre has been somewhat undermined.

Returning to the utility of Giddens's arguments, I believe that the notion of the urban, as distinct from the rural or the countryside, is of relevance in explaining the nature of modern environmental degradation, and that it is in relation to capitalism and industrialism that it must be explored. However in order to do so, we shall have to move beyond his predominantly cultural or experiential understanding of the created environment and put some flesh on the suggestion that there is a distinctive urban built environment. I shall pick up on this in the next section. Further, Giddens's account of the dissolution of tradition has some value in explaining the origins of environmental social movements. I shall examine this later in connection with his most recent work on the concept of risk. Where his arguments seem to offer least, so far, is in exploring the spatial nature of environmental degradation. The rise of the nation-state and the created environment would appear to have annihilated significant spatial differences in the transformation of the natural world. I shall argue that it is important to include a spatial dimension in social theory and shall do so in connection with the notion of globalization.

Environmental Degradation and the City

Contrary to Giddens's position I wish to make two arguments: (1) that the urban remains a conceptually useful tool for interrogating the history of environmental degradation, rather than simply a way of interrogating the psychological relationship between modern life and its physical surroundings, because the urban can be distinguished from the all-encompassing notion of the created environment; (2) that the relative roles of industrialism and capitalism in bringing about this state of affairs need to be rethought and a cultural and political dimension introduced.

Recalling my 'nagging doubt', we need to ask what remains specifically urban within the modern created environment. Urban areas can be distinguished from a created environment by three features: a very high density of people involved in collective consumption and productive processes; the proximity of people and economic processes to each other; and the massively reduced presence of features of the natural environment.[19] Rather than distinguishing the urban on the basis of being a built environment alone, urbanism is a combination of demographic, spatial, ecological and economic components. Furthermore, I wish to argue, recalling the terminology developed in chapter 1, that urbanism generates *direct causes* of environmental degradation, setting the possible types of degradation and providing the geographical locale in which society–environment interactions are concentrated. However, we must also trace the *structural causes* of degradation, the institutional constraints and opportunities that explain why potential degradation is actualized in urban contexts and forms. I shall do so by examining the relative roles of capitalism and industrialism. I shall also be concerned with the origins of urban growth, for if the urban is defined in part in demographic terms then we must seek to explain urban expansion as well as urban degradation.[20]

Environmental Degradation in the Premodern City

If we turn back to the advanced organic economies of England and the Dutch Republic, we can examine some of the clearest examples of rapid, non-industrial urban growth. In seventeenth-century England we find a static agricultural labour force and a rapidly growing overall population. These are the demographic preconditions of urban growth. This process was fuelled by an equally sustained bout of growth in agricultural productivity, freeing people from the necessity, and indeed the option of, working on the land.[21] We know that an increase in productivity was accomplished through the development of capitalist agriculture. The reasons why the people so 'released' concentrated in cities, rather than migrating or spreading out across the countryside, are historically more opaque. None the less, concentrate they did and there is evidence to suggest that they were as a consequence beginning to endure the specific problems of urban environmental degradation. The mortality rate in the cities remained obstinately higher than that of the countryside throughout the period, reflecting problems of disease, sanitation and proximity to economic activities.[22] The distinctive environmental problem of the period, coal-burning, occurred primarily in London.

This simultaneously demonstrates why preindustrial cities experienced rather limited degradation and why industrial cities would experience much more severe environmental problems. Urban growth in an advanced organic economy was limited for the same reasons that the growth of the economy as a whole was limited. Population growth and migration into the cities would eventually be curbed by ecologically induced rising food prices and shortages. Thus, whatever the specific environmental consequences of capitalist-driven urban growth, those consequences were necessarily limited in a preindustrial economy. Cities would, like those of the Dutch Republic, shrivel demographically under the pressure of organic constraints.[23] However, from the 1650s onwards, Londoners responded to one of those ecological limits – the spiralling cost of firewood – by using Newcastle sea coal as a source of domestic heating and fuel for manufacturing processes.[24] In switching to coal, Londoners began to outstrip the organic constraints that might have held their city, demographically and environmentally, in check. This delivered a portent of an altogether more fearful type of specifically urban environmental problem. For coal (among other things) multiplied the potential for economic and urban growth, magnifying the intrinsic environmental problems of proximity and density in a predominantly built environment. It also introduced the novel problem of the release of hundreds of tons of dangerous carbon and sulphur compounds into the atmosphere and people's bodies.[25] Once again, industrial energy sources had unleashed an organic capitalism; they were in turn unleashed on the enormously larger cities created by the capitalism those sources had rescued, magnifying old problems and creating distinctively new ones.

Environmental Degradation in the Nineteenth-Century City

In examining these changes I am going to focus on the record of nineteenth-century Western cities, where some of the most distinctive environmental consequences of modern urbanism can be demonstrated. In so doing we can disentangle the specific roles of urbanism (high density, proximity and a reduced natural ecosystem) from capitalism and industrialism, and emphasize the particular role of politics and culture in urban environmental history. Two direct urban causes of environmental impact, combining demographic, geographical and economic elements, suggest themselves. Reflecting Giddens's earlier insistence on industrialism's separation of the domestic sphere from the work-place, they are the consumption of housing and fuel, and factory production.

The central fact about the industrial cities of the nineteenth century was their explosive demographic growth, crowding people at densities and in absolute numbers of almost total historical uniqueness. That level of human congestion, when combined with the particular pattern of housing, spatial organization and consumption, resulted in a range of novel or greatly expanded environmental problems. These pressures bore heavily on what little was left of natural ecosystems within the built environment. Turning to consumption first, we have already noted the environmental problem created when coal as a source of domestic heating is combined with high population densities: intense and life-threatening atmospheric pollution. By the 1870s London was consuming over 18 million tons of coal a year, while 200 tons of soot a day damaged buildings and increased the incidence of respiratory disease.[26] The burning of coal also made hygienic conditions more difficult to achieve, contributing to the spread of pathogenic micro-organisms. Finally, coal smoke blocked out the sun and thus contributed to the spread of rickets. On the one hand, this appears to be a form of industrial environmental degradation since it is caused by the consumption of an inorganic energy supply – coal. However, the enormous expansion of coal consumption and its concentration in dense and expanding cities was fuelled by the expansion of a successful capitalism.

Equally important direct causes of environmental problems were the consumption of housing and food and the problem of sanitation. The latter is the most fundamental problem of high-density, stationary living: the relentless accumulation of human excreta and the by-products of consumption. Not only do these constitute a physical obstruction but, if not properly dealt with, pollute what remains of the ecosystem in a city and/or create new micro-habitats for a range of pathogenic micro-organisms, insects and mammalian vermin. It is hardly surprising, therefore, that the environment of the industrial city was so profoundly unhealthy, with its polluted water supplies and streets, cesspools, saturated land, garbage dumps and dirty human bodies.

The problems that both sanitation and garbage presented were magnified and complicated by the enormous presence of animals in industrial cities, ironically at higher densities and absolute numbers than in preindustrial cities. Huge numbers of cows, pigs and sheep and their accompanying pathogenic micro-organisms were driven through the cities and kept in urban markets.[27] Horses, although properly considered under the sphere of production, were synonymous with the newly industrialized city as a means of personal, commercial and public transport. Moreover, in the absence of the motor car they were indispensable. The railways and the physical expansion of cities had generated an enormous increase in trade and the demand for personal transport, but railways could not serve, for the most part, as a means of transport within cities.[28] Thus the horse population of cities actually spiralled with the initial advent of industrialization. Each horse produced some three to four tons of dung each year and around twenty gallons of urine every day. In addition, large numbers of animals were kept on a private and commercial basis within cities.

All these problems, with the exception of coal-burning, are common to preindustrial cities. They were all considerably magnified in the industrial city, which, having unleashed capitalism, reaped the dubious harvest of massive and rapid expansion in numbers and density. That growth, when combined with a specifically capitalist organization of urban space, ensured that expansion would result in longstanding environmental problems. Overcrowding and sanitation problems, for example, cannot, in themselves, be traced to industrialism alone; rather they were the consequence of a number of separate phenomena: a private and unregulated market in housing and land; the recurring problem of zero-priced environmental goods; the environmental dilemma of the economic free-rider; and the inapplicability of market mechanisms to the provision of public goods.

The working class and urban poor, who bore the brunt, if not the entirety, of the environmental problems in industrial cities had to consume whatever housing was available.[29] The housing stock that was available was rented by landlords interested, not surprisingly, in profit rather than in the provision of a service. Landlords therefore preferred the largest number of tenants possible at the highest rents in the smallest space, rather than healthy occupation rates or the provision of expensive and extensive water supplies and sanitary disposal methods. The first sanitary measures to be deployed simply involved pouring accumulated garbage into whatever water course was available – a zero-priced good that, if unregulated, would be used, as much as possible, by everyone. A great many people then paid the price of drinking and washing in contaminated water.[30]

Even if one landlord supplied WCs, against their immediate economic interests, there was no guarantee that other landlords would follow or that a network of sewers could be established to service them. Therefore, in the absence of political coercion or the public provision of goods, there was neither incentive for the provision of these services nor very much impact resulting from their sporadic implementation. Similarly, even if one street could pay for the removal of garbage by private contractors, there would be a limited environmental gain if streets around it did not follow suit.[31] Given that living standards of the working class did not permit such expenditures it is hardly surprising that most streets continued to live in a deep layer of their own garbage. Clearly, the provision of public services and public goods runs against the grain of the interests established in unregulated markets. No individuals are going to build sewers for themselves, while the benign environmental impact of their creation is radically diminished if they are built in the private sector and only made available to those who can or choose to pay.[32] Tracking the *structural causes* of environmental degradation has brought us to the importance of political intervention and, more often than not, its absence.

Urban production is a good example of the problem of industrialism's new externalities combined with capitalist economics. However, when these factors are combined with the enclosed factory working space and the problems of concentration and proximity, they create a novel form of urban environmental degradation. The nineteenth-century industrial city, in contrast to the preindustrial city, was marked by a much greater accumulation and concentration of old industries, the productive techniques of which had been transformed, and also entirely new industries. They released old and new pollutants at high volumes into the atmosphere, into water courses and eventually into human bodies. This had devastating health consequences and, in terms of productivity, severe economic consequences. These effects were made much worse by the intense geographical concentration of industries, the proximity of pollutants to workers inside the factory and their external proximity to densely packed populations. Arsenic was widespread in productive processes and consumer products, particularly printing, confectionary manufacture and paint-making. Matchmakers inhaled huge quantities of the necrotic phosphorous. Mercury was absorbed during the manufacture of barometers and mirror silvering. Lead was widespread in glass manufacture and paint production. Cutlery grinders breathed metal fragments, coal miners suffered silicosis, bleachmakers worked in a cloud of chlorine.[33]

These toxins spilled over into residential areas. That proximity was the consequence of the commodification of urban space. The absence of political control from the patterning of residential and industrial areas, combined with market prices, ensured that those working in the factory environment would also live in its shadow.[34] The steel industry released toxic phenols, benzene, tars, iron files and acids into rivers.[35] Paper mills flushed away sodium carbonate and lime. Slaughterhouses and their associated industries of glue manufacture, tanneries and canneries expelled fats and carcasses. Everything that required energy belched smoke from coal-burning into the air.[36]

Thus Giddens's notion of urbanism can only be made useful in investigating environmental degradation if, instead of cultural or psychological experience, we stress the importance of demography, density and proximity. This has allowed us to distinguish the urban from the created environment and to suggest how urbanism generates the *potential* for certain types of environmental degradation. Turning to the reasons why that potential was actualized, a more detailed historical investigation reveals that industrialism served first to unleash an organically constrained phase of capitalist-driven urban growth. Once unconstrained it has been the dynamics of capitalism, aided by the exercise of political power, that has *actualized* the environmental potential of unconstrained demographic growth and new economic processes in a spatially limited environment. Space therefore matters in environmental degradation. Moreover, Giddens's shift, in his most recent work, to industrialism as the root cause of contemporary environmental problems is undermined. I shall explore these last two points in connection with Giddens's discussion of globalization.

Globalization and the Historical Geography of Environmental Degradation

In this section I set out why a geographical approach is so important to any study of environmental degradation. Simply put, it matters where environmental degradation is generated and where it is experienced, what the physical constitution of the environment, created or otherwise, is, and how these differences overlap with social boundaries. On the basis of that analysis I shall argue that Giddens's account of globalization (an inherently geographical concept) is useful in explaining contemporary environmental degradation but retains a number of important limitations.

The constitution of the natural environment is spatially variable: flora, fauna, climate, soil, hydrology, all vary across space. The importance of this unremarkable observation is that the types of environmental degradation that an area can undergo and the consequences will be spatially variable. A semi-arid area will always be plagued by problems of water shortage and pollution more insistently than a temperate ecosystem. Boreal and desert ecosystems are more fragile than forests and can be disrupted at a lower level of human intervention. The capacity of a given area to retain air pollution will be related to its geological form and climate. Finally, despite their interconnections, ecosystems can and have developed in a degree of isolation from each other, caused by, for example, continental separation or sharp changes in geological forms. As a consequence, their internal constitutions can be astonishingly different and bringing them together at a pace faster than that of natural evolution can and does introduce the sharpest of ecological changes. Thus any sociology of environmental degradation must begin from a sound appreciation of the geographical variety of ecosystems.

Geographical difference becomes more important when one recognizes that the origins and consequences of environmental degradation may not share the same location. This has environmental and social causes. The materiality of the environment and the nature of the cycles that operate within it ensure that pollution, above all else, can be transmitted from its point of creation. Air pollution is carried by the wind, water pollution spreads itself throughout the hydrological cycle, heavy metals move and accumulate through the food chain. Similarly, while the origins of global warming are concentrated in the West, the climatic disruption it brings will not be predominantly experienced there. The environmental costs and economic benefits of economic activity are not equally distributed in space. The implications of demographic movements can also be lopsided when a swift transcendence of long-term ecosystem separation takes place, witness the exchange of micro-organisms between Europeans and indigenous Americans.

These spatial variations are not simply a consequence of underlying environmental differences, but also of uneven social processes. Giddens's discussions of system integration, regionalization and time-space edges acknowledge as much. However, we need to be more specific in describing what is uneven, why it is uneven and what level of geographical analysis we are considering. If my analysis so far has been correct then we need to examine the uneven spatial distribution of populations, types of economic activity and economic and political power. We should discuss this unevenness in the contemporary world in relation to the urban–rural divide, economic regions, nation-states and the major political and economic divisions of the world order of nation-states, such as the North–South divide and developed versus developing world. Explaining differences in economic and political power will allow us to understand why some areas take decisions with environmental consequences without necessarily experiencing those consequences, and conversely why other areas are powerless to prevent this happening. This is all the more important because the geography of environmental degradation is often only tenuously connected to social and jurisdictional boundaries. Pollution flows across nation-state boundaries; common environmental resources such as rivers straddle lines of sovereignty.[37]

The question remains why these social and environmental processes are so unevenly distributed. Here I only wish to touch on what is, after all, an enormous and complex topic. I am therefore going to focus on Giddens's account of world history and the globalization of the institutions of modernity to see if this will provide some purchase on the question. In confrontation with the model of world development offered by historical materialism and realist international relations, Giddens has attempted to theorize the interaction of different social orders and social types in time and space. His focus has been the dynamics of Western expansion, tracing the global spread of the institutions of modernity over the last five centuries. With regard to capitalism he notes that it is not the first social order to introduce a novel range of intersocietal connections. Class-divided societies and their empires had been interacting with tribal societies for many centuries before, but 'capitalism for the first time in human history initiates the creation of an inter-state system that is truly global in scope.'[38] However, the economic order ushered in by capitalism cannot be conceptualized separately from its original and continuing military and political dimensions, for 'the conjunction between the rise of capitalism and the absolutist state system produced a system of nation-states that . . . is integral to the world capitalist economy – which is at one and the same time a world military order.'[39]

This multidimensional approach to intersocietal relations in the modern world has been given a more specific form by Giddens, first in *The Nation-State and Violence* and amended in *The Consequences of Modernity*, where his adaptation of world systems theory has given way to a distinct concern with globalization.[40] In the former work, Giddens characterizes the current world system in terms of four interrelated phenomena: the global information system, the nation-state system, the world capitalist economy and the world military order. The economic system is marked not only by the global reach of international commodity markets but by the spread of international systems of production and finance, spreading patterns of accumulation, wage labour, debt, credit and trade. Giddens identifies transnational corporations and the separation of economy and polity in the capitalist core as the key agents of this process. This has been facilitated by the spread of the nation-state as the dominant geopolitical form and the simultaneous emergence of an interstate world system, in which the boundaries and sovereignties of those states have been reflexively monitored and managed. In withdrawing the political from the economic, the nation-state has unleashed the potential geographic reach of international corporations to markets beyond its borders; it has functioned to nurture capitalism at home and has accompanied its spread outwards through the mobilization of industrial power and military force in colonial enterprises.[41]

Giddens returns to this subject in *The Consequences of Modernity* and *Modernity and Self-Identity*, where he links globalization to industrialism and environmental degradation. This argument draws heavily on the concept of time-space distanciation and the idea of systems integration. He writes: 'Globalisation can thus be defined as the intensification of worldwide social relations which link distant localities in such a way that local happenings are shaped by events occurring many miles away and vice versa. This is a dialectical process because such local happenings may move in an obverse direction . . .'[42] Thus, once historically established, the structural essence of globalization is not simply that social structures and process are organized and co-ordinated across the globe, but that the impact of highly localized events can have dramatic causal impacts right around the world. By the same token, global scale changes can interact with and affect the smallest localities in any geographical area.

Once again Giddens considers the process in terms of four institutional dimensions. The analysis remains unchanged for the political, military and economic, but given the increasingly prominent role he has ascribed to industrialism, he subsumes the global information system of his earlier model beneath the rubric of a globalized industrialism. This generates an international division of labour, technologically transformed systems of communication and the spread of machine technologies in general. Thus the impact of industrialism is not limited to the sphere of production alone, but 'affects many aspects of day-to-day life, as well as influencing the generic character of human interaction with the material environment'.[43] That interaction is hardly benign. Not only is the natural world completely incorporated into the dynamics of the social world as one vast created environment, but 'the diffusion of industrialism has created "one world" in a more negative and threatening sense . . . a world in which there are actual or potential ecological changes of a harmful sort that affect everyone on the planet.'[44] My concerns are twofold: what light do these arguments shed on the geography of environmental degradation; and do they theoretically illuminate the environmental degradation that the globalization of Western institutions has brought about?

Let us consider the spatial dimension first. Giddens's understanding of globalization as the linking of macro- and micro-level social change is an accurate description of contemporary global-level environmental problems. Pollution generated in one specific location can have effects across the planet. Similarly a global-level shift in climatic patterns can and does impact on particular unfortunate localities. However, if my discussion of the spatial organization of environmental degradation is correct, then the contrast of global and local is an insufficiently precise conceptual pairing to grasp the full geography of contemporary environmental problems. Not all parts of the world contribute equally to the globalization of environmental problems and not all parts of the world receive equal levels of environmental degradation. Both are uneven. While not wishing to diminish the importance of global-scale problems, it is essential to look at unevenness within the global system.

That said, these arguments are probably not incompatible with Giddens's position. His discussions of the geographical divisions of the world in *The Nation-State and Violence* were marked by a concern with the inequalities of the world military and economic orders.[45] The discussion of the military, while perfectly valid in its own terms, is unsuitable for our purposes. Our concern is not primarily with the inequitable distribution of military power (now somewhat different from when Giddens was writing), since it does not necessarily correspond to the geography of environmental degradation. The power relations within the world economic order may have been a useful starting point for discussing the unevenness of environmental issues. None the less, Giddens did not pursue this tack; and in *The Consequences of Modernity* this route of explanation has been discarded. For while capitalism remains an important component of globalization, industrialism appears as an institutional order in its own right, generating ecological problems and its own international division of labour. Here, I believe, my arguments are not compatible with Giddens's position. I shall argue that Giddens's notion of a globalized industrialism simply cannot explain the initial spread of industrial technology, its subsequent organization into an international division of labour or the current forms of global environmental degradation.

Industrialism, outside its Western heartlands, was always actively imported and actively driven by local social forces and political institutions. This was accomplished first by colonial powers – albeit in highly uneven and inequitable forms – and then by independent postcolonial nation-states. The latter possessed economic systems that were either capitalist, with differing forms and degrees of state involvement (contrast Singapore with India), or state socialist (China).[46] Thus the emergence of a global industrialism must be explained with reference to the dynamics of both capitalist expansion and (as in the case of the former Soviet Union) defensive industrialization, orchestrated by national political elites. Similarly, the emergence of new technologies and industrialized systems of transport and communication may make possible a global network of production and an international division of labour, but it has only been actualized by the activities of multinational corporations and by politically orchestrated trading and investment relations.[47]

Though it is not directly discussed by Giddens, we still might infer from his argument that environmental unevenness could be explained in terms of differential rates of industrialization across the globe and different positions of industrialized nations within the international division of labour. I have, however, already argued that industrialism, once it has released economies from organic constraints, generates direct causes of environmental degradation that, along with population changes, are driven by the exercise of economic and political power. As such I find it implausible to suggest that industrialism *per se* is responsible for global environmental degradation.

Both the spread and current functioning of a global industrialism can only be explained by reference to other elements of the global social order. In any case Giddens's argument, on a positive reading, would tell us only where the industrial agencies of environmental degradation were located rather than where its consequences were experienced. Nor could it explain the current distribution of world population, which is a significant contributor to the extent of local pollution as well as to global environmental problems. I shall return to the uneven environmental implications of the global economy in chapter 3.

The Geography of Environmental Degradation and Environmental Politics

In this final section of the chapter I want to sketch a few points concerning Giddens's account of environmental politics and political movements. In general, his work on environmental degradation and ecological problems has given too little emphasis to political factors. His account constitutes little more than a sketch of the rise of environmental movements.

However, the range of political actors engaged in environmental politics is infinitely wider. In the case of urban environmental issues in the nineteenth century, it involved industrialists, trade unionists, ratepayers' organizations, etc. The outcome of their political struggles determined, at least in part, the environmental impact of market-driven, industrial and demographic agencies: the regulation or not of markets (control of food quality); the existence or not of urban planning and regulation (limiting industrial concentration); the pricing, control, prohibition or not of externalities and free goods; the provision or not of public goods such as infrastructure and services (provision of sewerage systems, water supply, garbage collection and disposal, bath houses).[48] In this sense the history of environmental degradation is at one and the same time the history of environmental politics and struggles, not simply of economic, demographic and technological change.

It is also a cultural history. Giddens has acknowledged as much in emphasizing the role of knowledge in the transformation of the environment.[49] But it would appear he is mainly, if not exclusively, talking about the impact of knowledge as technology. There are also other kinds of knowledge which impact on the environment, for example the way in which the epidemiology of disease was understood. One has to know that cholera is water-borne for the disease to be taken into account as an issue in the provision or not of water services. The fact that despite that knowledge water services were not instantly built attests to the importance of the differential power of different interests in environmental politics. Similarly, it was not only the resistance of capital and landlords to costs and taxes, or of local government to central government interference, that helped extend the reach of environmental damage. For years, smoke was associated directly with economic prosperity, rather than regarded as a painful cost to bear.[50]

None the less, within the limits of his work Giddens has offered two explanations of the rise of an environmentally orientated politics. Simply put, the created urban environment, originally the outcome of capitalist-industrialism, produced environmental movements born of the cultural alienation and spiritual vacuum that the contemporary urban landscape generates. In his more recent work this landscape is the product of industrialism alone, while the extended geographical reach of degradation in modern societies is ascribed to the globalization of industrialism. Under this scenario, environmental movements are primarily a response to the increased presence and perception of high-level material threats and risks that unchecked global industrial expansion has generated. I want to consider these arguments in more detail before summarizing my conclusions.

Environmentalism as a Response to Cultural Alienation

The causal pluralism of the four institutional dimensions of modernity was linked in *The Nation-State and Violence* to a political pluralism.[51] Each dimension throws up a distinctive type of social movement in response to the demand for a particular set of rights, and in the context of a particular crisis tendency, none of which can claim moral, structural or transformative primacy. In the case of industrialism and the created environment it produces, the demand is for moral imperatives in the face of a crisis of anomie.[52] Giddens appears to be suggesting that the alienating effects of the created environment of modern urbanism give rise to a crisis of anomie, although he is somewhat vague as to what precisely that constitutes. Though they are not directly discussed, he seems to be pointing to the cultural and psychological consequences of the dissolution of tradition and the suppression of many of the relationships to the natural world that premodern societies allegedly sustained. In the absence of those relationships, ecological social movements are orientated towards a recovery or a recreation of such alternative values and meanings, as well as the limitation of ecological threats. It is interesting that Giddens should argue that, in demanding the reshaping of the created environment, ecological movements are primarily a response to the impacts of industrialism, for this sits uneasily with the earlier, stronger argument: that the created environment and its moral vacuum are not simply the product of industrialism, but that rather capitalism and commodification are the key offenders.

There is, as I argued in chapter 1, an important moral-aesthetic component of environmental politics. Giddens had rightly highlighted this. I must however question his account, which turns on the contrast between the organic-natural experience of the premodern landscape and the alienated experience of the created environment in the modern world. I believe he has overstated the contrast between the cultural experience of individuals and their perception of the environment in the premodern and the modern worlds. That is not to disagree that the landscape of the modern city may often be alienating and day-to-day life within it morally denuded. Rather it is to emphasize the degree to which the natural world was profoundly alien or threatening for premodern human beings and to highlight the quite palpable truth that the modern city has also been an exhilarating civilizing landscape in which people have felt deeply at home.[53] Cities have, on occasion, also been bound by ties of community and civic pride of immense solidity.[54] Given the interpretive thrust of the theory of structuration, it is surprising that Giddens has been prepared to let such broad brushstroke descriptions rest at the level of theoretical speculation alone. The definitive argument for or against his position must rest with a careful interpretation of the actual experience of cities. At best the evidence for Giddens's argument is ambiguous.[55]

Environmentalism as a Response to Risk Perceptions

It is perhaps due to the degree of overstatement in his original argument that Giddens has subsequently changed his analysis of the origins of environmental movements. The account of ontological insecurity and the denuding of everyday life of its normative content has been replaced by the more broadly conceived arguments of *The Consequences of Modernity* and then reworked once again in *Modernity and Self-Identity*.[56] In both, the influence of Ulrich Beck's work on risk and the risk society is particularly important. In chapter 5, I will return to Beck's work. For the moment I shall consider the arguments of each of Giddens's texts in turn.

In *The Consequences of Modernity* insecurity is the product of the modern world's risk profile – the range and types of life-threatening problems that are characteristic of modern societies – rather than of the alienated urban environment. It is also the product of the ways in which post-traditional societies cognitively attempt to cope with that risk profile. The modern world's risk profile includes the threat of massive ecological problems, which Giddens claims have become globalized and thus increasingly problematic. The perception of those ecological problems has been transformed for three reasons. First, it has been transformed because of the *awareness of risk as risk*. By this Giddens means that the counterfactual possibilities with which modern societies are faced cannot be eradicated or sidestepped by the certainties of an unreflexive religious world-view. Second, it has been transformed because of the *well-distributed awareness of risk*. More human beings have greater access to a great deal more information about environmental problems, which reveals the risks they face with greater clarity. Third, the perception of risk has been transformed because of the *awareness of the limitations of expertise*. There exists a general recognition that expert systems of knowledge, however expert, are incapable of predicting the multiple unintended consequences of their actions: for example, environmental degradation.[57]

On the basis of this analysis, Giddens's explanation of the origins of environmental movements shifts. He now assigns primacy to the problem of ecological threats themselves and to their perception, and downplays the alienating effects of the created environment that he had previously emphasized. Ecological movements reflect 'the heightened awareness of high-consequence risks which industrial development, whether organised under the auspices of capitalism or not, brings in its train'.[58] Thus it would seem that an interest in environmental survival, nurtured by a transformation of the way in which the public perceives environmental problems, is the main causal factor in the emergence of environmental movements.

In *Modernity and Self-Identity* Giddens has developed these arguments and in so doing has combined the causal role of ideals and interests. Thus it is fair to say that he has actually produced a third model of the causal origins of environmental movements. Giddens places the politics of the environmental movement in the context of a broader swathe of new social movements and political agendas, which he refers to as life politics:

> life politics concerns political issues which flow from processes of self-actualisation in post-traditional contexts, where globalising influences intrude deeply into the reflexive project of the self, and conversely where processes of self-realisation influence global strategies.[59]

The emergence of a socially constructed but increasingly reflexive sense of self is the basis of this type of politics. In a post-traditional world, Giddens argues, the question of how one should live is incessantly posed by the conditions of modern existence. Therefore, environmental politics is not simply the outcome of increasingly perceived environmental risk. It is also fuelled by an increasing demand for the remoralization of abstract systems of social organization that have ceased to be accountable in any meaningful way to those they affect.[60] Thus, while acknowledging the importance of the risk of material threats in the emergence of the environmental movement, Giddens argues that 'much more decisive . . . are the alterations in human attitudes relevant to the issue.'[61] Those attitudes have been shaped by the spread of specialized ecological knowledge, the recognition of globalizing forces penetrating and transforming local environments and the understanding that contemporary (Western) lifestyles are instrumental in generating that environmental degradation.

Giddens is on stronger ground here than in his earlier attempts to explain the origins of environmental movements. His emphasis on the impact of an increasingly wide understanding of ecological issues is probably correct. Furthermore, I think he is correct in arguing that the emergence of the environmental movement must be explained by a combination of changing interests, commitments to new moral ideals and the impact of new cognitive interpretations of the impact of human activity on the environment. However, I am uncertain about the centrality of risk perceptions in the emergence of environmental politics. A great deal of environmental activism has been motivated not by the possibility of future environmental damage but by two other situations: protest arising from the experience of actual environmental damage (for example anti-airport expansion groups), or from the certainty of future environmental damage (proposed road-building plans). Even if we allow that the perception of environmental risk is a significant factor in the emergence of environmental movements, Giddens does not really help us to explain why only a very specific segment of Western publics are sufficiently moved by the perception of risk to engage in environmental politics. Why, given the social composition of the environmental movement, do the middle classes perceive risk more acutely and/or act on it more readily? In any case, it is one thing to identify the broad lines of political motivation, but another to explain their crystallization into actual social movements. Giddens's sketchy account of environmental politics leaves this issue unaddressed.

Conclusions

In this chapter I have examined four aspects of Giddens's work: (1) the importance of a spatial understanding of social processes in general and environmental degradation in particular; (2) the origins and environmental consequences of modern urbanism; (3) the origins and environmental consequences of the globalization of the institutions of modernity; (4) the ways in which both (2) and (3) have led Giddens to propose differing explanations of the origins of environmental movements. I am now in a position to offer some conclusions.

First, I believe that Giddens was right to place the question of space at the centre of social theory. However, it would appear that Giddens's proclaimed intention – to place urban sociology at the centre of social theory – is not a necessary condition of doing so. His own analysis of urbanism, while generating the useful concept of the created environment, did not sufficiently distinguish between the urban built environment and the created environment in general that exists under conditions of modernity. Nor did it manage to unearth specifically urban social relations. As such, the most plausible element of his understanding of urbanism – as the cultural and psychological relationship between human beings and the created environment – could not be located in any specific geographical locale. Giddens's powerful interpretation of the rise of the nation-state and the dissolution of the city resulted in the differing spatial locales of the premodern city and countryside being dissolved into the general notion of the created environment. Although hinting at the existence of a distinct urban built environment, that distinction was never substantiated.

My analysis of the urban as a geographically specific combination of demographic, economic, ecological and spatial factors was designed to transcend this impasse in his work. It also allowed me to specify, with greater accuracy than Giddens, the relative roles of industrialism and capitalism in actualizing the environmentally damaging potential of modern urbanism: industrialism unleashed the capitalist-driven urban growth of the advanced organic economy from its ecological limits. In so doing, it is the institutional dynamics of a capitalist economy that has shaped the environmental consequences of industrialism within urban locations. This has led to the magnification of older environmental problems and the creation of new ones. What made these environmental problems peculiarly intense was the combination of capitalism and industrialism with the essential elements of the urban: density of human beings, proximity of human beings to productive processes and the scarcity and vulnerability of what little remained of the natural ecosystems within the urban environment.

However, our analysis of those processes revealed that the environmental consequences of capitalism and industrialism cannot be understood separately from the impact of political and cultural struggles. It is also worth noting that Giddens has not pursued the likely consequences of environmental degradation beyond possible threats, perceived risks and the emergence of environmental politics. While these are not unimportant, Giddens's emphasis on these impacts tends to obscure the degree to which environmental degradation is currently having major socioeconomic consequences for many people, rather than simply posing a high-risk consequence at some point in the future. I shall take up these limits in chapter 3 through an analysis of the work of André Gorz. Gorz has placed the dynamic interaction between economics and politics at the heart of his account of environmental degradation and its broad socioeconomic consequences.

Giddens's analysis of globalization proved a more robust framework for considering the spatial dimension of social processes and structures. Thus my analysis of space and environmental degradation proved compatible with, rather than contradictory to, Giddens's approach. Where Giddens's work was at its weakest was in the claim that the globalization of industrialism was responsible for a global division of labour, the global diffusion of technologies and global environmental problems. In contrast, I argued that these phenomena cannot be understood by reference to industrialism alone.

Finally, we come to Giddens's analysis of the origins of environmental politics. As I suggested at the beginning of the chapter, Giddens offers two explanations of the emergence of environmental social movements. The first derives from his analysis of urbanism and emphasizes the causal importance of cultural alienation and unfulfilled ideal demands. The second derives from his analysis of globalization and risk, and emphasizes the causal importance of material interests in environmental survival. Both, as I argued above, have limitations. However, as we have seen, in *Modernity and Self-Identity* the two arguments seem to be combined in a description of a broader life politics motivated by material interests in environmental survival and by a demand for the remoralization of the relationship of humanity to a commodified and morally denuded natural world. Rather than attempt to judge these different theories and the relative weight of interests, ideals and cognitive understandings of environmental change, I shall pick up the origins of environmental politics again in chapter 4 in connection with the work of Habermas, while in chapter 5 the work of Ulrich Beck will provide a powerful counterpoint to Giddens in his writing on risk, environmental degradation and environmental politics.

3
The Political Ecology of Capitalism:
André Gorz

In considering Giddens's work I argued that he underplayed the role of
politics in creating and forestalling environmental degradation, and that,
apart from the development of environmental social movements, he did
not explore the broader socioeconomic consequences of environmental
degradation. In dealing with these topics I now wish to turn from the historical slant of chapters 1 and 2 to examine the interrelation between politics, economics and environmental degradation in contemporary capitalist
societies. To this end the work of André Gorz is an excellent starting
point.[1] He has addressed these issues in an idiom more suitable than historical sociology – that of political economy – and his work has become
part of the political currents we are investigating. Among contemporary
social theorists few have attracted so much interest from the environmental movements of the West.[2] This should come as no surprise. Gorz has
shared much of the intellectual lineage of radically inclined environmentalists.[3] Gorz has perceived the industrialized world in a similar frame of
reference, bemoaning its insatiable appetite for resources, its conspicuous
consumption and the dehumanizing consequences of technology.[4] Gorz
has therefore attempted to diagnose a parallel set of social and ecological
problems: the cessation of environmental degradation; the creation of
alternative notions of wealth and well-being; a radical overhaul of
patterns of consumption and production.[5] Finally, he has displayed, like
the greens, an antipathy towards the politics of European social democracy.

The tasks of this chapter are threefold: to explore the intellectual and
historical context of Gorz's work and outline the broad themes; to provide
a coherent reading of his work since the mid-1970s; to relate his work to
my concerns and subject it to a degree of critical scrutiny.

André Gorz: Context and Criticism

Gorz's work has attracted a growing body of scholarly analysis, as well as informing the substantive proposals of other writers. Yet considerable gaps remain in its critical reception. In particular, there is no comprehensive reading of the core of Gorz's work, or of its historical and intellectual context. Above all, no attempt has been made to properly assess the particular worth of his writings on environmental issues. The first has been effectively bypassed by the partial studies of his texts.[6] The second has been skimmed over by the comparative analyses published.[7] Environmental aspects of Gorz's work have as yet, despite the interest of environmentalists in his proposals for economic reform, only been considered superficially.[8] I want to clarify the context and broad sweep of Gorz's work before describing its distinctive environmental dimension.

I am going to focus on three aspects of the context of Gorz's work: the disjuncture between his early and later writings; its postindustrial aspects; and Gorz's peculiar Marxist appropriation of postindustrialism. The disjuncture is both political and theoretical. Throughout the 1960s Gorz sat on the intellectual left of French political culture. Although never a member of the French Communist Party, Gorz remained a reluctant and increasingly critical fellow traveller. Not surprisingly, his major work of the period, *Strategy for Labour*, despite its considerable distance from the conservatism of French communism, placed the working class at the centre of any future socialist politics.[9] There are clearly continuities between this period and Gorz's later work. Politically speaking, Gorz neither followed the broad swing to the right nor conducted the apolitical retreat of many of his contemporaries.[10] He has remained unequivocally on the left, albeit an unorthodox left, of contemporary politics. His early concerns with the political impact of technology, the analytical centrality of the division of labour in complex economies and the nature of commodification and consumption did not lapse, nor did the fervour of his search for socially responsible and socialized production diminish.[11] Yet in the end these continuities are somewhat tendentious.

From the early 1970s Gorz distanced himself from the traditional positions of socialist politics and some, though not all, of the tenets of his early Marxism. These shifts were indicated by his increasing co-operation with the non-communist union, Confédération Française Democratique du Travail, and his increasing theoretical borrowings from non-Marxist positions.[12] But perhaps most important was the self-ascription of the term 'postindustrial' to his work.[13] If we are to understand and accurately measure the distance he had moved by the mid-1970s, we shall have to explore the meaning of postindustrial theory. Clearly the term is parasitic on the terms 'industrialism' and 'industrial society', ascribing the main organizing principles of modern society to the use and organization of technologies of production. We should not, therefore, be surprised to find that it is the impact of technological development that postindustrial theory has tracked. I would point to four developments which postindustrial theory has been shaped by and with which it has engaged.[14] First, the last twenty years have witnessed a basic shift, in terms of numbers employed and percentage of economic output, from manufacturing industry to the service sector.[15] Second, a wave of new technological innovations has swept across every aspect of economic activity – above, all the deployment of computers.[16] Third and closely connected with the first two phenomena, the structure of the labour market and the experience of work have undergone significant changes. Not only have there been cyclically high periods of unemployment, but the goal of full employment has been quite impossible to achieve in any country in the West.[17] The generalized rise in unemployment has been accompanied by a progressive fragmentation or segmentalization of the labour force between full-timers, part-timers and casual labour, as well as between skilled and unskilled workers.[18] All these changes, whatever their causes, have had a profound effect on the conduct of a traditional socialist politics. A homogeneous political interest among the Western working classes, which European socialism had assumed, could no longer be said to exist, if indeed it ever had. Fourth, the intersection of these trends has made possible major changes in the practical organization of production and management.[19] For postindustrialists, it is the technological shifts of the last two decades that are at the leading edge of these changes.

Badham has suggested that two types of postindustrial response to these phenomena may be discerned:[20] hyper-industrializers and deindustrializers. The former argue that the logic of these developments should be seen through to their benign conclusion. Unpleasant manual labour can now be dispensed with, while the new communications technologies make possible new forms of self-learning and participatory politics; the factory and the slum can be abandoned for the more convivial environments of the 'electric cottage' and decentralized communities. Bell and Toffler, for example, argue that we are not witnessing the transcendence of industrialism but its final, evolutionary shift: the fulfilment of its Durkheimian promise.[21] By contrast, the deindustrializers are less hopeful about the future. Rather than focus on the benign qualities of technological and economic change, the emergence of a Weberian social order is charted; the technological and social transformations under way will progressively diminish the space of individual liberty and environmental stability. The future demands not the celebration of industrial change but a rejection of its premises and technologies.[22]

One of the virtues of Gorz's work is to suggest that these transformations open up both positive and negative futures. This has theoretical roots. He is, like all of these writers, a postindustrialist, to the extent that he accords to technological shifts a key causal role in social change and has abandoned the traditional programmes and assumptions of Western social democracy. Yet he remains close to certain Marxist positions. A measure of technological determinism and the rejection of traditional class politics is tempered by a reliance on relatively orthodox Marxist political economy and a characterization of the West as capitalist rather than simply postindustrial. Consequently, Gorz is not prepared entirely to disentangle technological change from the economic and political order under which it is mobilized. He has abandoned both the hyper-industrial and Marxist visions of a benign transformation of capitalism, but is no more at home with deindustrializers. He has remained enough of a Marxist to suggest that postindustrialism and its technology may not only serve as instruments of repression but, beyond the realm of necessity, as a means of liberation.[23]

Though the precise concerns of Gorz's work have shifted over the last fifteen years, a skeletal framework of analysis can be discerned. Above all, there is a claim that contemporary Western capitalism is in a state of crisis. It is not a crisis that derives from short-term problems alone (the dynamics of capital accumulation) but is intimately bound up with long-term, structural transformations (postindustrial automation). Nor is it comprehensible in economic terms alone; it has a significant environmental dimension. Gorz therefore investigates the origins of the crisis so as to assess its possible trajectories.

In *Ecology as Politics*, first published in 1975, Gorz's pre-eminent concern was with the economic and political implications of ecological damage.[24] Following the limits-to-growth debate, Gorz attempted to graft the implications of physical limits and environmental costs on to a more orthodox Marxist political economy. Simultaneously, he paid close attention to the impact of technology on the environment and social relations, indicating his drift towards a postindustrial position.[25] The question was whether capitalist economies could successfully overcome the ecological problems they had created. Would they internalize them through political repression and controlled consumption or would they burst the circuits of accumulation asunder?[26] In the latter case might environmental degradation facilitate a radical transformation of the mode and means of production? Gorz argued that the environmental consequences of capitalist economic growth would have to be quelled, but that this could not be achieved by the transformation of economic organization alone. The dominant cultural understandings of wealth, which fuelled economic growth, would have to be redefined as well.

Farewell to the Working Class, subtitled *An Essay on Post-industrial Socialism*, was first published in 1980. Again, the deepening crises of Western societies formed the backdrop to the study, but the focus had shifted. Gorz had moved from the dynamics of the crisis to the potentially liberating social forces unleashed. In a critique of Marx's theory of revolution, Gorz suggested that the working class could not fulfil its Marxist promise. The universality of the proletarian revolution was the product of Marx's Hegelian baggage rather than the outcome of careful empirical research of capitalist development. By contrast, Gorz argued that the working class had been successfully incorporated into the dominant order.[27] Moreover, the possibility of collective appropriation of the means of production, the socialization of production and the abolition of the division of labour were myths.[28] The forms of technology and consequent social organization ingrained in industrial societies made Marx's notion of communism quite redundant. Large-scale companies and complex manufacturing processes could not be efficiently managed without a multilayered and hierarchical division of labour. However, to abandon the latter would be to consign those societies to the same miserable poverty as preindustrial societies.

In the face of this intractable trade-off between wealth and alienation, the central political issue became not the abolition of the relations of production, nor the abandonment of the industrial means of production, but as far as possible the abolition of waged work itself. Work and consumption would be replaced by the expansion of free time and self-provisioning. The working-class would be unlikely to support such a programme. Thus the harbingers of the future society were the non-class of non-workers, the unemployed and unemployable, marginalized by the segmentation of the labour market, and unemployed through the irresistible rise of automation.[29] Duplicating the logic of Marx's argument, if not its contents, Gorz argued that their interests coincide with the abolition of work because, given their marginal status in the labour market, work ceases to have any intrinsic value to them. Indeed their active withdrawal from the labour market and the creation of a sphere of productive and consumptive autonomy in the informal economy outside waged labour presage the future utopia.

These arguments were developed in the 1982 book *Paths to Paradise: On The Liberation from Work*, refined in the 1989 *Critique of Economic Reason*, and pored over once again in a collection of essays published in the early 1990s entitled *Capitalism, Socialism, Ecology*. In all of these, the dominant concerns of the two prior works were integrated. Gorz reassessed the origins of the current crisis, subsumed his earlier account of environmental degradation into the wider notion of expanding and untenable social costs, and supplemented it with an account of the inevitability of structural mass unemployment induced by widespread automation of production.[30] Traditional socialist strategies could provide no solution. The Keynesian programmes of Western social democracy with their emphasis on a return to full employment were not deemed feasible, while a revolutionary politics and command economy had already been discounted.[31] In *Paths to Paradise* Gorz retained the utopian and darker possibilities of *Ecology as Politics*. Capitalism could survive automation and environmental degradation by expanding the sphere of commodified consumption and further marginalizing the growing underclass. Against this, Gorz put forward his most concrete proposals for a society beyond work: separating income and work, expanding free time and self-production, redefining wealth, appropriating amenable technologies and reassessing the boundaries and purposes of state and civil society.[32] This, then, is the outline of Gorz's programme; now we must proceed to its substance.

Gorz on Political Economy

Themes in Gorz's Political Economy

The core of Gorz's work is an account of a contemporary capitalist political economy moving in a postindustrial direction. I shall dissect the main elements of his argument below, but it is worth focusing on a number of themes with which he is preoccupied: (1) the failure of growing capitalist economies to alleviate poverty; (2) the morally questionable status of the dominant economic rationality; (3) the intersection of both of these issues with the necessarily finite limits of the physical world.

Gorz is initially not far removed from Marx's position. The primary dynamic of capitalist growth remains the insatiable chase for capital accumulation, inscribed in the competitive market economy and its capital-investment-capital cycles.[33] What distinguishes Gorz from Marx is his recognition that social democratic parties in Western societies are deeply implicated in the process.[34] Social democrats have argued that, given the political limits on major redistribution in democratic societies, it is only through the expansion of aggregate levels of production that problems of poverty and inequality can be solved.[35] However, for Gorz, the rush for growth is predicated on the dominant perceptions of welfare and well-being. Again, Gorz remains close to a Marxist perspective, reinvigorating the classic distinction between exchange value and use value. The Marxist argument of course runs that in a monetarized economy, driven by the imperatives of profit, economic decision-making will be gauged by exchange values, by the monetary costs and benefits to individuals and institutions involved in a given transaction, to the exclusion of non-economic or public criteria. This is unacceptable to Gorz. First, he finds the equation between 'more' and 'better' to be untenable. To put it another way, there is no necessary correlation between an increase in exchange values and an increase in use values. This may be because the expansion in production is due to products and services that are in some sense morally objectionable or superfluous (though it is by no means clear how Gorz can ground what a normatively acceptable form of production actually is). Second, Gorz writes: 'the growth of the underside of production can be seen in the growth of the environmental damage it causes.'[36] Thus the prevailing economic rationality of capitalist societies is not only morally unacceptable but incapable of adequately assigning exchange values to the real use values of the natural world transformed by economic activity. Indeed, Gorz rejects the possibility of this. As he sees it, economic growth fails, even on its own weak moral terms, to deliver long-term prosperity or environmental sustainability.[37]

The Mode of Consumption

Analytically, Gorz's political economy may be divided into the mode of consumption, the mode of production (comprising both the relations of production and technology), and their crisis tendencies. Gorz's focus on a distinctive mode of consumption is in itself worthy of comment.[38] Most Marxist political economy has focused on production as the central explanatory component of an economy and the primary determinant of other aspects of social life. While production is of central importance and the relationship between production and consumption is close, it is by no means clear that the latter is purely derivative from the former. The social organization of production does set limits on, and generates different capacities for, consumption. But, by the same token, consumption influences production. Goods that cannot be sold will in the end not be produced. Different forms of personal consumption, particularly education, will affect people's capacity to produce. Above all, the capacity to consume is not solely determined by a person's position within the productive process. The relationship between wage labour and income, production and consumption – the relationship that Gorz wishes to break – has already been mediated by people's capacity for self-production and their consumption of state sector services and benefits. The virtue of Gorz's approach is to try and distinguish the peculiar dynamics of consumption and production. Against the backdrop of the generalized drive for growth, Gorz argues that our current modes of consumption ensure that poverty is not eradicated but reproduced, that consumption is undergoing a progressive, indeed endemic, form of commodification, and that already substantial environmental damage is exacerbated.

The impracticability of social democracy's strategy of growth-led prosperity is tackled in Gorz's discussion of poverty. He is careful to distinguish between destitution, where basic human needs are not being met, and poverty, which is a culturally variable and inherently relative phenomenon. As one might therefore expect, it is not simply the volume of goods produced that determines the existence of scarcity or the experience of poverty, or even their distribution, but what is produced, how it is produced and how it is consumed. Gorz points to three phenomena that ensure, despite an increase in the aggregate level of consumption, that poverty persists: detrimental appropriation, monopolization or exclusive access, and distinctive consumption.[39]

Detrimental appropriation is the monopolization of otherwise abundant resources by a minority, thus creating an artificial rather than absolute scarcity. For example, an increase in food production and consumption does not automatically ensure the alleviation of starvation if prices remain high or production is concentrated in high value-added products. However, Gorz is less concerned with price/income differentials than with the ability of elites to translate political and economic power into the creation of scarcities. In environmental terms, the creation of protected and aesthetically valuable landscapes does not alleviate the experiential poverty of those in decaying urban environments if that land is held in private ownership. This overlaps with Gorz's second category. By monopolization he is suggesting that the intrinsic character of some goods and services cannot be distributed equally or used by all simultaneously without losing their distinctive value. The exclusivity of private landscapes is a good example. Landscapes lose their utility as unspoilt countryside if overpopulated and damaged by too many visitors. Similarly, the motor car cannot be made available to all without losing its utility as a convenient form of individual transport. In more conventional economic terms, the marginal benefit to each new motorist, as well as to existing motorists, declines. Finally, Gorz looks at distinctive consumption. An aggregate increase in the level of consumption may be accounted for by an increase in the consumption of products whose high exchange value is the outcome of their prestige or status value, rather than their superior use value – for example, opulent jewellery. As a consequence the overall level of human welfare, let alone that of the poorest, remains unchanged. Indeed, given the intrinsically relative nature of poverty, it may actually deepen the divide.

More disturbing for Gorz is the commodification of consumption. That may seem paradoxical. What is it that consumers consume but commodities? Gorz argues that the drive for growth extinguishes modes of self-provision, above all, leisure.[40] Free time and self-determined activities, outside commodified labour time, enjoyed and enjoined for precisely that reason, are converted into the consumption of commodities provided by the private sector. Consumption in capitalist societies undermines both the strategy of equality through growth and the virtues of self-provisioning, while exacerbating environmental degradation. First, economic growth is fuelled by increasing levels of consumption (of declining marginal benefit).[41] Second, the creation of an affluent, consumption-based lifestyle in the West has served as a goal of development for the rest of the world. Given an expanding world population, the industrialized path out of underdevelopment can only serve to hasten the contemporary ecological crisis without resolving the problem of endemic poverty.[42] Gorz can therefore argue that an environmentally sustainable future depends on transforming the nature of consumption as well as production.

The Mode of Production

The mode of production comprises the relations of production and the means of production or technology. Gorz's concerns are threefold: the political and social implications of technology, their ecological impacts, and the consequences of computer technology and the automation of production. His use of the concept of technology is not without ambiguity. He argues in *Ecology as Politics* that 'technology is the matrix in which the distribution of power, the social relations of production, and the hierarchical division of labour are embedded'.[43] What sort of claim is Gorz making about technology? It would seem that, though wary of any crass technological determinism, Gorz is not prepared to accept that it is completely shaped by the relations of production. The tension between the Marxist and postindustrial aspects of his work reappears, for he is arguing that technology establishes a framework around which the relations of production are organized. Technology thus has a causal impact on social organization.[44] The weight of empirical demonstration falls on nuclear energy. He goes so far as to argue that 'nuclear energy . . . whether "capitalist" or "socialist" – presupposes and imposes a centralized, hierarchical, police-dominated society.'[45] Why should this be? First, because it is technically complex and financially costly. It requires the mobilization of skills and resources that only large-scale bureaucracies can provide. Second, the size and delicacy of the multiple interconnected processes involved entail a high division of labour. Such an enterprise must have a complex stratification of command and management. Not everyone within the process has time or skills to acquire all the knowledge required to make key but routine decisions in the operation of a nuclear programme. Finally, the military significance of the nuclear industry requires high levels of secrecy and policing, trespassing both on civil liberties and democratic discussion of energy policy.[46]

Technologies thus have sociopolitical consequences. What then of their ecological impacts? Gorz is less specific here, but the thrust of his argument would appear to be similar to his initial argument: that certain technologies, irrespective of the relations of production within which they are deployed, are inherently ecologically damaging. Indeed, given the potential for ecological damage inherent in the most threatening technologies, their transformation is more important than any shift in the relations of production.[47] However, nowhere is the causal force of technology more fully explored than in Gorz's analysis of automation and its economic consequences. It is at this point that we must move from the static account Gorz has given of production and consumption, to the third, dynamic element of his political economy: the theory of capitalist crisis.

Environmental Degradation and the Crises of Capitalism

Five Theories of Crisis

We can discern five distinct but related notions of crisis in Gorz's work: an ecological crisis; two theories of a crisis of overaccumulation; a crisis of reproduction; and his own version of the fiscal crisis of the state. The notion of an ecological crisis, for all the importance Gorz ascribes to it, receives rather scant analytical attention.[48] If Gorz pays little attention to the specific biological and ecological changes that might constitute such a crisis, it is because his concern lies elsewhere: in the interaction of ecological change and economic development. Thus he writes: 'we are dealing ... with a crisis of capitalist accumulation, intensified by an ecological crisis ...'[49] What then is a crisis of overaccumulation?

Gorz has offered two possible explanations, the first in *Ecology as Politics*, the second in *Paths to Paradise*. In the first Gorz reiterates Marx's formula for the infamous tendency of the rate of profit to fall. The basic structural problem of capitalist economies is how to maintain rates of return per unit investment in an increasingly capital intensive and extensive economy. Gorz suggests that companies faced with such a dilemma may sell more products or produce higher value-added products. It is at this point that the dynamic of growth and the prevailing economic rationality collide with the physical limits of the natural world. The economic strategies for avoiding the downward recessionary spirals of overaccumulation are resolved, temporarily at any rate, by heightened levels of environmental damage. More products can be sold, for example, if their durability, reliability and reparability are curtailed. Thus they must be replaced more often, raising the volume of sales. In so doing, the use of natural resources, capital and labour are all intensified, without actually increasing the welfare of human beings.[50] Similarly, reusable containers are replaced by disposable containers, and the cheap repair of products is made impossible by low-grade production techniques.

In *Paths to Paradise*, the same Marxist model was qualified. Gorz accepts that 'the tendency of the rate of profit to fall' may be counteracted by other strategies related to the dynamics of class struggle. One such strategy would be to reduce unit labour costs, or raise output per unit wages. Alternatively, new markets might be sought. Gorz argues that from the mid 1960s to the mid 1970s these options were precluded in the West both by a levelling off of technological development and limits on the labour supply. New technology that raised output per unit capital to a level that offset the rise in unit labour costs could have offered a way out. However, the active resistance of the Western working classes to the imposition of the new technologies, together with their ability to drive up wages, in the context of labour shortages, made these options untenable. The crisis of overaccumulation – the inability of new investments of capital to reproduce themselves profitably – therefore remained.[51]

The economic consequences of environmental damage created by the crisis of overaccumulation were first explored in *Ecology as Politics*, as a crisis of reproduction.[52] Returning to his earlier analysis of the ecological crisis, there were two problems which had to be faced: the declining availability of urban land, air and water, and the gradual exhaustion of accessible mineral deposits. Both contribute to the declining rate of profit, for what characterizes them all is the fact that 'it is impossible to produce greater quantities of them no matter what price is assigned to them.' Thus the price of land will necessarily increase, encouraging at the same time the construction of skyscrapers and underground complexes, while air and water must be recycled and purified.[53] In order to continue the process of capital accumulation, industry must internalize the soaring environmental costs it had previously externalized. A similar cost inflation and capital intensity is experienced in the extraction of diminishing raw materials. More and more capital must be invested in exploration of distant and hostile environments, actual extraction becomes more hazardous and complex, ores are of a lower grade, requiring more expensive extraction and purification processes, and bulk goods must be transported over greater distances to industrial centres. The crisis of overaccumulation is therefore contained by the internalization of externalized costs and by the inherent cost inflation they generate. In terms of human welfare, Gorz is unequivocal: 'From the point of view of the final consumer, it is as if industry has to . . . consume more, in the form of wealth and resources – in order to maintain the same level of consumption for the population.'[54]

In *Paths to Paradise* this analysis is amended. Gorz shifts his focus away from the internalization of previously externalized costs to an explanation of the spiralling nature of ecological and social costs, and from their impact on the economy alone to the consequences of automation for economy and polity. In the terms of the neo-Marxist discourse Gorz argues that welfare states in contemporary Western societies are responsible for both the production of order, or social cohesion and consensus, and the production of the right kind of consumer demand; they match the productive capacities and economic expediencies of the capitalist economy to the potential for consumption and vice versa. The crux of the problem is that social and ecological costs, which result from the dynamics of capitalist accumulation, have risen faster than the aggregate level of production.[55] Therefore, societies must consume a greater proportion of their productive output simply to reproduce their conditions of existence. Why should this differential rate of growth have occurred? Gorz returns to the arguments of *Ecology as Politics*, pointing to the peculiar dynamic of consumption in capitalist societies:

> The explanation must be sought in advanced capitalism's own model of development. Essentially this model derives from the principle that all problems and needs – even collective ones – must be answered by *individual* consumption of marketable goods and services. Growth of production and consumption depends on this quest for individual solutions to collective problems. But these individual solutions are more expensive than a collective response, and moreover are increasingly ineffective.[56]

Gorz's focus is on housing, transport and health rather than specifically environmental problems, but the argument is worth pursuing. In the case of housing, suburban sprawl has been the answer to inner-city decay and lack of space. Yet it entails the use of large amounts of land, extensive road networks and, given the detached quality of the housing, the absence of communal facilities. This in turn encourages wasteful individual provision. Similarly, the cost of health services, even state-run and financed ones, expands because illness is dealt with on an individual curative basis, rather than tackling the collective social etiologies of sickness: pollution, poverty, smoking, etc.[57] All of this requires increasing levels of taxation to finance and maintain social order, deepening the problems of accumulation without resolving the social damage and environmental degradation it created in the first place. An impasse has been reached. How did Gorz envisage it might be transcended?

Resolving the Crisis

Gorz's argument consists of three components: the incapacity of Keynesian social democratic programmes to resolve the impasse; a possible right-wing response; a utopian, left-wing response that seeks to break with the dominant economic rationality of capitalism, transforming production and consumption.

Gorz's interpretation of Keynesianism is not exactly orthodox. The main mechanism of demand management for Gorz would appear to be the redistribution of company profits to the poor, via state taxation, thereby circumventing the flip side of overaccumulation, which is underconsumption. However Keynes, at any rate, would have argued that demand management operates by governments running up budget deficits in times of declining demand, counteracting the latter with public works programmes and the multiplier effect. Gorz would seem to be on surer critical ground when he suggests that the peculiar economic nature of automation makes Keynesian reflation (however orchestrated) impossible. He suggests that the introduction of computer technology into production not only displaces labour, but lowers capital and raw material costs. The latter occurs because energy costs are so low; the former because, given the efficiency of computer technology, 'The value of constant fixed capital per unit output diminishes rapidly . . .' Indeed such is the efficiency of the computer that 'it does not just bring down the value of total fixed capital per unit of output; it sets up a decline in the total mass of fixed capital employed to produce a rapidly increasing volume of commodities.'[58] Thus Keynesian reflation, given the postindustrial technological dynamic of the times, can only lead to unemployment, scrapping, and a decline in effective demand, and it thus reinitiates the cycle of overaccumulation. However, unlike the nuclear industry, this technology is politically more pliable: 'The mega-technologies were a one-way street, whereas micro-electronics is a crossroads . . . Nuclear energy or the space programme *can only* lead to hyper-centralization, whereas micro electronics can equally lead to self-management.'[59] If postindustrial change renders traditional socialist politics redundant, then it also offers the opportunity of a different type of progressive politics.

What then are the options? To the right, Gorz sees two possible developments. Social costs will be tackled by expanding the sphere of consumption, that is, by making profitable previously free activities and reducing the costs of producing consumers through microelectronics. Thus education will be based on commercially manufactured and supplied teaching machines.[60] This is particularly the strategy for the growing sector of the unemployed and unemployable, who in effect are paid to consume the goods which are produced. They must also be kept politically impotent by active spatial segregation and social marginalization.[61] Thus capitalism generates a society in which economic power is superseded by political and ideological power, exploitation by domination: 'what is being preserved *is not the capitalist system but capitalism's system of domination* . . . the goal of production is not . . . capital accumulation [but] . . . control and domination.'[62]

However, in the case of computers the equation between technology and domination does not automatically hold. It is on this basis that Gorz can propose his utopian alternative, which requires breaking the equation between 'more' and 'better', and thus recasting the rationality of economics to achieve the conceptual and social separation of the right to an income from the obligation to work, and an equation of wealth and well-being with increasing free time rather than increasing material income. The virtue of microprocessors is that they allow us to live at a given level of production while working less. Rises in productivity could be translated into a reduction in hours worked to produce the same amount of goods, rather than working as long to produce more goods. If, in addition, production is more socially orientated and collective solutions are sought to the problems of social costs, then the cyclic reproduction of poverty and spiralling social and ecological costs will cease. Moreover, Gorz envisages that a whole parallel economy will be established outside wage labour in people's free time. If appropriate decentralized technology can be made available, people will produce more of what they personally consume. Production outside the wage labour contract is not work but a self-determined free activity. The existence of an income separate from work ensures it is not a necessity. Of course, some work will need to be done; there are approximately twenty thousand hours a lifetime to be arranged as people find most convenient, perhaps two days a week, three weeks a month, etc. Moreover, the worst work should be shared more evenly. Gorz happily concedes that such an arrangement will require a central state to plan, co-ordinate, resolve disputes and provide the framework for this to happen.[63] Whether Gorz's utopia does offer the outline of an environmentally sustainable economy and polity will have to wait for the moment. With such a broadly conceived project, there is a need to make an initial assessment of where we stand and what we might find useful.

Gorz: an Initial Assessment

To help assess Gorz's work I want to sketch its virtues and dispense with some of its rather speculative elements. We can then focus on the arguments which bear on our concerns. As regards virtues, Gorz's eclectic theoretical borrowings have produced interesting results: a Marxist political economy that pays close attention to environmental issues, and a postindustrialism that attempts to grasp not only the social impact of technological innovations but the shaping of technology by social structures themselves. Gorz's key achievement, for our purposes, has been to integrate the economic, environmental and political trajectories of Western societies. The connections he draws between the dynamic of growth, the prevailing economic rationality and physical limits to growth are provocative. Gorz's dual emphasis on structural constraints in capitalist economies (the dynamic of growth) and the value orientation of economic behaviour (economic rationality) avoids the worst excesses of Marxian determinism, while continuing to place beliefs and attitudes in their material circumstances. Moreover, it leads to an equal emphasis on production and consumption in political economy, the virtues of which I have already stressed. Thus Gorz's 'critique of political economy' is aimed not only at the shortfalls of capitalism's relations of production, but attacks the cultural basis of affluence and consumerism. Gorz argues that changes in the ownership and structure of the means of production do not guarantee utopia; the means of production and the mode of consumption must also be transformed. Whatever the specifics of the relationship between environmental and economic change, there can be little doubt that they should be analysed together, given some quantitative perspective, and their sociopolitical consequences considered. Gorz, alone among social theorists, has done this.

Yet there remain some substantial problems with Gorz's work. The empirical accuracy and theoretical plausibility of much of the argument in *Farewell to the Working Class* has been seriously questioned.[64] It has been argued that Gorz's claims for the impact of automation are overinflated, that his account of the structural transformation of the labour market is exaggerated, and that the political potentiality of the non-class of non-workers has not materialized.[65] For our present purposes, the aspects of Gorz's work that bear specifically on our concerns are fourfold: (1) his account of growth and the problem of poverty; (2) his writings on technology; (3) his account of spiralling, crisis-inducing environmental costs; (4) his critique of social democracy and his postindustrial alternative.

Gorz's position on the environmental implications of capitalism is not dissimilar to the arguments established in chapters 1 and 2 above. He identifies the investment-profit cycle as the mainspring of accumulation and the pricing system as the origin of the market's environmental myopia. The consequences are an increase in externalities and diminishing supplies of raw materials. He argues that the political system of capitalist societies has been deeply implicated in maintaining growth. He has also argued that one of the major economic consequences of degradation is the internalization of environmental costs by capitalist firms, diminishing their capacity to accumulate capital. Where he differs from and supplements our argument is in his account of the problem of poverty and the logic of obsolescence. We have already suggested that social democrats have attempted to surmount the electoral limits to redistribution by increasing economic growth. Gorz argued that such a strategy, given the nature of consumption in capitalist societies, is self-defeating and in itself a major propellent of growth. Growth is all the more destructive since the logic of capitalist accumulation encourages the production of non-reusable goods with inbuilt obsolescence, or of higher value goods, and their production may require an increasing use of energy and materials and a corresponding rise in externalities without satisfying human need any more effectively.

In the next section I shall examine Gorz's account of political economy and suggest that, while illuminating, it offers an inadequate account of contemporary environmental degradation. In so doing I shall also examine our second concern, technology. Lying in the postindustrial camp, Gorz might well have been expected to offer us a clear definition of industrialism and ascribe a particular and intrinsic role to technology in environmental degradation. Unfortunately, he fails in the first task and responds ambiguously to the second. Technology for Gorz primarily affects the form of capital accumulation (the economic consequences of automation), the division of labour and political commitments (the fragmentation of the working class, the creation of the postindustrial proletariat) and types of political organization (the impact of nuclear power on civil liberties). I want, in the next section, to examine critically, and where possible extend, Gorz's arguments on the environmental impact of technologies.

Gorz's work helps us illuminate the way in which political power and decision-making have contributed to environmental degradation, but he has given little consideration to its opposite: how can politics limit the consequences of environmental degradation? Thus his account of spiralling environmental costs is somewhat deterministic. While we noted the market's incapacity to provide public goods, Gorz has emphasized the increasing and seemingly inevitable environmentally damaging consequences of the individualistic alternatives that have emerged: suburban housing, private health care, the car. However, these are presented without attending to the dynamics of public policy-making. Later in the chapter I shall introduce the distinction between environmental impacts and costs and examine the way in which the identification and understanding of environmental problems is highly politicized. In so doing I shall be able to argue that spiralling environmental costs and individualistic patterns of consumption are not inevitable, but contingent on the exercise of political and cultural power. This will allow me to go on to explore the ways in which political and cultural power can both stem the tide of environmental degradation and, more often than not, obstruct and limit environmental protests. Finally I shall return to one of the questions with which I began in the introduction to this book: what is to be done?

The Origins of Environmental Degradation: Politics as Facilitator

Whatever the merits of Gorz's eclectic political economy, it has some serious limitations. The most immediate problem is its limited concern with the international dimension of economics and politics and its implicit reliance on the notion of the nation-state as the centre of political decision-making. Gorz does of course pay a certain lip-service to third world issues and North–South inequalities.[66] That said, there is no concerted analysis of how the international economy operates and the environmental consequences thereof, and neither does he examine how the international political system affects environmental degradation, or the ways in which global and international forces, whether military, legal, environmental or otherwise, circumscribe the capacity of the nation-state to respond effectively to its consequences. As our discussion of globalization in chapter 2 should have made clear, no discussion of contemporary environmental degradation can afford to be ignorant of the enormous importance of international forces.

Gorz's political economy is not totally incompatible with these arguments even though he has clearly not addressed himself to them in any sustained fashion. Attention to them would, however, require some shifts in Gorz's position. I shall pick up some of these arguments below, when I discuss what it is that states can, cannot and will not do in the face of environmental degradation and environmentally orientated politics, and later I shall also examine the ways in which his utopian politics needs to be seen in an international perspective. Here I will consider how these issues undermine aspects of Gorz's political economy, and above all how the globalization of economic and politico-legal institutions have made the national economy and the nation-state very questionable starting points for a political economy concerned with environmental issues.[67]

The Globalization of the Capitalist Economy

Gorz's model of capitalist economies is, like his analysis of the state, implicitly an analysis of national economies. Any account of contemporary capitalism must necessarily recognize three important changes in the postwar world economy: the degree to which product and financial markets have become global in their scope; the enormous growth and power of transnational corporations; the successful industrialization of previously peripheral states.[68] Gorz does not engage with any of these issues and this has important consequences for the accuracy of his political economy. First, it undermines his account of the dynamics of capitalist crises, the limits of Keynesianism and the paralysis of social democracy. Second, his account of environmental degradation does not examine the degree to which environmental problems themselves have become globalized and uneven. Thus, third, he does not examine the ways in which economic and political decisions made in one part of the world have their main environmental ramifications elsewhere. Let us consider each in turn.

Gorz has argued that Keynesian demand management has been made redundant by the economic logic of automation: boosting demand and investment leads to a decrease rather than an increase in employment. Whatever the merits of this argument, it seems more plausible to argue that the demise of demand management strategies has come about due to the integration of national economies in the global economy and the enormous increase in global capital mobility. The linchpin of such strategies was always the reflation of depressed economies by a higher level of government expenditure, funded by increased government borrowing. However, this strategy has run into a number of problems. First, reflating national economies in the context of a global depression has often resulted in chronic inflationary and balance of payments problems: for example, the experience of the Mitterrand government in France in 1981–3.[69] Second, it has been increasingly difficult for governments pursuing such a strategy to maintain the confidence of the global capital markets from which they borrow. Given the ease with which capital can be exported from a borrowing nation, the sensitivity of capital movements to international differentials in interest rates and the aversion to deficit funding that dominates financial markets, such a strategy requires one of two options: high levels of interest rates to fund such deficits and maintain the exchange rate, which then cripple domestic economic expansion; or a declining exchange rate and low interest rates which may fail to attract sufficient funds and let inflation erode domestic economic performance.[70]

When discussing environmental problems, Gorz has tended to focus on issues of resource shortage and local pollution problems. These are the issues he addresses when outlining his theories of the crises of overaccumulation and the fiscal crises of the state. While clearly these are important, some of the most pressing environmental problems that we now face have radically different spatial and thus political characteristics: for example, global warming and ozone depletion, which have been exacerbated by the growth of Western economies and the progressive industrialization of the developing world. These are environmental problems in which the benefits and environmental costs of economic activity are spatially uneven. The existence of global environmental problems once again demonstrates the extent to which a focus on national economies and national environmental crises is problematic. Nations must often bear the environmental costs of economic activity that occurs beyond their borders. One of the responses of states has been the emergence of international regimes that attempt to regulate this problem.

The Role of International Environmental Regimes

The last twenty years have seen a significant proliferation in the number of multilateral environmental regimes and treaties, as well as an expanding corpus of international environmental law: for example, the Montreal Protocol on control of CFCs, conventions covering transboundary air pollution and marine pollution, and treaties covering the exploitation of Antarctica.[71] These political changes are not considered in Gorz's work. As such, he does not recognize the degree to which individual nation-states are required to bear the costs of environmental degradation. This is not necessarily because they choose to or simply in response to the kinds of costs that nationally based economic activity generates. Rather, the imposition of costs on nation-states may result from the outcome of international political conflicts and compromises, the negotiation of international treaties and the application of international law. In Europe, its most extreme form, the sovereign right to take decisions about environmental regulation and the distribution of environmental costs has been passed from individual nation-states to the European Union.[72]

To sum this up, we can state that the globalization of the capitalist economy and the enmeshment of nation-states in an increasingly dense network of international political and legal regimes demands that an environmentally informed political economy takes account of the following: unevenly distributed transboundary and global environmental problems and the consequent international political struggle over the distribution and consequences of environmental costs; the significant economic power that has accrued to global financial markets and the limits this places on traditional Keynesian economics. Gorz's political economy neither describes nor explains these phenomena.

Technology and Environmental Degradation

Moving on to Gorz's analysis of the mode of production, an important set of questions concerning technology lie unresolved. First there is a definitional question, for Gorz's description of technology as a 'matrix' is not very clear. Is technology to be conceived of simply as objects and machines or does it also incorporate skills, knowledge and combinations of machines and objects?[73] There are also causal questions to be asked: do socioeconomic circumstances determine the form and deployment of technologies or do technologies acquire an independent causal dynamic? Specifically, are some technologies inherently environmentally problematic or are their degrading effects a consequence of the socioeconomic context in which they have emerged?[74] Gorz has pointed to the independent dynamic of technologies when he discusses the inherent centralizing tendencies of nuclear power, and their malleability when he contrasts right-wing and left-wing uses of computer technology. Though Gorz has not made his position clear on the issue of technology and environmental degradation, the dual emphasis of his work points us in the right direction.

In a sense we are recasting our initial debate about the relative culpability of capitalism and industrialism. I concluded earlier that while industrialism had at a crucial historical moment *unleashed capitalism*, it was capitalism that unleashed the whirlwind of industrial environmental degradation. I have also suggested that the technologies of fossil fuel use are inherently environmentally problematic, given their reliance on a finite resource base. There is a good case for extending that problematic to all technologies that are reliant on non-organic raw materials, and to nuclear energy as well. In the case of the latter there are two reasons for doing so. First, the production of a range of extremely radioactive by-products is an inescapable consequence of nuclear technology.[75] While the pollutants associated with many technologies may conceivably, if at considerable effort and cost, be eliminated, this is not the case with nuclear energy. Second, the environmental consequences of reactor failure or waste product escape are considerably more devastating than with other pollutants. Whatever the technical details of the reactor safety debate, nuclear energy inherently carries a major environmental risk.[76]

If, then, we are suggesting that for certain technologies there are, independent of their socioeconomic context, problems of environmental degradation, where does this leave the role of political economy? In fact, the history of technology requires us to recognize the ineliminable presence of economic and political power in shaping the environmental consequences of technological change at a number of points: the assessment of technologies before they are actually deployed; the political economy of technological research and the move from technologies to production processes; and finally the subsequent investment of private and public capital in production and infrastructure. On the first two matters, Gorz's arguments, while not incompatible with those that I suggest, are rather thin on the ground. On the third, his position is valuable but requires elaboration. In each case, what is at stake are the consequences of the economic rationality that Gorz has tracked, even if he has not always followed it to its political conclusions: the dominance of profitability (and of military security) over short-term and long-term environmental interests.

Contrary to the experience of the early phases of the industrial revolution, new technologies have not just sprung from the hands of gifted amateurs. The majority of research takes place with the aid of advanced science and in the regularized context of public, private and educational research centres. While to an extent researchers set their own agendas and certain technological developments logically spring from earlier inventions, decisions over the allocation of research funds are controlled by public bureaucracies and private companies. In allocating funds a number of criteria are important: for governments, military security and the long-term buoyancy of the economy; for private companies, the creation of profitable products.[77] While other criteria may be important, there is one which has received little or no attention in defining the requirements for technological research and the nature of the product itself: environmental impacts. The refrigerator, for example, was developed without regard to the atmospheric consequences of its main coolant, CFCs. On occasion environmental consequences have been considered in the development stage, for example, the safety implications of nuclear energy. However, even when environmental impacts have been a factor in research, their salience has been outweighed by other requirements. Thus it is not that certain technologies are inherently problematic, but that the criteria for decision-making in the research and development stage has been either oblivious to environmental impacts or weighed them very lightly against strategic needs and profitability. Indeed, as Gorz argued, the design of products may not simply be oblivious to environmental impacts but actively encourage the increasing use of raw materials and energy in the pursuit of profit: unrecyclable containers, disposable pens, razors and nappies.

Capital Investment and Environmental Degradation

A similar myopia has been displayed in the design of, and investment in, production processes and infrastructure. Gorz has touched on only one of them. Their importance requires us to shift our attention from the production of technologies themselves to their actual deployment as instruments of production. Our analysis of the origins of environmental degradation has so far focused on already established markets and production processes, but it is at the stage *of major capital investments* that the really decisive choices in technological development are made and, with them, the environmental consequences of economic activity determined. In the case of production processes, the issue is simple: that the externalities of production, such as pollutants or excessive use of raw materials, have not only been ignored once the process is up and running but have not been incorporated into the technological choice and investment stage either. It has proved exceptionally difficult in capitalist societies to intervene politically in this, the heart of the accumulation process. Governments have on occasion been able to manipulate the boundary conditions of accumulation, altering overall levels of investment and regulating markets. They have, however, found it exceptionally difficult to intervene in the qualitative make-up of private capital investment.[78] Moreover, as Gorz has noted and the historical record grimly testifies, neither state socialism nor the nationalization programmes of social democracy have managed to create economic institutions whose attitudes to environmental impact assessment are any more respectable.[79]

With regard to infrastructure, we have already argued that the market alone is most unlikely, if not unwilling, to provide the large-scale, public goods that are so necessary to large complex economies: sewerage systems, dams, roads and transport, etc. The virtue of Gorz's argument is to suggest that even when these are directly provided by the state or indirectly funded, individualistic forms of consumption rather than collective models are pursued. As we have seen, Gorz casts the debate in terms of increasing social costs and diminishing social and individual benefits, of which environmental costs are a subgroup. Transport policy is a good example of precisely this problem. While the car and its attendant environmental impacts were not monitored at the level of research and design, they have been equally disregarded in the governmental transport policies that have made possible the enormous expansion of motor transport.[80] We have already dealt with the non-pricing of externalities, but equally important have been the provision of enormous road systems; tax relief for commercial motoring; the active dismemberment of public transport systems; and neglect of other transport users (especially cyclists and pedestrians) in the design of roads and urban centres.[81] This is not of course to suggest that governments have not had a great deal of help in pursuing these policies from a variety of interest groups.[82] What it does suggest is that the politically orchestrated provision of infrastructure and the public investment of capital have had environmental consequences as dire as those of investment by the private sector in production processes. However, for those environmental consequences to be registered in a way that affects the political process, they must be named and understood. It is to the politics of that process that I now turn.

The Consequences of Environmental Degradation: Environmental Costs and Environmental Impacts

The third of Gorz's arguments to be considered – the spiralling nature of social and environmental costs – will allow us to explore the incorporation of environmental impacts into the political process. Environmental impacts are made politically resonant as environmental costs. Once we have elaborated the distinction between impacts and costs we can turn to two further questions. Is Gorz correct in arguing that social costs and environmental costs constantly spiral upwards? Do they do so at a rate that increasingly outstrips the capacity of the state to fund their resolution? The answer to the second question, which underwrites Gorz's account of tendencies to crises in capitalist societies, will depend on the answer to the first. I shall return to the second question below. First, we shall need to clarify the meaning of 'environmental costs' and ask whether they inevitably spiral upwards.

To understand the political implications of environmental costs we need to be more careful in defining the term than Gorz has been. A distinction must be made between environmental degradation that is experienced and that which, in a strictly economic sense, is paid for: for example, a population may bear the implications of ill-health from pollution without there necessarily being any corresponding increase in the cost of health care. There is clearly a political process involved in converting social and environmental *problems or impacts* (see my discussion in chapter 1) to the financial implications of social *costs*. Moreover, there is a further distinction between costs that are being borne and are considered unacceptable by the public, and those which are actually incorporated into the political process. At that point those costs must be dealt with by the state in some way. In failing to make these distinctions, Gorz has obscured two important elements of environmental politics: the struggle to define impacts as costs, and the possibility that costs will not be recognized or declared legitimate, as a result of which governments may resist the inevitable upward spiral of costs.

The struggle to turn impacts into costs entails the identification of current and prospective environmental impacts and the claim that, in their current form, they constitute an illegitimately imposed cost. In some cases the identification of an environmental impact is not problematic. An impact may be recognized by lay actors directly affected by it: visibly smog-filled air. We should note that the designation of dirty air as a problem will depend on the culturally variable expectations about what constitutes clean or dirty, acceptable or unacceptable. However, other forms of environmental degradation are not so easily perceivable. Indeed they are only detectable and explicable through the application of specialized forms of knowledge and resources, as in the detection of traces of toxic heavy metals in drinking water. It is only by the application of sophisticated scientific knowledge and expensive technology that these phenomena can be detected, their origins tracked, and the connection between environmental change and ill-health drawn. Even so, when such arguments are made available, they are rarely conclusive. This imprecision allows for a great deal of political disagreement. That is not to say that threatened communities have not identified trajectories of environmental change that will be damaging, or that they have not made highly plausible arguments regarding the environmental impact of proposed socioeconomic change. The Amazonian indigenous peoples have had no difficulty in connecting Brazilian government policy and the economic actions of ranch owners with degradation and the collapse of their own precious relationship with the Amazonian ecosystems.[83] None the less, there are limits to lay knowledge. The full physical extent of environmental change, its social origins and social and environmental consequences are simply not always immediately perceivable. This is not to say that the Amazonian peoples have not subsequently absorbed and deployed these arguments themselves, but it does indicate a special feature of environmental politics: its reliance on contestable technical information.[84]

Gorz's account of cost spirals not only ignores this process of cost identification and definition, but ascribes the constant rise in costs to the pre-
dominance of individualistic and profit-orientated service provision over
collective consumption. He is correct to draw attention to this problem,
but in doing so he has overstated his case and ignored some of the other
main contributors to rising costs. First, demographic change, both quantitative and qualitative, can push social costs upwards.[85] Second, the provision of services like health, or indeed environmental protection, may
increase at a rate of inflation faster than the rest of the economy, for the
former are labour intensive rather than capital intensive and therefore less
susceptible to improvements in efficiency. Third, social costs may
increase, not because the situation has got any worse (increases in the volume of pollution) but because the subjective experience of those costs
leads to demands for their control (people are less prepared to put up
with pollution – the issue of rising expectations).[86]

Thus where we must decisively depart from Gorz's work is in assuming the inevitability of increasing social costs as opposed to ever increasing environmental impacts. Population increases may raise the level of
environmental impacts, but these problems may remain financially unaddressed. Pollution may worsen, but its translation into stiffer taxes or regulations on businesses is not a foregone conclusion. If anything we should
expect the opposite. The translation of these changes into costs is an inherently political process. That fact that for the last forty years or so in the
West we have conducted a politics in which rising expectations of social
provision, if not the cessation of environmental degradation, have had a
decisive effect in raising state expenditure should not blind us to the contingent nature of that outcome, or make us assume the necessity of its
continuation or the smooth application of that model to environmental
issues. Once we acknowledge these arguments then some of the strategies
available to governments wishing to curtail increases in social/environ-
mental costs become apparent: they may ignore them; they may challenge
the validity of arguments that demonstrate their existence; they may
argue that current impacts are not illegitimate or unjustifiable; they may
refuse to compensate or respond, or they may deny the possibility of
intervention.[87]

Before we can assess whether costs will accelerate at a rate that outstrips the capacity of states to deal with them administratively and of capitalist economies to fund their resolution, we need to do two things that
Gorz has not done: examine what states and governments actually do
when faced by environmental degradation; and consider the ways in
which environmentally orientated politics, inside and outside the public
policy process, can act so as to curtail environmental degradation. In failing to attend to these political processes Gorz has limited his capacity to
understand the actual dynamics of environmental degradation and the
pivotal role of politics in facilitating or stemming it.

Public Policy and the Consequences of Environmental Degradation: Environmental Politics as a Brake

If the transformation of environmental impacts into environmental costs and their subsequent incorporation into the political process are not foregone conclusions, and if governments have the capacity to ignore demands for costs to be recompensed, then we need to turn to the broader politics of environmental degradation. Gorz has argued not only that environmental costs inevitably spiral upwards, but that they fall in a very particular way on the polity and economy.[88] However, the situation is rather more complicated. In this section I want to look at how, once environmental costs have been placed on the political agenda, Western democratic polities act. Here we are on the classical territory of public policy analysis and I shall draw on that literature to supplement Gorz's work. This is essential because, despite the reliance of Gorz's argument on certain directions of state policy and action, he includes no discussion of how policy is actually made and executed. Moreover, in the absence of any theory of policy-making, Gorz does not allow for the capacity of environmental political movements to intervene in the policy process and place a brake on the process of environmental degradation. Having established the outlines of what happens, we can turn to Gorz's account of the consequences and crises of environmental degradation. But we shall not be able to do so until we have understood precisely what it is that states do, or do not do, in the face of environmental degradation and environmental movements, and why.

Traditional public policy analysis leads us to look at a number of interconnected features of the environmental political process:[89] the construction of policy agendas; the members of policy communities and their differential capacities to affect the nature of the policies produced; the forums within which those debates and conflicts are resolved; the range of interests and ideals motivating that politics; and the implementation of policy and the options available for redressing the problem of costs. In this section I shall sketch the importance of these features and demonstrate why Gorz's inattention to them undermines his account of environmental degradation.

Policy Communities and Policy Agendas

As already noted in my discussion of Giddens's work, environmental movements are but one set of social actors in the complex mesh of environmental politics. In this section my focus is restricted to the role and capacity of environmental movements to influence the political process and to control environmental degradation, first by forcing the recognition of environmental costs, and then by demanding their cessation or transformation. However, we can only calibrate the capacity of these movements and the scale of political difficulties they face if we look at them in the context of a broad range of political actors.

The definition of costs constitutes one essential moment in the construction of the environmental policy agenda.[90] Equally important is the capacity of environmental movements to force these issues of environmental costs high up on the broader policy agenda. It is one thing to demand a policy response to global warming or resource depletion, another to get Western publics and politicians to prioritize these over economic growth, welfare spending or job preservation. Gorz, by contrast, does not acknowledge the existence of such policy communities or agendas. These absences allow him to paint an untenably deterministic picture of the consequences of environmental degradation. As we saw when discussing Gorz's account of crises of reproduction and the fiscal crisis of the state, costs appear automatically out of the operation of capitalist production, consumption and technology. They are then laid at the door of states, which must then respond. The peculiar role of environmental movements does not merit a mention in his work.[91]

Sites of Conflict and Policy-Making

Although we are predominantly concerned with policy-making by state institutions and the responses of states to environmental costs, conflict and action over environmental issues are not confined to state institutions. This is a particularly important point when discussing environmental politics, for there is a significant component of the environmental movement that rejects incorporation into the policy-making process and the snares of bureaucracy. The transformation of impacts into costs is primarily conducted outside state institutions in what we might call the cultural or public sphere. This includes the highly specialized spheres of technical journals, scientific research departments and educational institutions, and the wider public sphere of mass communication and decentralized networks of personal contact. Environmental politics has also been conducted within the economic system, where conflict has been more muted. However, two phenomena are worth noting: the rise of the 'green consumer', and the occasional strikes in industries over environmental issues. Finally, the legal system has been an important site of environmental conflict, although its use will depend on the existence, if any, of environmental legislation.[92]

None the less, the most important point of conflict so far has been the political sphere proper, above all the state, or rather, given the international nature of environmental politics, nation-states and the international organizations within which they are represented. Moreover, it is public policy that ultimately deals with the existence and resolution of environmental costs. Within Western polities the sites of policy-making are highly variable depending on the internal constitution of the state and the ways in which it has historically responded to the problems of environmental costs. This affects the capacity of environmental movements to engage in the policy process. For example, the capacity of environmental movements to make their position heard will depend on the existence of a government department with specific responsibilities for environmental protection. In the absence of the former the environmental movement will have to deal with policy-making institutions that have, and represent, interests that may well be fundamentally opposed to environmental protection.[93] Another important factor for environmental movements is the existence or otherwise of freedom of governmental information, without which it becomes extremely difficult to track and monitor government policy.[94] However, as with the struggle over impact identification and cost establishment, differential power and resources ultimately determine the policy influence of actors.

We have already touched on the reasons why political combatants have such differential political power in these struggles and why those with most power have the most environmentally problematic interests. I shall return to these issues below. We need, however, to focus on the reasons why political opposition should then be mobilized on such issues at all.

The Mobilization of Environmental Politics

As I suggested in the introduction and chapter 2, we may tentatively distinguish between ideals and interests as motivating factors in the mobilization of environmental politics. The distinction can be overstated, for someone may object to the destruction of wildwood on a number of counts: because their own interest in visiting it is affected; out of an ideal or moral concern for the interests and opportunities of future generations; as well as out of a more diffuse moral sense for the preservation of the countryside irrespective of material consequences. A more comprehensive set of concerns might include personal economic, health and aesthetic interests. The ideals that motivate environmental politics include issues of justice, especially intergenerational justice, the moral-aesthetic significance of the environment and the moral rights of living things.

The ways in which interests motivate environmental politics are relatively easy to recognize: householders mobilizing over the drop in property prices caused by local pollution emissions; residents near nuclear power stations organizing in opposition to leaks in radioactivity and increasing levels of child leukaemia. The connections in these examples between interests and mobilization are common to most types of politics. However, environmental politics incessantly raises the question of justice: is it just that local residents should bear the costs of leukaemia caused by electricity production from which a whole population benefits? It is this type of moral question that gives environmental politics, on occasion, a political edge over the brute mobilization of dominant political and economic interests.[95]

Why should the question of justice be so central? As Rawls has argued, the first requirement of legitimate institutions and social arrangements in contemporary Western societies is that they are perceived to be just.[96] The legitimacy of Western societies routinely hangs on the pragmatic achievement of economic success for sufficient numbers and the perceived justness of political decision-making procedures. That is not to suggest that all forms of environmental degradation which are objected to are indeed unjust. For example, the objections of the rural middle classes to new housing developments may, on a certain reading, be perceived as the protection of an already unjust distribution of open space access and quality housing. Rather, it is to suggest that the successful political transition from perceived impacts to borne costs entails a definition by participants of the former as unjust. The scope of injustice has been extended by environmental politics to the predicament of humanity, future generations and the natural world itself. To pursue such a politics is to claim and define the genuine common interest. That environmental politics can do so is a testament less to its capacity for moral inquiry and more to the very real way in which contemporary patterns of environmental degradation have consequences for the entire planet. Future generations, given the cumulative and often irreversible quality of environmental change, will necessarily bear the costs of current environmental degradation in terms of resource depletion and diminished environmental resources.[97] The natural world, though traditionally excluded from Western moral inquiry and concern, is being drawn within it, by radical environmentalists at any rate. I shall explore the conditions under which these ideals can mobilize a significant political force in chapter 4.

Policy Options and Implementation

Given his account of the crisis of capitalism, Gorz should have examined the options for altering the current imposition of costs. Where he has considered the imposition of costs he has argued that industry must absorb them as increasing costs of production and pass them on as higher prices, or that the state must take responsibility through increased taxation. Clearly the former only occurs when resource shortages have reached a critical point – when there is simply no clean water left for manufacturing processes and it must be purified before it can be used. However, this is an exceptional rather than routine occurrence, at the moment at any rate.[98] Gorz's grasp of governmental action, it should now be clear, is equally limited. Governments have the potential to intervene in the determination and allocation of environmental costs in an immense variety of ways: taxation of consumption (reduced tax on lead-free petrol); legislation (on land use, wildlife preservation); regulation and inspection (the Health and

Safety Acts); monitoring and research; and subsidies for pollution abatement.[99] In failing to consider this, Gorz's account of the dynamics of capitalism under environmental stress must be questioned. His analysis rests on the assumption that costs will be recognized, that they will be imposed, and that they will fall directly on industry and the state. The reality is somewhat more complex and, as yet, uncertain.

However, even the best informed environmental political struggles, with the most legitimate claim to recompense for costs imposed, the most articulate demonstration of the injustice of a situation or the most sophisticated battery of policy instruments, will not necessarily result in a shift in political decision-making. We have already considered the political constraints on the control of externalities and the regulation of private and common property.[100] What then of the additional processes that we have identified in Gorz's work: technological development and public and private capital investment. As we argued above, it has as yet proved difficult to intervene from an environmental perspective in the development and deployment of technologies and in the investment of capital by private and public agencies. That the former should have been so resistant is not exactly surprising, given the insulation of the economy from the polity and the degree to which both business and investment institutions have jealously guarded the right to dispose of capital as they see fit.

The intransigence of public agencies in the face of manifest injustice is no less surprising. The mechanisms that have existed for incorporating environmental concerns into infrastructure planning have at the best of times been opaque: public inquiries have almost uniformly proved to be cosmetic exercises;[101] cost–benefit analysis has rarely been able to incorporate environmental costs in any significant fashion.[102] Above all, the lobbying organizations that have most significantly shaped the political agenda on infrastructure provision have combined both the most powerful political resources and the most environmentally problematic interests: the road lobby towers over the public transport lobby in transport policy; electricity generators and fossil fuel suppliers have consistently greater political resources than the energy efficiency and renewable energy lobbies in energy policy; farmers and fertilizer companies dominate the agricultural policy debate.[103] I shall pick up on the intransigence of public agencies and the political reach of polluters again in chapter 5 in connection with Ulrich Beck's work.

So far I have focused on collective political action. I now want to turn briefly to one further important site of environmental political conflict: consumption. Public policy has some limited purchase here. If Gorz is correct in saying that the social organization of consumption is one source of environmental degradation, then consumers must be informed about the origins and environmental implications of consuming the products they purchase. Left to itself, it is well known that the market will not provide that sort of information with any degree of honesty or regularity. Just as there have been political conflicts in trying to force the investment and research strategies of public and private agencies into the public realm, so the provision of information for consumers has been a political struggle. However, once that information is available there is no guarantee that individuals will consume in any more responsible fashion (or that if a small minority do, that private corporations will alter their production processes accordingly). Private consumers, like private corporations and public agencies, have a range of conflicting interests to attend to, but must also contend with a range of moral positions of varying degrees of coherence. Consumers may consider the cessation of environmental degradation to be both in their interest and a laudable moral ideal. That they possess such an interest or accept such a moral claim, should they do so at all, has not as yet ensured that they prioritize it over an interest in obtaining certain goods at a certain price, with a certain convenience. That they find ways for making those decisions differently is at the core of a successful environmental politics. It is now, on the basis of a sharper understanding of the origins and politics of environmental costs and environmental policy-making, that we can turn to the consequences of those costs and the political options available to cope with them.

Conclusion: the Consequences of Environmental Degradation and the Environmental Limits to Social Democracy

In this final section I intend to pick up some of the loose ends from earlier in the chapter. First, I shall examine Gorz's investigation of the consequences of the increasing environmental costs of economic growth in connection with his account of the 'crisis' of capitalist societies. I shall then return to his critique of social democracy and ask what we might do politically in the face of contemporary environmental degradation. In particular I shall want to assess the merits of Gorz's own utopian proposals for a society beyond work, asking whether this is politically feasible and environmentally sustainable.

The Consequences of Environmental Degradation and the Crises of Capitalism

It should be clear that Gorz's proposition – that the environmental costs of economic growth increase at a rate faster than the capacity of that growth to pay for them – is at best a possibility rather than an inevitability. What is and what is not a social cost, and which social costs are actually dealt with by a society, are all, politically, up for grabs. However, there are good reasons for suggesting that in the absence of any countervailing force there are significant pressures for the intended and unintended consequences of economic and political decision-making in contemporary capitalist societies to continue to generate substantial environmental degradation. These include the economically and politically driven process of economic growth; the environmental and generational myopia of unregulated markets and private property; the environmental blindness of technological development and capital investment; the inherent environmental consequences of fossil fuel and inorganic raw material technologies; the political, economic and ideological resources available to the most environmentally problematic social interests; the continuing likelihood that short-term economic interests will prevail, for individuals and institutions, over longer-term interests and moral positions.

Our quarrel with Gorz, then, is not that capitalist societies will *probably* have to face the environmental consequences of their own making, but whether these pressures will, in the long run, generate a socioeconomic crisis of the type he suggests, with the options for solving it that he poses. Gorz's two theories of overaccumulation sound like 'business as usual' rather than crisis situations. It does not require the spur of any tendency of the rate of profit to fall for capitalist economies to use more resources and create more pollution. Whether profits are rising or falling, the pursuit of economic growth, and increasing profitability, are inscribed in the practices of competitive markets and the political demands of electorates. Gorz's crises of reproduction and social costs are a little more promising. In the former, the consequences of increasing resource use and pollution are a spiralling of costs to industry and the necessary internalization of previously externalized costs. In the latter, the weight of increasing social and environmental costs, combined with the economic logic of automation, debar any solution but an authoritarian control of consumption or a utopian transformation of society.

However, as we have noted, the industrial internalization and rising tide of costs are politically contingent. Should this occur it is by no means certain that capitalism cannot live with them, or precisely how and why cost inflation would result in the types of major social crises Gorz suggests. It is not inconceivable that increasing costs to industry will be overcome, in the short to medium term, by increasing productivity, or technological innovation, or both. This may not resolve the problems of environmental degradation and its human costs, nor put off the problems indefinitely, but it may well serve to maintain, on its own peculiar terms, the operation of the economy. The question then becomes what the relevant time-scale is within which to view environmental politics. Similarly, increasing social costs could be borne directly by those on whom they fall, without any demand for taxation of the offender and recompense for the sufferer being successfully made on the state or any other institution. This is particularly so from an international perspective. The costs of contemporary environmental degradation do, and will, fall very differently across the globe. The major impacts of global warming, caused predominantly by emissions from the industrialized world, will fall in the South. The political capacity, and even the strength of the moral claim, of the states and peoples so affected may well be incapable of forcing those costs back on to the economies that have actually generated them. Alternatively, within capitalist economies, the brunt of resource shortage and pollution increases could be borne by a minority of the population. The increasing costs of governmental measures and economic price rises to curb or compensate for major environmental change could well fall most heavily on the poor and the marginalized. For example, increased taxes on consumer goods and on energy could be raised to cover depletion and pollution costs, as well as to curb certain forms of environmentally problematic consumption. Most consumption taxes are flat rate, and will therefore fall most heavily on those least able to pay and those least capable of articulating their opposition.

None of this should suggest that environmental impacts will not continue to bear upon the population of the world, or that they will not be perceived as costs, or that they will not have major economic and political consequences. All three will happen. None the less, we should recognize that the detailed trajectory of any such predictions cannot be more than highly tentative. Prediction in politics is epistemologically problematic. As Giddens has argued, the circularity of knowledge in modern societies ensures that predictions not only attempt to interpret the future but, by influencing actors' expectations and understanding of the world, help shape the future as well.[104] This epistemological instability is particularly acute in the case of environmental predictions. I argued earlier that predicting the outcome of environmental change even on the basis of the collection of specialized data and the use of specialized knowledge is open to question. While it is central to a successful environmental politics to consider the implications of current and future environmental degradation, we should be wary of trying to extrapolate too far into the future with any degree of precision. There are simply too many political and environmental unknowns. In this respect our predictions must be tempered not only by their inherent epistemological limitations, but by a relevant time-frame. I would suggest that we can only stretch our moral concern and political imagination so far, perhaps two generations (to our children and grandchildren as points of moral reference). I do not have space here to pursue that argument in depth, though I shall return to it later.[105]

Yet even on this minimal concern for intergenerational justice, the depth of our moral concern almost certainly outstrips the epistemological limits of our capacity to predict the future coherently and accurately. What we can know with some degree of certainty are not the details of the future trajectory of environmental degradation and its consequences, but the sorts of options available to us in the face of such uncertainty. Gorz recognizes that different political options exist. However, given the epistemological uncertainties of this kind of prediction, I believe that he has been too specific in outlining the choices that face us. Rather than focusing on the details of possible forms of social organizations, we should begin from a more abstract set of choices.

Consider the example of global warming. Despite the wealth of evidence and research available, it would be foolhardy to say that the mechanisms, causes and consequences of global warming are definitely understood. There is good cause, however, for very serious concern should our current understanding of global warming be correct. We can assume that the future course of environmental change will lie somewhere on a spectrum between the most pessimistic and the most optimistic outcomes. Optimists have suggested that the impacts of global warming, if it is happening at all, may be quite minimal and in many parts of the world actually induce beneficial climatic change. Pessimists have suggested an altogether different scenario: major climatic change and agricultural dislocation on a global scale, famine, rising sea levels, huge migrations and political turmoil.[106]

We in turn can take up a position of political response somewhere on a spectrum between 'business as usual' and extreme caution. In the case of the latter, faced with an optimistic outcome, we will no doubt have wasted time and energy controlling our economy and tempering our consumption – wastage that we might have avoided had we pursued business as usual. However, business as usual carries with it the most enormous risks because of the peculiar qualities of environmental change: that it can be quite irreversible; that it can pass points of no-return long before its most devastating consequences become apparent; that it is often a cumulative phenomenon, the consequences of which increase at an accelerating rate; that the interconnections of biological systems allow the impact of one type of environmental change to multiply rapidly and unexpectedly throughout an ecosystem. Therefore, in the event of the pessimistic course of environmental events, not to have taken pre-emptive action at an earlier stage may have pushed patterns of environmental change so far as to make their remedy and control either enormously expensive, or even quite impossible. Faced with such a dilemma (in a way a far more complex and difficult one than Gorz's self-assured prediction offers us) it would seem prudent to choose the strategy of pre-emptive caution and immediate action. This disposition, like the commitment to the interests of future generations or a long-term perspective on economic development, is not a virtue with which Western political cultures are blessed in any great amount. Developing this virtue, making it the common sense of our political culture, will be a necessary if not sufficient condition of limiting the worst consequences of environmental change. The question remains, what strategy of action might actually inform such a disposition? In attempting a partial answer to this question, I want to consider Gorz's critique of social democracy.

Gorz's Critique of Social Democracy

There are three elements to Gorz's critique of social democracy. First, that its commitment to growth in a capitalist society generates environmental degradation and fails to resolve the problem of poverty. Second, that its Keynesian-based strategies of reflation and full employment are incapable of delivering growth, even were it desirable. Third, that the fragmentation and incorporation of its core constituency, the industrial working class, has denied it the political muscle to pursue such a strategy, irrespective of the coherence and validity of its programme.

Gorz is, I think, correct to argue that economic growth is both environmentally problematic and, as yet, provides no answer to the problem of poverty. If poverty is a relative phenomenon, then there can be little doubt that our current arrangements for production and consumption will ensure that enormous disparities will continue to exist in Western societies. In fact Gorz has missed an important unintended consequence of the egalitarian politics of social democracy. For not only has economic growth failed to eradicate poverty through the provision of jobs and/or income, but the welfare state (that was supposed to remedy the failings of the economic growth) has often subsidized the middle classes to the disadvantage and cost of the poor.[107] He is correct, I believe, in arguing that classical demand management, in the context of the international financial system and resistance by both capital and labour, is of limited use in generating long-term economic growth.[108] He also has a point in arguing that the political muscle of the organized working class in the West is, if not eradicated, certainly past its peak.[109] The question does, however, remain as to whether his own political and economic arguments are any more practicable and environmentally beneficial than those he has criticized.

Those who wish to limit the baleful consequences of environmental change should focus on winning and maintaining political power. The currently appalling state of environmental degradation, the degree to which politics and the execution of political power are implicated in that process, the likelihood of it getting worse, the limited capacity of the environmental movement to influence the policy process, and the need for caution all suggest that whatever else is proposed, the wielding of state power is of the utmost importance. On this count Gorz's invective against social democracy is somewhat misplaced. Given the truly appalling record of the radical left in Western societies in winning mass ideological support and power, and, on the rare occasions that they have done so, in maintaining power and executing its politics successfully, it behoves a writer like Gorz, to the left of social democracy, to be a little more measured in assessing its political potential. For we are unlikely to be able to rely on the parties of the right to stem capitalism's capacity for environmental degradation, nor on historical and current performance should we expect those further to the left to be in a position to do so. Furthermore, important as the environmental movement and green parties are, it would be foolhardy to expect them to deliver the political goods in the near future.[110] Our preference for caution and immediate pre-emptive action makes any short-term reliance on these forces particularly questionable. The first virtue then of social democracy is that it at least has the opportunity of obtaining the first prerequisite of effecting change – winning elections and forming governments. Though, by the same token, we would be equally foolhardy to place our political trust exclusively with the leadership of contemporary social democratic parties.

If Gorz's critique of social democracy is strategically unwise, his condemnation of the policies it has pursued may be cogent. The real test of his cogency is not simply whether his objections are correct, but whether the alternatives he proposes are feasible and at least no worse in their outcomes than current social democratic practice. Politics, in the face of environmental degradation, can only choose between the lesser of two evils. If my analysis of the structural origins of environmental degradation is correct, then the central political dilemma for environmental politics is to socially and environmentally curb capitalism. I write curb, rather than transcend, for no alternative mode of production is visible on the intellectual or economic horizon. This argument is in no sense an active approval of capitalism; rather it is the sobering consequence of the total failure, environmental and economic, of its only rival, state socialism, and the limits of our own economic and political imagination to envisage anything else.

Given the premises of caution and immediate anticipatory action, the task for environmental politics must be, for the moment, how to live with capitalism. Gorz berated social democracy for fruitlessly pursuing economic growth. However, growth, though central, is not the only problem we face. A stationary economy, organized along capitalist lines, would still face a series of problems: resource depletion, externalities, the non-provision of public goods, unregulated investment and technological development, the dominance of business interests in state policy. Here, surely, is the natural territory of an aggressive and competent social democracy: the regulation of markets; the opening up of decision-making processes; and the attempt to articulate the common good and translate it into collective action and public goods.[111] Furthermore, social democracy is not unsuited to the environmental and political task presented to it by industrialism: diminishing reliance on finite supplies of fossil fuels. Whether we can maintain a level of consumption currently enjoyed in the West on the basis of renewable energy supplies is a technical question that I shall not discuss. What is clear, however, is that with sufficient intervention in the design and research of renewable energy and energy-efficient technologies, and the investment of public capital in the energy infrastructure, a substantial start can be made.

Environmental problems associated with growth and the issue of poverty and unjust distribution of costs would, however, remain unaddressed. It is here, if anywhere, that Gorz's critique of social democracy bites. Once again, it is a question of the distribution of costs. For the cessation of environmental degradation will entail both substantial transitional costs, as our current forms of production and consumption are shifted, and a final settlement on a distribution of different costs and different levels of consumption and standards of living. It will, moreover, when viewed in an international perspective, require somewhat more than the regulation of growing Western economies based on non-fossil fuel. Thus this is not simply a domestic issue for the West, but first and foremost an international one. Even if we were to temper the process of economic growth, then what are we to make of the enormous disparities of wealth and power that will remain between North and South? Whatever the West makes of them, there can be little doubt that the governments and the peoples of the South will continue, as best they can, to expand their economies, energy and resource use in pursuit of a measure of the affluence currently enjoyed by large numbers in the West. If that disparity is not addressed it is all the more likely that whatever action is taken within the West, it will be made irrelevant by the capitalist industrialization of states containing huge numbers of people with environmental appetites as voracious as ours. Although it is in the final analysis a technical question, I would suggest that it is prudent to claim that a world population that will double in the next quarter of a century cannot live at the level of affluence, even a regulated one, of the average citizen of the United States or Western Europe.[112]

Two of the questions facing environmental politics are therefore: how might one persuade the electorates of the West to accept a slowing down or cessation of economic growth and the environmental degradation it brings, as well as a degree of resource transfer to the South; and second, how economically might one go about doing so in the context of a capitalist economy and liberal democratic polity. It is on these issues that Gorz's utopianism is at its most effective, if not as yet at its most feasible. Let us consider the politics of the West. Not because the politics of the South is irrelevant, but because any resolution of the problems of the relations between North and South and the inequitable distribution of wealth between them, in the absence of open international conflict, will be resolved only by a fundamental shift in the politics and opinions of Western publics and their politicians.

Gorz's Utopia and the Prospects for Environmental Politics

It is clear that, at the moment, Western publics consider the maintenance of economic growth and a rising standard of living to be a necessary, if not sufficient, condition of political support for political parties. In such a context it is most unlikely that a political party promising limited growth will be successful. The virtue of Gorz's argument is to suggest that we will only control our demand for growth if we begin to redefine our meanings of welfare and well-being and consume differently. We must break the cultural equation between more and better. Given that material interests tend to mobilize political support somewhat more effectively than our ideal concerns, there is surely a case for trying to redefine our material interests in the light of our moral concerns. However, no political programme that calls for Western publics to reduce consumption and accept stationary standards of living, given contemporary attitudes to what constitutes wealth and well-being, has any chance of political success. Social democracy has not mustered, and in its present form is unlikely to muster, the intellectual resources to transcend this problem. The singular achievement of Gorz's work is to suggest that such a redefinition might be founded on breaking the link between income and work, or a massive reduction in individual working time and a consequent redistribution of working time from the overemployed to the underemployed and unemployed, as well as a massive increase in free, self-determined activity and the creation thereby of a thriving, enlarged and increasingly autonomous civil society.

The choice, in simplistic and compressed terms, for the electorates of the West would be something along the lines of earning £20,000 a year and working a three-day week, or earning £30,000 a year on a full week's work. In economic terms, increases in productivity would be translated into shorter working hours to produce the same volume of goods and services, rather than increased production of goods on a full working week. The trade-off, of course, is somewhat less appealing for those on £5,000 a year. In that sense, it is a programme that is only morally acceptable, if not politically feasible, if it also entails some sort of redistribution of wealth, be it by income or public service provision, or redistribution of work. In fact Gorz takes the argument so far as to suggest the allocation of a basic income to all adults independent of work and related to dependants' needs.[113] The strategy is, in effect, not the control of the market (social democracy) or its abolition (state socialism) but its circumvention. It involves the creation of a sphere of non-market consumption and, should people choose, production as well, which would be freed from the environmentally problematic imperatives and rationality of other economic systems. The overall size and environmental consequences of a regulated market sector would be controlled. The strength of Gorz's position and its capacity to transcend the limits of social democracy rest on the answers to a number of questions.

First, we must ask whether Western publics are prepared to accept such a programme and thus whether well-being can be defined in terms of free time and autonomous production for a substantial majority of the population. Moreover, can it be accepted within an appropriate time-scale given the proximity and implications of catastrophic levels of environmental degradation? The evidence so far, while not conclusive, is not greatly encouraging. There is little doubt that Western publics are capable of enlightened redefinition of self-interest and political action on the basis of public interests. However, environmental problems and the major types of social transformation that their resolution demands have as yet not been capable of permanently occupying the commanding heights of public policy agendas. Indeed they have shown a disturbing propensity to slip from sight during periods of economic downturn. It may be that the impacts and costs of environmental degradation will have to directly affect a larger number of people in the West in a more profound way before they are prepared to contemplate and vote for major social change to deal with environmental problems. However, as the question of time-scale reminds us, by this point not only may patterns of environmental degradation be irreversible, but millions of people in the South will already have been bearing the brunt of these costs for some time. One of the reasons that Western publics may take so long to respond politically to the dilemmas they face is the difficulty in redefining wealth and well-being in the way that Gorz describes. Again, there is some evidence from union campaigns that shorter working hours are being negotiated in preference to higher wages. The size and importance of the informal economy is significant in a number of Western countries and there is some evidence of dissatisfaction with consumerism.[114] However, as yet, this hardly amounts to a significant cultural revolution.

Second, the question remains whether such a socioeconomic system would be environmentally sustainable. Gorz has not considered whether autonomous production would be environmentally benign or whether the traditional economy that remained would be of a form and size that did not entail major environmental problems. How could we ensure that the overall consequences of free time and self-production would not be environmentally problematic? People may choose to consume more in their free time should it be available. Would they want to engage in self-production anyway? What of the politically destabilizing implications of boredom? Similarly, what size would the rest of the economy be? How big would it need to be in order to provide a level of basic income for a population otherwise reliant on their own efforts? Even were we to stall the level of growth in the formal economy at current levels and divert all subsequent productivity increases into the expansion of free time and autonomous production, we would be left with an enormous level of formal economic consumption. Diminishing this rump of the formal economy would no doubt prove even more politically problematic than simply checking its growth. In any case, we have yet to determine whether capital can be forced to accept controls on the level of overall production. Given the capacity of capital to derail the policy process over regulation, how much more powerful would the resistance be to the controls that Gorz's work implies? In an open international economy, where capital is increasingly mobile, the political prognosis is not optimistic.

It is even less optimistic for the third question that Gorz's proposal has to face: can such a model can be accompanied by sufficient levels of resource transfer from North to South to limit population growth in the South and generate sufficient economic prosperity to make managed and limited environmental resource use possible? If it can, what are the appropriate institutional forms for doing so? On this, Gorz is in effect silent.

Conclusions

In the introduction to this chapter I argued that an examination of Gorz's work would allow us to explore two important issues that Giddens's work had raised but had not adequately dealt with: the intersection of economic and political power in the production and control of environmental degradation, and the socioeconomic consequences of environmental degradation. We can now summarize the strengths and weaknesses of Gorz's work in tackling these issues.

As I have already argued, Gorz's integration of environmental issues into a broad political economy is an advance in itself. His focus on consumption, cultural interpretations of wealth and well-being and technology have all advanced our understanding of the political economy of environmental degradation. Similarly, his discussion of cost spirals and capitalist crises has allowed us to perceive the ways in which environmental degradation may have system-wide effects on capitalist societies rather than just individual impacts on health and well-being. However, it is fair to say that his account suffers from a number of limitations which this chapter has tried to highlight: (1) his inattention to international economics and politics; (2) an overdeterministic understanding of the consequences of environmental degradation which stems from his failure to distinguish between environmental impacts and costs, and thus his inattention to the political struggles of converting one to the other; (3) an overdeterministic understanding of state action, which stems from his inattention to the institutions and dynamics of public policy formation and the extent to which those political struggles can both aid and restrain the environmentally problematic consequences of economic action; (4) a rather overoptimistic belief in the capacity of prediction of the social sciences.

None the less, Gorz's predictions are not without value. They have helped to demonstrate the environmental limits of social democracy, while not always acknowledging its strengths. Moreover, he has clearly articulated the necessity of a transformation of cultural attitudes and interests in the West towards work, wealth and time without which an environmentally sustainable future is unlikely to materialize. Thus, for all the uncertainties of prediction, it is certain that, in the absence of a cultural revolution of the magnitude that Gorz suggests – of a redefinition of material interests and an elevation of our moral concerns in the conduct of our individual consumption and collective politics, of a commitment to the long term and of the acquisition of a more careful political culture – we in the North, and even more so those in the South, will pay the very high costs of our lack of caution and our demand for growth.

4
Social and Cultural Origins of Environmental Movements: Jürgen Habermas

In my discussion of classical social theory I argued that environmental politics is mobilized by the interplay of structurally determined interests, cognitive understandings of the world and ideal-moral values. I argued that Giddens offered two explanations of the emergence of environmental politics. On the one hand, environmental politics was characterized as a response to high-risk ecological threats and is thus *a politics mobilized by interests* in self-preservation. On the other, Giddens described environmental politics as a response to the normative emptiness of modern urbanism and thus as *a politics mobilized by ideal values and moral imperatives*. The importance of the latter was highlighted in my discussion of Gorz and the model of environmental politics which I established in connection with his work. What remained unclarified in Giddens's work and inadequately discussed in relation to Gorz were two theoretical issues: the precise structural origins of political interests, cognitive understandings of environmental change and cultural values and ideals; and the relationships between these sources of mobilization.[1] I intend to develop these issues through a critical assessment of the work of Habermas, in particular his *Theory of Communicative Action*.[2] Habermas's theory of modernity, elaborated in this work, has been shaped with these issues in mind: 'In assessing the Greens, what is significant . . . is whether the potentials they represent are structurally generated or just contingently thrown up. *My view is that there are systematic reasons why these potentials are still expanding.*'[3] These systematic reasons can be traced in Habermas's work to changes in and interconnections between political ideals, knowledge and interests. At the core of Habermas's position is the notion of the *colonization of the lifeworld*. To explore the strengths and weaknesses of this concept I shall sketch some aspects of his earlier work.

The Theory of Communicative Action: Origins, Contexts and Arguments

The Theory of Communicative Action has attracted a great deal of critical attention. Some studies have sought to illuminate its internal arguments;[4] others have linked those arguments to the broad sweep of Habermas's earlier work.[5] Without wishing to duplicate the existing literature, we must clarify three themes in Habermas's work. First, I shall examine his use of linguistic analysis and the inherent rationality of communicative action. Second, I shall look at the way in which the latter serves to illuminate the notion of the one-sided or pathological development of modernity. This is pursued from the perspective of moral philosophy in *The Philosophical Discourse of Modernity*[6] and taken up sociologically in *The Theory of Communicative Action* in connection with Weber's theory of rationalization. Finally, I shall examine how, in drawing on the theory of social evolution in *Communication and the Evolution of Society* and the critical theory of late capitalism in *Legitimation Crisis*, Habermas has attempted to resolve the issues thrown up by his reading of Weber.[7]

Linguistic Analysis and the Theory of Action

Since he abandoned the attempt to ground a critical theory in terms of quasi-transcendental human interests, the philosophy of language has assumed an increasing significance in Habermas's work.[8] Its role has been twofold: Habermas has pursued the place of language in a sociological theory of action, and sought to demonstrate that the structure and function of human language provide the foundations of a universalistic and democratic ethics.[9] I do not intend to account for all the turns that these arguments have undergone.[10] It is the structure of the argument that concerns us. Habermas has argued that linguistic analysis, supplemented by speech-act theory, can, through rational reconstruction, reveal the universal and unavoidable presuppositions of everyday language.[11] Thus all speech acts potentially raise a series of validity claims. Certain validity claims, if raised, can be rationally justified through argumentative discourse. This discourse can be clarified in terms of the conditions that constitute an ideal speech situation.[12] In his recent work two important additions have been made to these arguments: an ontological specification of the possible worlds which can be known and a reassessment of the knowledge we deem valid for each; and the recognition that human action may be orientated to many goals, but linguistic action, given its rationally reconstructible basis, is orientated towards the co-ordination of action achieved by mutual understanding. Habermas specifies three worlds towards which speakers orientate themselves: the external world of physical objects, the social world and the personal, inner world.[13] He can therefore differentiate conceptually between *communicative action*

(action orientated towards mutual understanding in the social world), *instrumental action* (orientated towards success in the external world) and *strategic action* (orientated to success in the social world).[14]

Habermas fuses this line of argument with those relating to universal pragmatics. He claims that, in uttering speech acts concerning any one of these worlds (external, social, internal), speakers use a distinctive type of speech act (constative, regulative, expressive) and raise a distinct set of appropriate validity claims (truth, correctness, sincerity). These validity claims may be judged against distinctive forms of rationality (cognitive-instrumental, moral-practical, aesthetic-expressive) through appropriate modes of argumentation, where rationality is understood as openness to objective appraisal, and argumentation is deemed valid under the conditions of the ideal speech situation.

Habermas and Weber's Theory of Modernity

Habermas's use of this model can only be grasped in relation to his concern with modernity. If *The Theory of Communicative Action* is an attempt to comprehend modernity sociologically, then *The Philosophical Discourse of Modernity* approaches the same subject from the standpoint of philosophy. In tracing the course of post-enlightenment Western philosophy Habermas identifies a perennial moral paradox. The paradox which marks the philosophical discourse of modernity, indeed heralds its arrival, is the recognition that its self-understanding is only made possible by its severance from tradition. In making that break, modern philosophical argument also generates a demand for an unshakable source of moral justification. With the loss of traditional ethical foundations and the rise of an internally generated demand for sure foundations, the paradox of modernity is 'the necessity of creating normativity out of itself'.[15]

Does modernity have the capacity to solve its own moral paradox? Habermas is sensitive to the criticisms of the dominant enlightenment notions of reason that originally promised to do so.[16] Communicative rationality is to serve as an alternative. His argument, in short, is that the structural and cultural transformations that constitute modernity not only generate the demand that morality be rationally founded, but are made possible by the historically unique unleashing of the rational potential of communicative action. Modernity simultaneously demands rational justification and furnishes the cultural resources by which that demand can be actualized. The questions remain why modern societies should unleash the rational potential of communicative action, and, more pressingly, why that rational potential is so rarely actualized in the institutional organization and cultural practice of modern societies. Habermas refers to this as the one-sided development of modernity. We have thus moved from the territory of philosophy to that of sociology, from rationality to rationalization.

It is hardly surprising that Habermas should conduct a rereading of Weber, reconstructing two separate but historically interconnected dimensions of his historical sociology: cultural rationalization, entailing the disenchantment of world religions and the emergence of modern structures of consciousness; and social rationalization, entailing the emergence of institutionalized, formal domains of purposive-rational economic and political action.[17] In so doing he has two intentions: first, to make the cultural dimensions of Weber's historical sociology explicit and thus explain why modernity unleashes the rational potential of communicative action; second, in explaining its one-sided development, to clarify the meaning of Weber's 'pathologies of modernity', the loss of meaning and the loss of freedom. Weber argued that the former resulted from the collapse of modern reason into irreconcilable spheres of distinct cultural values, among which no overarching sureness of meaning could be constructed. The latter was a consequence of the irresistible dynamics of the purposive-rational action let loose by social rationalization. The means–ends rationality of the modern bureaucracy would engulf those realms previously subject to value orientations.

Habermas detects two limitations to Weber's work:[18] first, that his notion of rational action is exclusively bound to the idea of strategic or instrumental rationality; second, that the nature of social rationalization remains too unclarified to provide a normative standard against which to judge its actual progress. As a result, Weber misdiagnosed the pathologies of modernity as inevitable rather than contingent and the rationalization of the modern world as inherently problematic rather than historically one-sided, and lost sight of the rational kernel of modernity that is worthy of preservation.[19] Habermas therefore attempts to establish a theory of social rationalization which captures the different forms of rational action he made explicit and which is sharp enough that it might normatively denounce its pathological forms and historically explain their development. If Weber is Habermas's starting point for considering the trajectories of rationalization, an alternative model of social evolution and late capitalism is required.

Social Evolution and the Rationalization of the Lifeworld

An alternative model of social evolution was first elaborated in *Communication and the Evolution of Society*.[20] Habermas had earlier criticized Marx for reducing his conception of human action to labour alone, and supplemented it with the notion of interaction.[21] The equiprimordial status of human beings as language users as well as producers demanded a reinterpretation of Marx's 'motor of historical development', the forces of production. Habermas argued that the development of human societies should be seen along two autonomous but interdependent axes: success in material reproduction, and advances in moral development. Indeed, advances in material success remained dependent on the evolution of advanced stages of moral consciousness.[22] The latter is characterized by an increasing ability to assume the perspective of other participants, to reflect on one's own interests and to assent to the correctness of moral norms on the basis of argument and consensus. All these rest on an increasing capacity for the utilization of the rational potential embedded in communicative action. In this case the correctness of the social evolution argument would provide an explanation of why the unleashing of the rational potential of communicative action generated both the historical emergence of modern societies and a normative standard against which to judge its development. Durkheim is Habermas's point of departure in pursuing this.

Durkheim traced a line of development from segmentally differentiated societies to ones composed of functionally distinct units.[23] It is a transition that is marked, not only by an increasingly complex division of labour, but by differing forms of social solidarity: mechanical and organic. Habermas describes the argument: 'Whereas primitive societies are integrated via a *basic normative consensus*, the integration of developed societies comes about via the *systemic interconnection of functionally specified domains of action.*'[24] However, Durkheim did not intend to conceptualize organic solidarity as a form of system integration decisively separated from the value orientations of actors. Moral and legal rules remained at the heart of the integration of modern societies. Habermas argues that there is no causal explanation of the connection between functional differentiation and integrating morality in Durkheim's work. This leaves his normative claims regarding the abnormal divisions of labour unsubstantiated.[25] This absence can only be redeemed by abandoning the unitary concept of society on which Durkheim relied. Rather than attempt to explain the emergence of new forms of moral regulation with reference to the differentiation of the economic system, Habermas writes: '[The] distinction between a *social integration* of society, which takes effect in action orientations, and a *systematic integration*, which reaches through and beyond action orientations, calls for *a corresponding differentiation in the concept of society itself.*'[26]

This differentiation rests on the distinction between system and lifeworld.[27] Habermas describes the lifeworld as a domain of communicative action in which social reproduction is accomplished by the achievement of uncoerced mutual understanding through the medium of language.[28] Systems, by contrast, are systematically integrated contexts of action. They are the domain of instrumental and strategic action, in which system reproduction is achieved by the functional intermeshing of action consequences disengaged from the perspective and orientation of individual actors, mediated by delinguistified steering media: money and institutionalized political power. Habermas makes the role of communicative action in the reproduction of the lifeworld more explicit by breaking down the lifeworld into three structural components and three processes of symbolic reproduction: culture, society and personality; and cultural reproduction, social integration and socialization.[29] Each of the processes of symbolic reproduction, working through the medium of language, makes a contribution to the maintenance of each of the structural components of the lifeworld.[30]

This model underwrites Habermas's theory of social evolution based on *the rationalization of the lifeworld*, which has normative implications and evolutionary consequences. Habermas equates the rationalization of the lifeworld with the progressive unleashing of the rational potential of communicative action.[31] Ethical advance can be demonstrated by judging the rationalization of the lifeworld against criteria of moral-practical rationality: advances in cumulative learning capacity; increasing universalism and generalization of moral norms; and an increasing openness to the peculiar force of consensually orientated argument. This is because 'the further the structural components of the lifeworld and the processes that contribute to maintaining them get differentiated, the more interaction contexts come under conditions of rationally motivated mutual understanding, that is, of consensus formation that rests *in the end* on the authority of the better argument.'[32]

The evolutionary consequence of the rationalization of the lifeworld derives from Habermas's contention that moral advance is the precondition of developments in the material reproduction of societies.[33] In *The Theory of Communicative Action*, however, he refers not simply to material reproduction but to advances in systemic complexity, calibrated by the increasing capacity of a society to respond to its environment.[34] The decisive modern advance in system complexity is the emergence of non-linguistic steering media: money and power. Once established, economic and political action can be co-ordinated without the constant necessity for complex and risky negotiation and processes of common will formation.[35] In order to be effective media, capable of co-ordinating action and reproducing their respective economic and political subsystems, both require the development of systems of modern law and morality. Modern constitutional and contract law are the *sine qua non* of the establishment of systemically integrated contexts of action. Freed from the normative burdens of communicative action, actors may act strategically or instrumentally within the newly created economy and bureaucracy.[36] System and lifeworld, system and social integration, communicative action and strategic/instrumental action are uncoupled.

Habermas can now offer an answer to the normative paradox of modernity. The rationalization of the lifeworld, which brings modern societies and its separate media-steered subsystems into being, simultaneously provides the normative criteria against which to adjudge their subsequent development. The question remains why should that development of polity and economy have been so morally problematic or one-sided? Habermas answers this by drawing on *Legitimation Crisis*. The main lines of the text are well known,[37] but three points are important. First, the distinction between the mode of reproduction of the economic and political systems and the cultural system had already been made, albeit with less precision. Second, the failure of politico-economic crises to develop along Marxist lines could be explained by the fact that the disequilibria of each system are first dealt with by the other and then shunted into the realm of social reproduction; economic stability is bought at the price of political instability, political stability is bought at the price of cultural disfigurement.[38] Third, in an earlier formulation of the rational potential argument, Habermas suggests that sociocultural changes are undermining capitalism. An increasing capacity for rational discourse among the population brings rejection of the imposition of system reproduction on social reproduction. Moreover, the declining purchase of bourgeois and pre-bourgeois world-views in the face of such rational discourse makes ideological mystification increasingly transparent. Given that the current distribution of power and wealth, and their impact on the reproduction of socio-cultural life, could not be assented to under rational analysis, a legitimation crisis is likely to occur.[39] The reformulation of these arguments in the light of the bi-level concept of society leads us to Habermas's theory of modernity and the source of its pathologies: the colonization of the lifeworld.

The Theory of Modernity and the Colonization of the Lifeworld

I want to focus on four elements of Habermas's theory of modernity: first, his description of the structural organization of modern societies; second, in his own words, 'the theoretical deficits detrimental to Marx's attempts to explain late capitalism . . . a model that explains the compromise structures of late capitalism and the cracks within them';[40] third, his reading of the origins and consequences of contemporary crises in modern societies and how they result in what he calls – rereading Weber's loss of freedom – the colonization of the lifeworld; fourth, the detailed arguments through which he attempts to substantiate this claim.

The main components of Habermas's structural model of modernity are outlined in figure 1. The central distinction is between media-steered subsystems and the lifeworld. Habermas subdivides each into public and private domains: the polity and communication networks, and economy and families respectively. The centrepiece of the model is the relationships established between system and lifeworld, crystallizing around four social roles. These are the points at which the actions of individuals can be orientated and organized through the steering media on which the differentiated subsystems rely. Habermas distinguishes between organization dependent and independent roles. Into the former category fall the roles of *employee* within the economy and that of a *client* of state institutions. In both cases the roles individuals assume are legally constituted and enshrined in specific institutional locations. By contrast, the organization independent roles of *consumer* in the private sphere and *citizen* in the

Institutional orders of the lifeworld	Social roles	Interchange relations	Media-steered subsystems
Private sphere	Employee Consumer	────────→ Labour power ←──────── Income from employment ←──────── Goods and services ────────→ Demand	Economic system
Public sphere	Client Citizen	────────→ Taxes ←──────── Organizational accomplishments ←──────── Political decisions ────────→ Mass loyalty	Administrative system

Figure 1 Habermas's model of modernity (adapted from figure 39 in Jürgen Habermas, *The Theory of Communicative Action, Volume 2*, Beacon Press, Boston, 1987; Polity Press, Cambridge,1987)

public sphere rely on self-formative processes within the lifeworld. Consumption preferences and political allegiances are rooted in its communicative practices. Individuals bring these with them when encountering the systemic mechanisms of the market and the modern polity.[41]

Habermas is now able to chart the limits of Marx's model of late capitalism:the limited rather than revolutionary nature of economic and political crises; the containment of the contradiction between democracy and private accumulation rather than their insoluble conflict; and the countering of the threat of an organized working-class politics. Government intervention in the economy has secured the first by influencing the business cycle and manipulating the boundary conditions of accumulation. In addition, military and politico-legal force has been used to ensure the maintenance of accumulation in the face of organized opposition. Infrastructural support and spending have filled the gaps left by the dysfunctioning of the market.[42] The contradiction between democracy and capitalism recalls the arguments of *Legitimation Crisis*. Simply put, under the conditions of a rationalized lifeworld, only democratic processes of will formation will be accepted as legitimate. There is, argues Habermas, a fundamental tension between the normative principles of a democratic polity and the functional requirements of capitalist accumulation. The former places primacy on the integrity of the lifeworld, and the latter reaches its legitimate limits at the point at which the social integration of the lifeworld is threatened. However, the process of capitalist accumulation requires that 'the propelling mechanism of the economic system has to be kept as free as possible from lifeworld restrictions as well as from the demands of legitimation directed to the administrative system.'[43] Thus, in functional terms, capitalism requires that the value orientations of the lifeworld (towards use) be detached from action in the economy (orientated towards exchange values), while in normative terms the demand for democracy unleashed by the rationalized lifeworld finds these consequences of capitalism unjustifiable.

This demand for rational justification, placed on the administrative system by a rationalized lifeworld and articulated through the role of citizen, is dammed by the advent of mass democracy. Mass loyalty is manufactured by the administrative system: positively by delivering social welfare programmes, and negatively by systematically deforming the process of public, democratic will formation, which would render capitalist accumulation and the contemporary distribution of political power illegitimate.[44] The role of citizen has been reduced to the casting of votes, choosing between political elites uncoupled from the processes of will formation on which the legitimacy of that process should normatively rest.[45]

The advent of the *welfare state* not only shores up the manufacture of mass loyalty but is instrumental in neutralizing the political threat of class conflict. Habermas argues that the welfare state heads off the protests that arise from the costs of untrammelled capitalist economic development. Neutralization of conflict is ensured by upgrading the role of the consumer.[46] If alienated labour is obtained at the price of an expanded consumerism, then alienated political participation is equally 'compensated' for by goods and services received from the polity by the clients of welfare systems.

Habermas can now rediagnose the loss of freedom as *the colonization of the lifeworld*. In short, he argues that the dynamics of late capitalism channel their compensations for alienated labour and political participation through the roles of consumer and client. However, their consequences are ambiguous. They entail the conversion of socially integrated action to systematically integrated contexts of action – which Habermas calls *systemically induced reification*. This is, in effect, a return to the arguments of *Legitimation Crisis* at a higher level of theoretical specificity and with a renewed interpretation of the cultural shifts that accompany this process. Rather than the disintegration of bourgeois ideologies, Habermas now writes of the fragmentation of consciousness and the consequences of *cultural impoverishment*.

The theoretical explanation of systemically induced reification is relatively clear. Processes of social integration are converted to system integration, displacing communicative action orientated to mutual understanding with strategic action orientated towards success. This is *both normatively objectionable*, when measured against the demands of a rationalized lifeworld, ('dimensions of evaluation' in figure 2 below), and *functionally problematic*.[47] Habermas has argued that disturbances in the domain of lifeworld reproduction processes call forth social pathologies. Although, as Habermas admits, these arguments are conducted at a high level of theoretical generalization, he provides more substantial arguments against which his position might be tested.[48] In particular, he attempts to clarify the process of colonization through the notion of juridification and the pathologies of personhood; to give a sharper sense of the structural origins of societal pathologies; and to recast the loss of meaning in terms of cultural impoverishment.

Juridification and Pathologies of Personhood

Juridification allows Habermas to explore the way in which the dynamics of the administrative system and the historical constitution of the client role impinge on the reproduction of personality within the lifeworld. Juridification usually refers to the general increase of formal law in modern societies. Habermas distinguishes between two types of juridification: the expansion of law to codify and regulate a previously informal form of social organization; and an increasing density and specialization of law in an already regulated area. The normative implications of this argument turn on the distinction between legal institutions and law as a steering medium. Legal institutions are norms that cannot be justified by reference to positivistic or procedural criteria alone. Rather, they require substantive rational justification.[49] Law as a steering medium is relieved of the problem of justification since its execution is grounded in procedural criteria alone. Habermas can thus argue that the juridification of informally regulated areas of life is not automatically problematic. The early waves of juridification were characterized by new legal institutions, 'restrain[ing], in the interests of citizens and of private legal subjects, the political and economic dynamics that had been released by the legal institutionalization of money and power.'[50]

The emergence of the democratic-welfare state entails both forms of juridification. Within the realm of the wage-labour contract and the role of the employee, already constituted by formal law, we see an increasing density of legal regulation, on hours, conditions, benefits, etc. But, with the provision of state welfare itself, there has been a loss of freedom at the interface of system and lifeworld, where public welfare policy is tailored to the peculiar demands of bureaucratic implementation and monetary redemption which require a redefinition of the client in individualistic and technical, legal terms.[51] The paradox is that 'the legal institutions that guarantee social compensation become effective only through social-welfare law used as a medium.'[52] The use of law as a medium of intervention in social reproduction can only be executed at the cost of pathological consequences.

Habermas illustrates these consequences with reference to school and family law. Drawing on the institution/medium distinction he argues that education and socialization are processes reproduced by communicative action. Juridification may take the form of supplementing these socially integrated contexts through the creation of legal institutions, or, as is more often the case, converting them over to systemic integration through the imposition of law as a steering medium. So, for example, the constitution of the family as a legal institution is not in itself a pathological problem. It may be beneficial if it secures children's rights and more gender-equitable property and divorce laws. Rather, it is when procedures of legal decision-making displace the processes of consensual negotiation that we have a pathological situation.[53] The creation of educational law is not in itself a problem; it may guarantee the rights of students and parents and limit the capacity of schools to carry out corporal punishment. But these are gained at the cost of bureaucracy and juridification penetrating deep into the teaching and learning process.[54]

Social Pathologies

Habermas's comments on the pathologies of society are more cryptic. He argues that the systemic disequilibria of economy and polity become steering crises when the performances of economy and state manifestly remain below a common level of aspiration.[55] Those steering crises are neutralized by recourse to the resources of the societal component of the lifeworld. It is here that the media-steered subsystems are anchored in the lifeworld and where they are legitimated. The complete breakdown of social institutions, through generalized anomie, is forestalled by the displacement of systems effects into the peripheral dimensions of culture and person. This leads to alienation and unsettled collective identity. More serious steering crises eat away at the contribution of cultural reproduction and socialization to societal maintenance, leading to a withdrawal of legitimation and motivations. Only when these resources have been exhausted and deformed is societal integration under attack.

The Loss of Meaning and Cultural Pathologies

Finally, there is the colonization of the cultural component of the lifeworld. I want to explore two aspects of this: first, the wider question of cultural impoverishment; and second, the more restricted pathology of

Structural components / Disturbances in the domain of	Culture	Society	Person	Dimension of evaluation
Cultural reproduction	Loss of meaning	Withdrawal of legitimation	Crisis in orientation and education	Rationality of knowledge
Social integration	Unsettling of collective identity	Anomie	Alienation	Solidarity of members
Socialization	Rupture of tradition	Withdrawal of motivation	Psycho-pathologies	Personal responsibility

Figure 2 Pathological consequences of the disruption of lifeworld reproduction processes (reproduced from figure 22 of Jürgen Habermas, *The Theory of Communicative Action, Volume 2*, Beacon Press, Boston, 1987; Polity Press, Cambridge, 1987)

the loss of meaning. The question of cultural impoverishment arises since Habermas must explain why, when faced by colonization, a rationalized lifeworld remains politically powerless and culturally indifferent. In most societies, ideology and myth have served to render the illegitimate acceptable. Habermas suggests that myth is incapable of masking the consequences of system expansion, and the totalizing ideologies of modern societies are in irreversible cultural decline.[56] However, modern societies have found a functional equivalent for ideology. Rather than generating positive legitimatory ideologies, a negative function is fulfilled by modern culture, preventing the articulation of any coherent oppositional world-views. Everyday consciousness is not deceived but fragmented. Only then are the conditions for the colonization of the lifeworld met.[57]

The processes by which consciousness is fragmented remain somewhat opaque, but the loss of meaning is made explicit. The rationalization of the lifeworld, we will recall, was calibrated in terms of its internal differentiation. This entailed the cultural and conceptual separation of worlds towards which knowledge could be orientated, and distinct types of validity claims. Combined together these give nine possible formal-pragmatic relations that actors can assume within the lifeworld. Habermas argues that in the course of cultural rationalization only some formal-pragmatic attitudes have been drawn on to generate standardized forms

Worlds / Basic attitudes	1 Objective	2 Social	3 Subjective	1 Objective
3 Expressive	Art ↓			
1 Objectivating	↑ Cognitive-instrumental rationality Science Technology	Social technologies ↓	X	
2 Norm-conformative	X	↑ Moral-practical rationality Law	Morality ↓	
3 Expressive		X	↑ Aesthetic-practical rationality Eroticism	Art

Figure 3 Rationalization complexes (reproduced from figure 11 in Jürgen Habermas, *The Theory of Communicative Action, Volume 1,* Beacon Press, Boston, 1984; Polity Press, Cambridge, 1987)

of expression and discourse. These are the basis of modern forms of rationality and argumentation that have been reproduced through permanent institutionalization (see figure 3). The separation and irreconcilability of cultural value spheres were, for Weber, essential to the rationalization of culture and lay at the root of the loss of meaning. Habermas argues that his formal-pragmatics provides a standard against which a non-pathological cultural rationalization can be deduced. To do this, we must distinguish between those knowledge complexes that can and cannot, on epistemological grounds, be rationalized, institutionalized and made fruitful for cumulative learning. Further, we must subdivide those complexes that have the potential to be rationalized into: (1) rationalization complexes that emerged successfully as specialized discourses; (2) rationalization complexes whose underdevelopment can be traced to secific historical conditions rather than epistemological unsuitability. The epistemological distinction rests on the difference between those formal-pragmatic relations that can be worked up into specialized knowledge systems, open to reflective criticism and the growth of knowledge, and those that cannot. The former are the three rationalities identified earlier by Habermas: cognitive-instrumental rationality, institutionalized in the scientific enterprise; moral-practical rationality, institutionalized in the specialized discourses of jurisprudence and moral philosophy; aesthetic-practical rationality, institutionalized in the artistic enterprise and critical tradition. Those relations which are unsuitable for rationalization and institutionalization are the Xs in figure 3. Box 1.3 with its X is incapable of rationalization because 'nothing can be learned in an objectivating attitude about inner nature qua subjectivity.'[58] Similarly, the X in box 2.1 suggests to Habermas that we should be sceptical of giving our relationship with the natural world a rationalized moral dimension. This is because moral discourse must be based on communicative action, and the natural world is, it would appear, incapable of engaging in such a discourse. The X in box 3.2 indicates an expressive attitude towards society, characteristic of some countercultural forms of life which 'do not form structures that are rationalizable . . . but are parasitic . . . on innovations in other spheres of value.'[59]

Habermas suggests we may now state 'the necessary conditions for a nonselective pattern of rationalisation'.[60] Historically contingent, pathological cultural rationalization can occur for four reasons. First, when any one of the rationality complexes is insufficiently institutionalized. A system of learning cut loose from any institutionalized foundation can neither be adequately transmitted across the generations, nor have its learning potential adequately exploited. Second, when any one of the rationalization complexes comes, in its wider 'structure-forming' effects on society, to dominate the others, or any one complex is so inadequately 'worked up' that its own structure-forming effects are minimal. Third, when any one of the rationalization complexes intrudes into a formal-pragmatic domain for which it is epistemologically unsuited. For example, when scientific models of rationality are consistently applied to domains, like the social, for which they are epistemologically and ontologically ill-suited. Fourth, pathologies arise when specialized systems of knowledge become separated from everyday communicative action and are appropriated by the expert cultures in which they are primarily produced and reproduced.[61] It is on the basis of his account of the pathologies of modernity that Habermas constructs a theory of social movements.

New Social Movements

Habermas's position on new social movements is, at one level, simple to state: they are the response of the lifeworld to its colonization. On the basis of this causal argument Habermas is able to develop a typology of modern social movements; offer an account of their structural and cultural origins; supplement this with an account of why specific sectors of modern societies are more responsive to the threat of colonization; explain what political form they take and the issues that they address. However, Habermas's arguments are not fully fleshed out and I shall therefore seek to reconstruct them sympathetically. I shall consider each of these arguments with particular reference to the environmental movement.

Habermas is responding to a widely perceived but poorly understood process of political transformation in the postwar West: the secular decline of class-based politics and the emergence of a variety of newer social movements which differ from the labour movement, not simply in their social composition, but in their organizational forms, methods of political action and political aims. In contrast to the dominant forms of social democratic politics: 'The issue is not primarily one of compensations that the welfare state can provide, but of defending and restoring endangered ways of life. In short, *the new conflicts are not ignited by distribution problems but by questions having to do with the grammar of forms of life.*'[62]

That grammar entails the defence of the reproductive processes of the lifeworld, functionally threatened by systemically induced reification. Habermas can now distinguish between two categories of social movements: emancipatory, and resistance and withdrawal. The women's movement is the emancipatory movement *par excellence*, while the ecological movement falls into the second category.[63] The resistance movements can be subdivided into 'the defence of traditional and social rank (based on property) and a defence that already operates on the basis of a rationalized lifeworld and tries out new ways of cooperating and living together'.[64] This distinction allows Habermas to separate middle-class protest groups and movements for regional autonomy from his main concerns: youth, peace and ecology movements. He suggests that these movements are united by the *critique of growth*.[65] This phrase describes the ways in which the perception of growing system complexity and its unchecked effects on the lifeworld have been articulated. On the basis of this critique, resistance to colonization and demands for the decolonization of the lifeworld are mounted.

However, these movements, initially at any rate, are not directly engaged in the defence of lifeworld integrity, but are sensitized to the problem of colonization. Habermas focuses on three contemporary issues which sensitize actors. First, the problem of *excessive complexity*, in which the dynamics of economy and polity have reached a scale and complexity which have become quite uncontrollable: for example, nuclear power and genetic engineering. The nature of technical change and organizational expansion has outrun, temporally, spatially and socially, the capacity of the lifeworld to take responsibility for the risky and morally problematic processes unleashed. These function as catalysts for a more widespread recognition of the colonization of the lifeworld.[66] Habermas would appear to be suggesting that the environmental movement's opposition to the consequences of unrestrained economic and technological development and morally unhindered political and economic action provides it with a cognitive perspective from which otherwise invisible processes of colonization can be detected and resisted.

Second, the tangible, material destruction of the natural and urban environment accounts for the emergence of an environmental politics. In wrestling with environmental degradation, 'developments that noticeably affect the organic foundations of the lifeworld', the ecology movement is simultaneously made 'drastically aware of standards of livability, of inflexible limits to the deprivation of sensual-aesthetic background needs'.[67] Habermas is drawing a connection between the ecology movement's concern with non-material values and experiences and a peculiar concern for the social reproduction of the lifeworld. In ensuring the integrity of the lifeworld, the need for those experiences can be met and the articulation of those values sustained.

Finally, Habermas links aspects of the ecology movement's politics with a response to what he calls an *overburdening of the communicative infrastructure*. Fragmented consciousness, the loss of totalizing understandings of the world and the bureaucratization of the will-forming process in the public sphere lead to characteristic features of environmental movements: 'The revaluation of the particular, the natural, the provincial, of social spaces that are small enough to be familiar, of decentralized forms of commerce and desegmentalized activities.'[68] Forums are thus created in which undistorted communication and democratic will formation are made possible.

At the core of these political movements is a particular segment of modern societies. Drawing on the work of Ronald Inglehart and others, Habermas argues that the young, the more formally educated and the new middle classes are most susceptible to this politics.[69] Habermas cites three reasons for this: first, because they are further removed from the productivist core of modern capitalist societies. While the traditional working class, employers and those he calls 'middle-class tradesmen' remain engulfed in the trade-offs of welfare state politics and the bureaucratized political negotiations of mass democracy, the new middle class has less to gain from such trade-offs, and its interests are not incorporated into decision-making systems. Second, these sectors have been more strongly exposed, through the three catalytic mechanisms elaborated, to the potential consequences of unchecked system growth. Finally, these groups have felt those consequences, as pathologies, most acutely.

In this way, the political demands, organization and targets of protest for the new social movements lie at some distance from the older politics. Demands are based around the quality of life, individual self-realization, participation and human rights. They are expressed through challenges to the conventional definitions of the four roles at the interface of system and lifeworld. Thus the role of the employee is rejected. The profit-dependent instrumentalization of one's labour which characterizes formal employment is contrasted with more benign modes of co-operative, decentralized work and demonetarized barter. The role of consumer is rejected for its commodification of lifestyles, properly produced and defined within the lifeworld. Unconventional political protest subverts and ridicules the dominantly strategic quality of conventional political participation and rejects the mass party/representative democracy formula in favour of looser political organization and participatory democracy. Finally, the role of the client and the client relationship to the public sector has been criticized in line with the juridification argument, and new modes of self-help and participatory control have been advocated. There is in all these protests a demand that the colonization of the lifeworld be stemmed, but also an attempt to evacuate system imperatives from the lifeworld and recreate spaces in which the lifeworld can operate according to its own dimensions of normative evaluation. At the risk of repetition I shall restate the argument as ten theses.

1 Economic and political steering crises oscillate between their respective subsystems. The emergence of government intervention has substantially facilitated the control of these processes.
2 The core of the lifeworld is its societal component and the process of social integration. These come under threat when steering crises are of such magnitude that problem oscillation between subsystems proves ineffective and economy and polity perform substantially below expectations. Capitalist societies have not, as yet, come to such a crisis.
3 Those subsystems have, for over a century, been under threat from the labour movement and the movements for democratization. As employees and citizens, Western publics have threatened to dismantle capitalism and bring unaccountable power to public account. These protests were rooted not simply in direct material interests, but in values and ideas as well.

4   Both threats have been countered. The role of employee-based con-
    flict has been controlled by corporatist bargaining and compensated
    for by the expansion of the role of the consumer. The role of citizen
    has been neutralized by the advent of mass democracy and the com-
    pensation of client status in the welfare state.

5   However, the compromises created – corporatism, consumerism, the
    welfare state and mass democracy – have brought segments of the
    lifeworld under renewed attack: in the realms of culture and person-
    hood and in the constitution of the public sphere.

6   The welfare state has created pathologies of personhood and social-
    ization through processes of juridification. Mass democracy can only
    maintain the current political system by systematically distorting the
    process of democratic will formation and fragmenting consciousness.

7   The environmental movement is part of a wider swathe of new politi-
    cal activity, united by a shared defence of the lifeworld and articulated
    as the critique of growth. *In this respect it represents a politics underwrit-
    ten and motivated by moral values.* The inevitable technization of the
    lifeworld functionally fails if reproduction processes are disrupted.
    However, resistance to this process ultimately rests on normative
    commitments generated by a rationalized lifeworld.

8   A non-productivist core of the young, middle-class and well-educated,
    gaining from or responding least to the compromises on offer, experi-
    ence those pathologies most acutely and are most sensitized to their
    existence. Their capacity to perceive the colonization process stems
    from their response to ecological and complexity problems. These
    demonstrate the disengagement of economic and political decision-
    making from democratic control and value orientations. *Material
    interest in survival opens participants to the more general impact of strate-
    gic action systems* which are now penetrating the lifeworld.

9   We can therefore explain the recent intersection of environmental
    issues with radical political and moral positions. In mobilizing
    against the environmental impact of economic and political decision-
    making, the environmental movement has argued that the problematic
    quality of those decisions is rooted in the decision-making process
    itself. This has led to a demand for a restriction on system imperatives
    and expansion of the lifeworld's capacity to order action. The struc-
    tural preconditions of a sustainable society are therefore an expansion
    of civil society and a diminishing sphere of state authority; participa-
    tory democracy over representative democracy and self-help over
    welfare; and the expansion of an informal, non-monetary economic
    system, though without the complete abandonment of a formal eco-
    nomic sphere.

10 If the environmental movement can be explained in terms of its resis-
    tance to a pathological colonization process and its motivations in
    terms of the lifeworld's self-generated normative criteria, we should
    expect the cultural standards that it defends to tally with the account

of a non-pathological culture; preference for the three rationalizable complexes over the non-rationalizable; commitment to their equal structure-forming effects; and the demand that their cumulative learning be made available to the public sphere.

Habermas on New Social Movements: an Initial Assessment

If I have characterized Habermas's views correctly, then he has not explained the origins of the environmental movement. Rather, *the strength of his argument is in its account of a particular fragment of contemporary environmental politics*: its more radical wings like the green parties. Within these confines, his argument has had some successes. Habermas has tried to explain why these elements of the environmental movement have acquired their particular 'world-view' by connecting environmental politics with the defence of a rationalized lifeworld (thesis 9). We would expect Habermas to be, morally speaking, broadly in agreement with this defence (theses 7 and 10). Habermas's characterization of protests over the four dominant social roles, the alternatives proffered and the democratizing demands of the greens ring true. There is no doubt that the environmental movement has undergone a political radicalization and a broadening of concerns. Thus the suggestion of a sensitizing shift from a purely environmental politics to the politics of the lifeworld may be plausible (thesis 8). In addition, Habermas has, like the classical social theorists, offered an explanation of political mobilization against the backdrop of broader shifts in contemporary societies (theses 3–6), and investigated the relative political roles of moral values and interests (theses 7–10).[70]

Moreover, Habermas's work is in a number of significant respects an improvement over competing theoretical perspectives. Habermas does not, like Neil Smelser, reduce social movements to irrational outbursts of collective action.[71] Despite his Marxist affiliations he does not repeat Manuel Castells's political reduction of social movements to class interests.[72] In contrast to rational choice theory, Habermas's concept of rationality and action orientations is sufficiently broad to suggest that moral imperatives and non-strategic motivation remain at the core of social movements.[73] Despite these strengths, I believe that Habermas's work is to be found wanting in four key areas: its definition of the environmental movement; his theory of modernity; the relationship between cultural change and the growth of environmental politics; and the degree to which his account of change in contemporary societies and the colonization of the lifeworld thesis can actually explain the development of environmental politics. I will explore the first three of these problems in this section and offer some alternative positions in the next. Then I will take up the strengths and limitations of the colonization thesis.

Defining Environmental Movements

Habermas has focused on a subject of inquiry both too narrow and too broad. It is too narrow in that his explanation of the world-view of radical environmentalism does not constitute an explanation of the environmental movement in general. It is too broad in that the core arguments of Habermas's work are concerned with the emergence of 'new social movements' in general rather than the environmental movement in particular. Habermas attempted to simplify these issues by focusing his inquiry on those elements of the environmental movement (and other new social movements) which most closely correlate with the theoretical explanations he has offered. The elements of the environmental movement that Habermas wishes to explore are defined by their motivation in defence of the lifeworld.

> Within resistance movements we can distinguish between the defence of traditional and social rank and a defence that already operates on the basis of a rationalized lifeworld . . . This criterion makes it possible to demarcate the protest of the traditional middle classes against threats to neighbourhoods . . . from the core of new conflict potential . . . *It is possible to conceive of these conflicts in terms of resistance to tendencies toward a colonization of the lifeworld.*[74]

In making this argument, the explanation of the emergence of the environmental movement lies parallel to that of the peace and alternative movements. I believe this to be an unacceptable theoretical position on two counts: first, because even if one were only concerned to explain the rise of the radical environmentalists, it would be unwise to dissociate that process from the emergence of less radical environmentalism. The two are likely to have some common historical roots. Second, while there are clearly connections between the new social movements, and their simultaneous emergence cannot be ignored, we should not consider these connections to be evidence of identical causal origins. In contrast to Habermas's broad-brush explanations we need to disentangle the common roots of the peace and environmental movements, their interconnections with each other, and their distinct and separate causal origins. In any case, it is unwise to classify social movements exclusively in terms of their causal origins. We might, for example, claim that the socialist and communist movements of the twentieth century both spring from the shared origins of working-class struggle and organization. It hardly helps us to understand why they have emerged at different times, in different places, with different levels of political success. The questions therefore remain. What in general is a social movement and what in particular is the environmental movement? To what extent are the origins of the contemporary environmental movement shared with or different from other social movements? To what extent are these movements 'new'?

Habermas's Theory of Modernity

Habermas's theory of modernity, while uniquely suited to rediagnosing Weberian pathologies, pays the price for such a particular focus. For while Habermas retains Weber's preoccupations with rationality and broad theoretical generalizations on the relationship between political mobilization and long-term trends in modern societies, he undoubtedly lacks the historical sensitivity of Weber's work. Habermas's model is too insensitive and abstract to grasp the complex history in question for three reasons.

First, his depiction of societies as systems and their lifeworlds remains oblivious to the interactions between societies, and the peculiar form that modern societies have taken. The site of environmental politics is historically rooted in particular nation-states and is increasingly a product of the interaction of global economic and political systems. Environmental issues have on a number of occasions constituted a major element of a broader nationalist politics: for example, the role of environmental degradation in energizing nationalist protest in the Baltic states.[75] The interaction of nation-states, in the context of global systems, is central to the production and character of environmental degradation. Such interaction shapes the problems to which environmental movements have responded and the ideological positions they have assumed.[76]

These points illustrate a second limitation of Habermas's model: it is oblivious to the interaction of societies with their natural environment. Consequently his account of the causal importance of environmental degradation in the emergence of environmental politics is too simplistic. In Habermas's model, the perception and experience of environmental degradation functions primarily as a factor in the sensitizing of individuals to the colonization of the lifeworld. However, it should be located at the very core of any explanation of the origins and development of environmental politics.[77] In the absence of sufficient emphasis on this unique and distinctive causal factor in the emergence of environmental politics, it is little wonder that the latter can be collapsed into a very general explanation of all new social movements.

Third, Habermas's model displays a similar problem to Giddens's work: its insensitivity to historical periodization. Giddens did not conceptualize the key shifts in the nature of capitalism and industrialism. Habermas is also apparently unconcerned with the clearly periodic quality of environmental politics. Rather than displaying a constant level of mobilization, its political profile has been jagged. Environmental politics emerged in Britain and America in the late nineteenth century and continued into the early twentieth century, making some impact in Western Europe, before effectively disappearing after the First World War. It re-emerged in Britain and America in the late 1950s and early 1960s, spreading more rapidly across Western and Eastern Europe, where on many counts it outstripped its precursors. It has also, in the closing decades of the twentieth century, become a point of political mobilization outside the

West. Faced with such a history, Habermas's work is of little immediate explanatory value. One could, it is true, argue that Britain and America have experienced a harsher colonization of the lifeworld than others or have been culturally more attuned to the problem, but the really important questions remain. Why was the experience harsher in Britain and America in the 1890s and 1960s? In any case, the decisive shift in the colonization of the lifeworld would appear to coincide with the emergence of mass democracy, consumerism and the juridification of the welfare state. This might explain the post-1945 upsurge of environmental politics, but it hardly helps us to explain the upsurge experienced at the turn of the century. At the root of this problem is Habermas's focus on major moments of system–lifeworld change. This focus obscures other momentous forms of social change which have had equal, if not greater, import for the emergence of environmental politics, for example, changes in technology and forms of environmental degradation, and changes in the class composition of societies (particularly important given Habermas's reliance on a notion of the new middle classes).[78]

Environmental Politics and Cultural Change

Habermas's account of cultural rationalization is geared to the reconstruction of the main lines of cultural change in the West since the Enlightenment and has been developed with a particular purpose in mind: to demonstrate the enduring validity of the cultural resources of modernity.[79] However, this focus generates a model of cultural change that is unsuited to historical explanation or to assessing the role of cultural ideas and values in the mobilization of environmental politics. These charges require some explanation.

If I am correct in stressing the role of cultural perceptions and changing moral values in the mobilization of environmental politics, then any account of the emergence of the environmental movement is as much a cultural as a political history.[80] Habermas is not oblivious to this problem, indeed it is at this level that Habermas finds the common causal origins of new social movements (thesis 7). However, he neither specifies the types of knowledge and value systems that underpin the emergence of environmental politics nor, beyond a general account of the epistemological and moral consequences of a rationalized lifeworld, explains why and where that knowledge has emerged and how it has been used. Once again the problem appears to be that there is both too much and too little of Weber in Habermas's work: too much, in that the presence of Weber's macroprocesses of directional cultural change obscure the peculiarities of different national cultures and subcultures of class, region, ethnic group, etc.; too little in that Weber was never oblivious to those problems, as his writings on nationalism and cultural conflict testify.

These are surely some of the issues on which an adequate explanation of the cultural dimension of the emergence of environmental politics turns: for example, why should nineteenth-century American culture have generated such a distinctive and positive evaluation of the aesthetic and moral worth of wilderness, while French culture was quite oblivious to the issue? How have those who have opposed cruelty to animals challenged those who are indifferent or opposed to their concerns? Why have some groups of scientists elaborated the environmental implications of their work and communicated that knowledge to a wide audience? Habermas could suggest that an aesthetic evaluation of the natural world is the inevitable outcome of the culture of a differentiated, rationalized lifeworld. He might, through this theory of argumentation, tell us under what conditions some of those disputes might be rationally resolved. He might even let us argue that a failure of scientists to transmit their findings to a wider public is morally pathological. But he cannot tell us why these cultural changes happened when they did, or where they did, and why they met with varying measures of cultural success and political impact. The answers to these questions are a necessary, if not sufficient, condition of any plausible account of environmental movements.

Habermas's theory of cultural change, to be fair, does not explicitly deny the importance of these questions. However, because his theory is cast at a such a high level of generality and orientated towards epistemological and normative issues, it cannot adequately explain specific forms of cultural change (like the emergence of environmental ethics and aesthetics), and nor can it tackle causal questions with any plausibility (such as the greater impact of environmental aesthetics in American culture).

With the broad model of cultural change found wanting, there are also more specific theoretical deficits in Habermas's work. As I argued in the introduction to this book, cultural change turns to political mobilization when new ideas and arguments lead to a redefinition of interests on which people act politically, or when the emergence of new moral ideals and values are able to elicit a political response. The notion of interests, both individual and collective, is problematic, and their connection to political behaviour equally so.[81] None the less, the notion remains central to political discourse and in broad terms refers to the motivations and goals that drive political and economic actions. Habermas has himself tackled the problematic nature of interests in a number of works and his use of the term has shifted over time.[82] In *The Theory of Communicative Action* he explains the motivation of communicative action in terms of orientation to understanding (assent to the correctness of different types of validity claims, including the rightness of normative positions), and the motivation of strategic and instrumental action in terms of orientation to success (in ordering the social and non-social worlds in accordance with the actor's perceived needs). However, this shift in terminology does not make the notion of interests redundant; rather it seems to repackage them in the language of Habermas's newly developed theory of action.

Recalling my ten-point outline of Habermas's argument, the emergence of the environmental movement can be explained in terms of interests (or orientation to success in instrumental-strategic action) and ideals (orientation to understanding in communicative action). Thesis 8 argues that an emergent material interest in survival generates political opposition to environmental degradation, but also sensitizes actors to the extent to which the same processes that threaten their material survival are responsible for colonization. Thesis 7 argues that the normative ideals of those living in a rationalized lifeworld come into conflict with the pathological exercise of strategic and instrumental action in the domains of culture, society and socialization.

My objections to Habermas's argument are twofold. First, regarding thesis 8, it is not clear from his work how Western publics, or those sections of Western publics that are committed to the environmental movement, have recently come to redefine their material interests in terms of survival. Or rather, it does not make clear why Western publics have reprioritized their material interests, giving greater weight to health considerations and standards of environmental quality over increasing personal consumption. The threat and impact of environmental degradation are, after all, hardly new. Habermas has not investigated how new types of knowledge about the environment have transformed our perception of the threats we face and the political and economic decisions we should take to avert them, or how these threats have transformed our individual and collective economic and political interests.

Second, there is a certain confusion in Habermas's work on the relative weight of interests (however arrived at), ideas and ideals in the generation of environmental politics. On the one hand, it would appear that the emergence of material interests in environmental survival has opened Western publics to a new set of ideals (thesis 8) and that moral values drive the new politics. On the other hand, Habermas approvingly quotes Weber's switchman metaphor, in which ideals and values transform the perception and direction of interests.[83] We must therefore ask whether new interests lead to the emergence of new values that then mobilize environmental politics, or whether the emergence of new ideas and moral arguments leads to a reshaping of interests that then underwrite the development of environmental movements. We shall need to specify the interrelation between understandings of the environmental, moral values and interests more clearly than this.

Political Mobilization, Cultural Change and Environmental Degradation

In this section I shall try to remedy some of the deficits exposed by my critique of Habermas. First, I shall return to the problem of defining social movements and offer a sharper definition of what the environmental movement is and how we should conceptualize its relationship to other movements. In so doing I shall be able to explore the role of environmental degradation and cultural change in the emergence of environmental movements, focusing on the role of ideals, ideas and interests. I shall then expand on these arguments, sketching some of the ways in which changing forms of environmental degradation, interpretations of degradation and the moral implications of those interpretations have underwritten the emergence of the environmental movement in the postwar West.

Defining the Environmental Movement

Defining the environmental movement raises three interrelated questions. What is our working definition of a social movement? Should we consider the environmental movement to be part of a distinctive set of 'new' social movements and, if so, how do they differ from prior movements? If such a phenomenon exists, should we seek to examine the environmental movement in tandem with the contemporary peace and alternative movements, or consider a quite distinct set of explanations for its emergence? Rather than, as Habermas does, exploring the new social movements in terms of their relationship to colonization processes, it is helpful to begin with a more general understanding of social movements: simply as forms of collective action, with a degree of organizational continuity, committed to some form of basic social change.[84] As regards the environmental movement, basic social change might be defined as *the cessation or limitation of environmental degradation, as defined by movement participants, and the creation of social structures and cultural perspectives which keep that degradation within tolerable limits.*

This definition allows us to a counter the unacceptable narrowing, widening and historical unspecificity of Habermas's model. In terms of the movement's goals, this definition analytically separates the environmental movement from other social movements, yet allows us to include diverse organizations within its parameters: for example, Earth First (engaged in non-violent direct action), Friends of the Earth (engaged in government lobbying and public information campaigns), the National Trust (engaged in land management and conservation).[85] Habermas's focus on radical groupings and responses to colonization processes would have probably excluded all but Earth First. I would suggest that any explanation of the environmental movement requires, at the very least, an understanding of groups as significant as Friends of the Earth. In focusing on a commitment to the limitation of degradation, my definition also allows us to recognize historical continuities and discontinuities. The identification of tolerable limits and appropriate cultural attitudes and social structures is historically cumulative and variable. Thus the British and American conservation movements of the late nineteenth century as much as the green parties, for all their differences, can be considered elements of different historical phases of the environmental movement.

However, we would be as guilty as Habermas of historical insensitivity were we to leave our definitions there, for there are major differences between the early conservation movement and the contemporary environmental movement. This brings us to our second question: the nature of 'new' social movements. The 'newness' of the alternative, environmental and peace movements is usually based on a contrast with the labour movement. The contrast is defined, not only in terms of the obvious differences in goals and aspirations, but also of their site of political operation (civil society and culture over the state and politics), organizational structure (open, fluid and participatory),[86] social composition (aligned along non-class cleavages), motivations to participation (morally and ideally as opposed to interest based politics),[87] unconventional forms of political activity (direct action, symbolic protest, mobilization of public opinion)[88] and core aspects of their ideological positions.[89] That said, it is true that the newness of the movements has been overstressed. Participation is often interest based, structures tend towards permanent bureaucratization, and political activity is often orientated to lobbying and corporatist negotiations as well as direct action and symbolic protest.[90] None the less, there would appear to be sufficient difference between the old and new social movements to merit some form of distinction and some form of collective historical explanation.[91]

However, if we are correct both in separating the environmental movement out as a distinct object of study, with specific and unique causal origins, and in identifying a distinct shift in the organization and operation of 'new social movements', how might we reconcile these positions? What historical factors account for the emergence of environmental politics in particular and what wider social processes account for the simultaneous historical emergence of a range of new social movements? I shall consider the specificity of environmental politics below. Here I shall examine a possible explanation of simultaneous social movement development that connects to the general importance of cultural change outlined in the previous section.

Defining the Role of Culture

In a sense, Habermas offers an argument on this issue. He links the new social movements with the colonization of the lifeworld and the latter to the epochal shift in forms of juridification experienced under welfare state capitalism. Thus a general causal factor can be discerned to account for the simultaneous proliferation of new social movements in the postwar West. However, the decidedly non-corporatist quality of the US polity and its powerful environmental movement renders the connection suspect. In Europe, links between levels of corporatism, bureaucratic welfare state provision and levels of new social movement activity are almost non-existent.[92] Moreover, the emergence of environmental movements in the developing world suggests that the link between corporatism and social movements is suspect.[93]

In any case Habermas's arguments would be unable to account for the emergence of environmental movements that preceded the Second World War. The same is true for the peace and alternative movements. The peace movement, while having nineteenth-century organizational and cultural roots, achieved a degree of mass mobilization around the turn of the century and retained a numerical significance into the 1930s.[94] Similarly, alternative movements, committed to alternative value systems, lifestyles and cultural practices, have historical precursors. The 1830s and 1840s saw the emergence of Fourierism, Owenism and a surge of commune building, while the turn of the century saw widespread cultural revolt in Germany, Britain and America.[95] Therefore, while the welfare-state/jurid-ification/colonization thesis may be a contributory factor in the emer-gence and character of postwar social movements, it is in itself insufficient. A more promising approach would seem to be based on cycles of cultural change and protest.[96] Karl Werner Brand has argued not only that there have been cycles of social movement mobilizations which preceded those of the 1960s and 1970s, but additionally that the mobiliza-tion of these movements is concurrent across Britain, America and Germany, as is their dissolution. Moreover, he has suggested as an alter-native explanation that these cycles of mobilization are accompanied by 'an emergent, persuasive mood of cultural criticism'.[97] However, a num-ber of questions remain unanswered. Why have waves of cultural criti-cism risen and fallen? What precise form do these waves take? Above all, how does the cultural mood contribute to the emergence of all of these social movements?

Brand's arguments are not incompatible with elements of Habermas's work. Brand suggests that waves of cultural criticism and protest can be thought of in terms of three, overlapping, responses to modernity: cri-tiques rooted in premodern cultural residues; critiques that simultaneously abandon premodern cultural perspectives and engage in negative re-evaluations of the cultural resources of modernity; and protest from the distinctively modern perspectives of aesthetic and intellectual alien-ation or moral-idealistic positions.[98] We see here an outline of the argu-ments of *The Philosophical Discourse of Modernity*. In Habermas's terms the normative paradox of modernity can be met in three ways: (1) recourse to metaphysical-religious world-views; (2) the declining purchase of these views can lead to a Nietzschean-anarchist rejection of modernity, which in the absence of an alternative and coherent normative perspective col-lapses into a generalized dissolution of truth claims and universal moral positions; and (3) pathological forms of cultural rationalization can be countered by the cultural resources of modernity itself. The latter is based on the demand for a reassertion of the truth claims, institutionalization and wider social impact of moral-practical and aesthetic-practical reason and a defence of the integrity of the lifeworld.[99] That Habermas has not really pursued such an explanatory, though compatible, strategy can be explained by the fact that his model of cultural rationalization, while capable of describing modes of cultural resistance, is too descriptive and static.

A further element of Habermas's position which might allow us to explain the simultaneous emergence of new social movements in terms of a broader shift in cultural sensibilities is the notion of a unifying critique of growth. However, if Habermas is referring to the growth of system complexity and systemic invasions of the lifeworld, then in what sense is the peace movement, for example, critical of growth? One would be hard pushed to explain the Cold War and the nuclear arms race, which Habermas would no doubt acknowledge as central to the growth of the peace movement, in terms of the growth of system complexity. The harsh dynamics of the balance of power in the international state system are not unique to the postwar era. In any case, Habermas does not explain the conditions under which such a critique can be actualized, whatever the amount of system growth.

Even if Habermas's position is compatible with Brand's explanation, whether this position is useful remains to be seen. Brand has suggested that the temporal coincidence of waves of cultural criticism and social movement mobilization is unlikely to be simply contingent. This temporal overlap is in itself a compelling piece of evidence, though I cannot offer a full investigation of this proposition here, nor shall I attempt to explain the cultural and historical origins of each particular wave. However, it would seem plausible to suggest that the emergence of such waves of cultural criticism is a necessary if not sufficient condition of the emergence of social movements for two additional reasons. First, if our characterization of social movements is correct, then cultural beliefs and moral positions are at the core of their political mobilization. Such a politics, whether orientated towards alternative lifestyles, the environment or pacifism, can thrive only in the context of new and widespread beliefs which disrupt dominant ideological perspectives, challenge contemporary value systems and posit alternative goals and values. Second, the strong overlap in personnel, organizational contact and ideological positions suggests that these movements draw on a similar stock of cultural argument.

The question remains, do waves of cultural criticism actually contribute to the rise of the environmental movement? I shall expand on this issue in my sketch of postwar environmental politics. Habermas's work is of minimal use in this area. One could sympathetically argue that the moral universalism demanded by a rationalized lifeworld has been actualized in the form of arguments for global and intergenerational justice. However, this has not been a smooth evolutionary development. In Habermas's terms, the cultural resources of modernity are not drawn on automatically, but are only converted into political principles and actions under the most specific historical conditions, and it to those that we must pay closer attention. To continue the Habermasian metaphor of modernization, not only is the path of one-sided modernization a historical and contingent phenomenon, but so too is the realization of the cultural potential of modernity. The point that I wish to make is that if we are to understand the historical dynamics of that process, we need to pay closer attention to the actual production of knowledge and to those who produce it: intellectuals and the institutions within which they operate. In this regard, one necessary condition of the development and mobilization of the environmental movement has been the existence of a sufficiently large body of intellectuals with the scope, motivation and resources to examine environmental issues and present conclusions that may be highly problematic for vested political and economic interests.

Environmental Degradation and Environmental Perception

I have argued that the histories of environmental degradation and politics are deeply intertwined.[100] Moreover, they are linked to the history of cultural perceptions and valuations of the environment, to the way in which the existence of environmental change and degradation is established, the way their future consequences are assessed, and to judgements as to whether those consequences are unjust. The intention here is to demonstrate why Habermas's cursory remarks on environmental degradation are a serious limitation on his capacity to explain the origins of environmental politics. I will also attempt to remedy some of those limitations. Since different nations and social groups have experienced different levels and forms of environmental degradation at different times and dealt with them with radically different cognitive and intellectual capacities, we can perhaps begin to explain the historical and geographical variations in environmental politics and link them with the broader shifts in cultural climate and attitude that we identified earlier. I do not aim to provide a comprehensive historical investigation here. Rather I intend to highlight some of the key areas for discussion and suggest a conceptual framework which might allow us to accomplish that investigation. I shall therefore consider some of the specifics of environmental degradation undergone in the West in the last forty years and the changing forms of moral values, interests and cognitive capacities with which Western publics have attempted to grasp them.

In tracing the trajectory of environmental degradation, I suggested that we consider aesthetic, health and economic impacts.[101] While this is a useful analytical classification, it does not necessarily correlate with the environmental experience and vocabulary of Western publics. Whatever the limits of actors' perceptions of environmental change, the conceptual vocabulary with which they make sense of environmental problems should not be ignored. This vocabulary informs their political action.[102] For example, the destruction of small forests in Britain would, in my initial classification, have a predominantly aesthetic impact. However, those people who oppose such a development would not be thinking about the problem in terms of aesthetics. Rather, they would do so through the conceptual framework of 'the countryside', with all its attendant values and meanings.[103] Thus, to understand why environmental change is interpreted as degradation and is then politically opposed, one needs to grasp what the countryside means to those actors and which values and images have been generated around it. Therefore, I would suggest a fourfold division of postwar environmental degradation and perception: the toxic environment, the urban environment, the countryside and wilderness, and 'global concerns'.

As noted in chapter 1, both capitalist and state-socialist industrialized economies have since 1945 unleashed an expanding volume and range of increasingly toxic matter into the environment. Quantitative changes have resulted from the expansion of key industries under conditions of historically high economic growth, and from their spread to an increasing number of industrializing countries. Qualitative changes have resulted from new industrial processes, in particular from the world-wide expansion of the nuclear industry. The absolute growth of fossil fuel electricity production has contributed to notable increases in the levels of acid rain. Similarly, the chemicals industry and its products have generated a very wide range of novel chemicals in the postwar period: pesticides, CFCs, dioxins, carcinogens, heavy metals, non-biodegradable plastics.

Equally important in explaining the re-emergence of environmental movements has been the increased capacity of those societies to detect and monitor their release and impact. In contrast to Habermas's gloomy prognosis on the state of Western public spheres, that knowledge has reached an expanding public, increasingly capable of registering and interpreting it.[104] The increasing recognition of these threats and the subsequent political mobilization around their release can be traced to a number of sources. First, the postwar world has seen a rising number of specific environmental disasters with major political repercussions, rather than simply the unseen cumulative release of toxins: for example, Chernobyl and Three Mile Island, the Love Canal waste site, the chemical plant disasters in Bhopal and Seveso, and rising numbers of oil spills.[105] Second, an increasing volume of scientific energy has been brought to bear on the problem. The scope of toxicology has enormously expanded in the last forty years and the resources available to the discipline have grown. Third, the publics affected by the problems of toxins have had increasing access to the work of toxicologists. Such knowledge is, of course, uneven and often fragmented, but there can be little doubt that Western publics have learnt to register the impact of pollution more acutely, mentally tracing the passage of toxins from initial dispersal through biological systems to food, air, water and their own bodies. Thus the numbers of people who see their direct health interests bound up with any one type of pollution are massively increased from those who are directly and immediately affected. Individual charismatic scientists have played an important role in this process of revelation and diffusion, as have the higher profile of health and safety issues in the work-place and the role of lobby groups. Fourth, popularly held notions of the body and health have shifted in content and increased in importance in postwar Western cultures, and the threat of pollution has thus achieved a greater political salience.[106]

A similar process of increasing degradation, perception and protest has been experienced in the urban environment. As noted in chapter 2, 'urban environment' is not a term free from ambiguity, primarily because dominant interpretations of the environment have usually referred to the natural world. In this respect the increasing importance of the notion of the urban environment is significant. The idea of the urban as part of the environment has, of course, long historical roots: the garden city movement of late Victorian Britain was a significant cultural innovation in this area.[107] The perception of urban environmental degradation has been of increasing import in political mobilization, for the vast majority of support for environmental movements has come from urban areas. It is improper to generalize too far about urban degradation, but a number of common trends and experiences can be noted: the impact of the motor car; the costs of postwar urban planning and design; major infrastructural developments; problems of air quality, water quality and waste management. We reviewed some of the costs of the motor car in chapter 3. Suffice it to say that the massive expansion in levels of urban car use has had a significant impact on living in urban areas, affecting air quality, noise levels, city design and the general quality of life. Moreover, proposed urban road schemes have formed a crucial point of collective mobilization.[108] Here, the role of knowledge of toxicity has been important. In addition, the idea of 'quality of life' has assumed a decisive significance in environmental politics. Similarly, political campaigns against certain types of urban design and redevelopment, as well as over the siting of large infrastructural projects with major environmental impacts (airports, industrial estates, waste dumps, refuse centres), have relied on a developing political discourse regarding quality of life.

Although more physically distant from urban populations than their own built environment, the transformation of the countryside has attracted the most consistent – if non-radical – protest. In part this is due to the longer history of political organizations related to the countryside and wildlife, and to an even older symbolic and cultural valuation of the countryside.[109] However, in the postwar era the pace of environmental degradation has grown, its forms have shifted and the political opposition has widened. In part this is no doubt due to the middle-class exodus, in most Western countries, from the cities to commuting belts.[110] The latter constitute the bedrock of local amenity societies and ad hoc local interest-based coalitions protesting over the siting of housing developments and infrastructural projects which destroy sites of scenic beauty.[111] The problem of rural degradation has become particularly acute, not just because an increasingly articulate middle class has occupied these areas in rising numbers, but because with a fixed quantity of land the process of rural degradation is cumulative. That fixed quantity of land has had to accommodate increasing population, the decentralization of manufacturing plant away from urban centres, increasing demands for large-scale projects such as river developments, irrigation and reservoirs, and increasing demands for recreational use by urban dwellers. Finally, the nature of agricultural practice has shifted in the postwar years with increasing environmental impacts: fertilizer and pesticide use has contributed to soil and water pollution as well as to the disturbance of balanced ecosystems, and the rationalization of land use has resulted in the removal of scientifically and symbolically important elements of the landscape such as hedgerows and wetlands.[112]

These changes have been opposed for a broad set of reasons. Direct interests have been at stake: property values, local amenity access, demand for recreational use. However, moral values have also been central, particularly for the urban dwellers who may not even visit the countryside. These include an aesthetic appreciation and, in some cases, a spiritual reverence for the natural world, and increasingly the ascription of a moral quality to the natural world: a value system that has both informed and been drawn on by the animal liberation, anti-hunting and anti-cruelty movements.[113] These values are not exclusive to the postwar period and can be discerned in periods of previous environmental mobilization. However, they have been newly articulated and developed in this period and reached a wider audience then before.

Probably the most decisive shifts in forms of environmental degradation, perception and politics have been at what I shall call the global level.[114] Once again we are concerned with simultaneous changes in degradation, its perception and evaluation. The postwar world has seen a massive upswing in rates of species and ecosystem extinction, in resource use, energy consumption and population levels. It has also begun to experience the effects of environmental degradation such as global warming, oceanic pollution and ozone depletion at a truly global level. The changing forms of degradation are rooted in the increasing levels of world economic production, the industrialization of agrarian societies outside the West, their consequently expanding populations and the cumulative impact of pollution since the first industrial revolutions.

Of greatest significance, however, are the new kinds of knowledge by which these problems are revealed, and the emergence of new cultural and moral attitudes towards them; for example, the recognition of depletion problems has required advances in data collection and forecasting; the impact of population change has required increasingly sophisticated demographic work; global warming and ozone depletion have been made cognitively accessible by advances in climatology. Perhaps more importantly, these phenomena, once recognized, have begun to elicit distinctive moral perspectives among segments of Western publics. Global environmental problems have stretched the normative time-horizon of political discourse and introduced the notions of intergenerational justice and sustainability into our politico-moral vocabulary. Similarly, the threats faced by the developing world have been increasingly traced to the economic and political activities of the West. This in itself is a shift in perception which has begun, falteringly, to elicit a shift in the geographical horizon of moral and practical concern.

It should be clear that, in contrast to Habermas's model, new types of knowledge, made accessible to the public sphere, have led to a redefinition of self-interest (response to pollution) and a narrowing of distance between self-interests and the common interest due to the shared necessity for ecological survival and environmental quality (in relation to global warming and quality of urban life respectively). Similarly, while, as Habermas seems to be suggesting, interests however defined and arrived at do form a significant mobilizing force in environmental politics, moral issues and values have an equally powerful resonance. These do not just appeal to movement activists after they have redefined their interests in the pursuit of ecological survival. They may have a long historical pedigree and may be rearticulated in new circumstances (as in the case of countryside preservation). Moreover, they may, among movement activists, be infinitely more important in motivating action (wildlife protection and anti-cruelty movements). A final point, hinted at but not expanded on above, is that the take-up of environmental information, the appeal of new moral arguments and the redefinition of interests in the light of such arguments has not been uniform across Western publics. Rather, they have been concentrated within the middle classes. It is this phenomenon that I now wish to interrogate, and in so doing I shall examine the strength of the colonization thesis.

Environmental Politics, the New Middle Classes and the Colonization of the Lifeworld

Theses 7 and 8 demonstrated that at the heart of Habermas's explanation of the emergence of radical environmentalism was a morally based defence of a rationalized lifeworld by the new middle classes, sensitized by an emergent material interest in environmental survivability and the problems of system complexity and growth. As the discussion in the previous section made clear, moral values are not the only mobilizing force behind environmental movements, but they do remain significant. However, it is one thing to note the emergence of new moral arguments, but another to explain why they should have any degree of political purchase. Habermas has argued that the new middle classes are most receptive to these moral arguments and act on them politically for three main reasons: they gain least from corporatist political bargaining; they are excessively burdened by the colonization of the lifeworld; and they are peculiarly sensitive to its pathologies. I intend to challenge these assumptions. In the last section we left the origins of waves of cultural criticism unexamined. I shall turn to some of the work on new political movements on which Habermas has drawn to see if this can provide any empirical defence of his position.[115]

The Burdens of Colonization

Habermas has cited social security bureaucracies and family and educational law as examples of juridification. One point is immediately worth noting: any pathological effects experienced due to the abstractions enforced by social security bureaucracies can hardly be said to fall on the middle classes, old or new. If there were a link between client status in such bureaucracies, juridification of the lifeworld and a commitment to the latter's defence we might expect a higher proportion of the long-term unemployed, single parents and the disabled to be active supporters of the new politics. This is not the case.

Similarly, in the case of family law, although the middle classes are affected by divorce law, social work, etc., it would seem that the brunt of intrusive legal organization falls on those on low incomes. The incidence of state intervention in the domestic sphere because of domestic violence and children at risk is highest among lower income groups. Again, educational law has an impact on children and parents of all backgrounds. This does not mean that the imposition of bureaucratic constraint and the demands of economy and polity fall equally across the educational system. Those who suffer most from the demands of the examination ritual are children from lower income backgrounds who are in general more alienated from the prevailing cultures and discourses of the classroom.[116] The impact of labour market demands, through low-paid and compulsory training schemes, do not generally fall on the children of the middle classes, who tend to move into higher and more academically orientated education. Whatever the impact of these various forms of juridification, the middle classes are not suffering them more acutely than others.

In short, we must argue that the experience of the client role, like that of employees, is structurally variable. Habermas's model of modernity is insufficiently sensitive to these differences. Welfare states do not provide all goods and services on a universalistic basis. Indeed they are marked by some sharp divisions of service provision. The most disabling and intrusive services are often provided on a means-tested basis, and as such they will generally not affect the middle classes. Social security is an obvious example, but it also applies to residualized public housing and publicly funded care for the elderly and disabled. Furthermore, not all clients come to the welfare state equally capable of negotiating its bureaucratic channels. Once again, the middle classes have the edge over lower-income groups in successfully dealing with public institutions; individually and collectively they are able to exert a more significant degree of power and protest and are capable of articulating their demands more effectively. Because Habermas does not attend to the social divisions of welfare provision he probably overstates the degree to which the middle classes suffer from its intrusions. In any case, it is difficult to square the predominantly middle-class composition of new social movements with the juridification–colonization thesis on the basis of the claim that the middle classes disproportionately suffer from its pathological consequences.

The Existence of Pathologies

The problem with this aspect of Habermas's argument lies in his discussion of pathologies – or rather the lack of discussion – for they are theoretically derived categories the validity of which rely on the accuracy of his characterization of the lifeworld. The concepts he deploys, such as the loss of collective identity or the rise of pyschopathologies, are, because of their broadness, difficult to examine empirically. This is not incidental to Habermas's work. If his work is to have any purchase, it must be possible to identify the existence of these pathologies, let alone account for political and moral responses to them. I shall not make an exhaustive survey of this problem here, but a number of points are worth noting.

It would appear that the pathologies of society are more significant than those of culture and personality. Habermas claims that systemic imperatives eat away at culture and personality before affecting the social component of the lifeworld. Social solidarities, however, come under attack more easily, for example, the loss of legitimations and motivations being experienced by the 'underclass'. As Habermas has argued, these pathologies occur when the polity and economy fail to deliver a certain level of jobs, income, political representation, etc. In short, enduring poverty and political disenfranchisement will engender a withdrawal of legitimations and a fraying of social solidarities.[117] Habermas's focus on juridification not only misplaces its most vulnerable targets, but obscures the most obvious pathologies of capitalism and bureaucracy: their impact on the poor.

In explaining protest from the new middle classes, Habermas might have put more stress on commodification and the deformation of the public sphere as agencies of colonization rather than on juridification. Responses to both these phenomena are more significant in the emergence of radical environmental politics than responses to juridification. Indeed, two of the primary goals of the environmental movement are, first, a response to the systematic strictures placed on the public sphere, forcing the environmental issue on to a political agenda predominantly controlled by organizations that have no immediate interests in responding to the issue; second, the demand that the environment and environmental resources be accorded a central place in the economic decision-making of institutions and individuals that have until now responded only to the imperatives of profit-making and the rewards of material consumption. However, neither of these problems can easily be characterized by any of the nine pathologies Habermas has derived (see figure 2 above). Thus the colonization thesis, while suggesting interesting avenues of investigation, does not offer a decisive explanation of environmental movements.

The Distribution of Corporatist Benefits

The suggestion that any fraction of the middle classes has seen a significant decline in the benefits received from the contemporary organization of political power and distribution is simply not sustainable. Habermas pays the price here for too general a model of corporatism, which focuses on the institutionalized negotiation between capital, labour and the state. In Western countries since 1945 the benefits of welfare and public spending have fallen disproportionately on the middle classes.[118] The middle classes make more use of universal, tax-funded services such as health and education, and invariably consume a larger percentage of the most expensive elements of those services. For example, middle-class families have a much greater take-up rate of higher education funding than lower-income groups.[119] They also receive a very significant percentage of the tax breaks that are made available on company cars, commuter rail subsidies, arts funding, housing costs, private pensions and savings plans.[120] Similarly they are exceptionally well represented and catered for within the party systems of Western polities. The focus in *The Theory of Communicative Action* on corporatist or tripartite bargaining relationships, which are on the decline everywhere in the West, underestimates the degree to which middle-class protest and interests are included in the programmes and electoral calculations of political parties.

Why then should the new middle classes remain dissatisfied with corporatist politics and welfare compensations? Some writers, albeit tortuously, have suggested that the politics of the new middle classes can be sociologically explained by their predominant location outside of the private sector. The new middle classes are therefore committed to extending their power base within the institutions of the welfare state, which they staff.[121] The private–public distinction is a useful one. We shall see below how it offers a plausible starting point for explaining the division in middle-class politics. However, this account is hardly in line with the politics of lifeworld defence, for it remains tied to a view of interest rather than value-oriented politics. Moreover, on this reading, the new middle classes would be defenders of the current welfare state rather than alienated from it. It is surely the case that the aspirations and values of the new middle classes have changed, and thus that the rewards of corporatist bargaining and the nature of these processes, rather than the quantity of rewards, become problematic. The questions remain, who are the new middle classes, why have their values shifted and why are they most sensitized to the process of colonization? This is precisely the direction pursued by Habermas in his most recent work, where he acknowledges the exhaustion of the political compromises and institutional forms of the postwar welfare state and the degree of middle-class alienation from the form and delivery of state welfare services.[122] To explain these shifts we must turn to the work of writers on the new politics on which Habermas has drawn.

Inglehart and Postmaterialism

The history of the concept of the 'new middle classes' has been confused and contested.[123] For our purposes the key use of the term has been in connection with the work of Ronald Inglehart, on whom Habermas would appear to be heavily reliant.[124] Inglehart seeks to describe and explain two phenomena: first, he describes a major and enduring shift in the value orientations of Western publics since the Second World War, and second, he argues that the level and form of political skills available to certain segments of that public have massively increased. Thus his concern is with the educated middle classes and their engagement with new political issues and organizations, such as the environmental movement.

Inglehart attempts to explain the systematic origins of those changes and the longer-term consequences for the political life of the West. The shift in values is conceptualized in terms of materialism and postmaterialism. The former is registered by a greater preference or concern with the more traditional interests of Western politics: economic security, social stability, the fight against crime. Postmaterialists show a greater concern for personal satisfaction and self-realization, and place greater weight on the quality of life and aesthetic values. Using extensive data and a variety of statistical techniques, Inglehart attempted to determine whether such a shift can be discerned, who the postmaterialists are and the reasons people become postmaterialists.

In explaining the rise of postmaterialism, Inglehart's key argument concerns the distinctive cohort experience of the postwar generation. This rests on two assumptions. The first is that there exists a hierarchy of human needs each of which must be fulfilled or satisfied before human beings will be concerned with higher-order desires. Priority will therefore be given to questions of material and personal security before aesthetic ones.[125] The second is that socialization and other aspects of childhood experience are the key factors in establishing basic value orientations in an individual.[126] Inglehart does not, of course, suggest that values do not change over an individual's lifetime, but he does argue that early influences are the most determining and long-lasting. Given those premises, the absence of total war and the immense increase in personal disposal income for the majority of people in the West since 1945 have allowed the development of postmaterialist values in a wider swathe of Western publics than ever before. Further, Inglehart finds statistical correlations between increasing penetration of postmaterialist values and greater wealth.[127]

Inglehart argues that economic success can be traced to the technological developments and profound structural economic changes of the postwar period. These changes have also diminished the numbers and importance of the traditional working class and created a distinctive stratum of professional, middle-class, white-collar workers, who have fuelled the expansion of education in general and higher education in particular. Inglehart suggests that the experience of education has also shifted the priorities and perception of priorities of this new middle class in a postmaterialist direction.[128] For Inglehart, education leads to a diminished concern with self and a moral and political perspective that is more universal: a perspective increasingly concerned with one's environment, one's aesthetic needs and with the needs of others. This is not dissimilar to Habermas's view of discourse. The role of education brings us to the second element of the 'silent revolution': the diffusion of political skills. The structure of contemporary society has thrown up a populace that is more capable of engaging in complex political discourse and increasingly demands a bigger role in decision-making and agenda-creating than before. Education is decisive in generating the skills and confidence to do so.

When the argument was initially formulated, Inglehart did not address the issue of postmaterialism and its correlation with the emerging environmental movements head on. However, later formulations of his own work, as well as that of others influenced by him, have associated postmaterialists with anti-nuclear activities and more generally with the 'unconventional political participation' that appears to characterize new social movements.[129] Inglehart has suggested that postmaterialists constitute the core recruiting ground of the new environmental movements. Such an argument is not difficult to discern from the consequences drawn in *The Silent Revolution*. Clearly, if the characterization of postmaterialism is correct, then issues of environmental quality, long-term ecological thinking and the aesthetic import of the environment will achieve greater prominence and importance in the hierarchy of needs and political outlooks of postmaterialist publics.

What support does Inglehart's work actually offer for Habermas's position? On the positive side, it would appear to offer an empirically informed sociological account of the value change on which lifeworld politics is based, that is, the increasing sensitivity of the middle class to colonization, which prevents the realization of higher-order needs, and the diminished importance of the material rewards of corporatist bargaining. Similarly, his emphasis on the effects of education and political skills suggests a mechanism whereby members of this class can overcome the fragmentation of ideology, while the potential power of mass media used by counter-elites suggests how the stultification of the public sphere might be broken. However, Inglehart differs on three important counts from Habermas, and thus Habermas's citing of Inglehart does not amount to conclusive support for his case. First, Inglehart argues that postmaterialism predates the emergence of environmental politics, a point that tallies with our thesis concerning the impact of waves of cultural criticism. Habermas, however, has suggested that environmental concern engenders a sensitivity to lifeworld pathologies. Second, the specific conjuncture of peace and prosperity in the postwar West are central, positive, causal factors in this value shift. This argument would allow us to explain the North American and European environmental movements, whereas Habermas's focus on corporatism would not. Thus from Inglehart's perspective it is not simply the negative consequences of affluence that generate the new politics (consumerism and commodification, for example). In addition, affluence generates the psychological space for the emergence of less self-centred, survival-orientated value systems.[130] Third, this value shift is based on a theory of human need rather than the defence of the normative demands of a rationalized lifeworld.

Inglehart's work has been extended by Steven Cotgrove and Andrew Duff, who have asserted that the experience of peace and affluence in adolescence is an insufficient explanation of postmaterialism. Moreover, they have provided the most plausible explanation for why it is not the middle classes in general that are highly postmaterialist in their values, but a specific fragment thereof. Rather than focusing on the general public, their research has examined the values held by specifically targeted groups, and compared them to those of the wider public.[131] Cotgrove and Duff have looked at members of environmental organizations, trade unionists and industrialists. By controlling for age and affluence, they found that there still persisted significantly higher postmaterialist orientations among environmentalists. This difference from Inglehart's work was explained by reference to the failings of the Maslovian needs theory, which does not allow for the dual existence of material and postmaterial concerns, found to some extent among trade unionists. Moreover, Inglehart's work does not examine the degree to which values are actively shaped by ideas, precisely the fault we discerned earlier in Habermas's work. A closer examination of value orientations reveals that postmaterialism is not simply a collection of values.[132] Rather it is a collection of values which has been articulated into a broad vision of an alternative social order. Such a vision cannot be derived from socialization alone, but must have been modelled and shaped by the broad range of cultural argument and political alternatives developed in the West over the last twenty to thirty years. In contrast to Inglehart and Habermas, we must then take account of the way in which cultural change moulds, redefines and articulates personal value systems into political goals.

What is most striking in the research of Cotgrove and Duff is the precise occupational status of environmentalists, who are not simply affluent, middle-class and well-educated, but are a particular segment of that class. Environmentalists are massively engaged in occupations which are not directly engaged with the market: 'In particular they tend to choose occupations which do not involve direct commitment to the goals and values of industrialism and are congruent with their generally anti-industrialist sentiments.'[133] Cotgrove and Duff argue that occupations in the arts and in welfare institutions remain carriers of non-economic values and goals – in a Habermasian sense, they carry and practise the values of the lifeworld, precariously holding at bay those of the economic subsystem. Where, however, their argument comes closest to Habermas is in the explanation of such sentiments prior to career decision-making. Suggesting the limits of Inglehart's peace and prosperity model in statistical terms, they retain the importance of socialization in value formation. In particular they focus on the evidence concerning student radicals, who tended to come from families where a similar scepticism for traditional authority and dominant values was displayed. The work of Flacks suggests 'the emergence of a new kind of middle-class family, less authoritarian and hierarchical; more child-centred and democratic. It is in such families that the new character structures have been moulded, encouraged to pursue individuality and personal autonomy.'[134] Of course, given their educational background, environmentalists are in a position to choose their occupations much more selectively than the general public.

Conclusions

How does the colonization of the lifeworld argument and its connection to environmental politics now stand? First, it should be clear that the middle classes of the West do not bear the brunt of the pathological consequences of the colonization process. Nor do they receive insubstantial benefits from, or limited political representation within, current sociopolitical arrangements. Quite the opposite – the only really plausible element of the argument is that there is a greater sensitivity to the pathologies of colonization amongst sections of the middle classes and a greater dissatisfaction with the very nature of the rewards and compromises on offer. This, however, is a relatively strong argument. Postmaterialist arguments offer an explanation of why the middle classes are more sensitive to these problems and more sceptical of the compromises on offer – affluence, peace and particular patterns of socialization have created basic value orientations among the middle classes that prioritize 'higher-order' needs over material rewards. Such value orientations have been shaped by the cultural alternatives and criticisms produced in the West since the 1960s into political concern for the environment and the possibility of radically reorientated social relationships. However, peace, security and cultural ideas are the most significant factors in creating a constituency for radical environmental politics rather than the colonization process itself. This is not to deny the existence of colonization or its pathological consequences. Nor is it to deny, more generally, that the pathological consequences of colonization have diminished the legitimacy of and support for current welfare institutions. Rather it is to suggest that the pathological consequences of colonization have played only a marginal role in creating environmental political movements. Once created, these movements have, as made clear in thesis 9, responded to those pathologies, but the pathologies are not themselves a pivotal factor in the development of environmental politics. In conclusion, and in contrast to Habermas's work, I would tentatively suggest that the following factors are of greater significance in the emergence of environmental politics.

1 I would maintain that the levels and forms of contemporary environmental degradation are the central causal factor in the development of contemporary environmental movements. The development of new forms of technical knowledge has allowed degradation to be recognized and its implications calculated. It is worth noting that the postwar West has seen an enormous expansion in the diffusion of this information through expanded higher education and mass media and the activities of the environmental movement itself. This has forced a redefinition and recalculation of material interests among segments of Western publics: material interests must be judged on the basis of survivability and quality of life as well as on the more usual calculus of personal consumption. These changes have resulted in a significant broadening of the already existing environmental movement left over from the previous wave of late nineteenth-century cultural criticism, and accounts for the growth in the less radical elements of the environmental movement as well as its more radical wings.

2 In addition, environmental politics has been mobilized by the articulation of and appeal to a range of moral values. These have emerged partly in response to the nature of the environmental problems being faced, but have deeper historical roots in the whole set of post-enlightenment cultural transformations: for example, the emergence of more universalistic moral positions which can comprehend and respond to the needs of the common good, ultimately at a global level of planetary survival. However, those moral arguments initially found their most effective expression through the wave of post-1960s cultural criticism (alternative movements, countercultures, feminism, critiques of consumerism, etc.). The latter enabled arguments to be articulated in the public domain and alternative social arrangements to be offered. Only then could diffuse values be turned into political programmes and possibilities.

3 These moral arguments and redefined interests have found, in the last thirty years, a sizeable constituency to whom they can appeal. This is the new middle class, who, because of postwar social changes, have been taken up into the expanded public and voluntary sectors. However, it is not only the socioeconomic location of the new middle class that predis-

poses them towards environmental concerns; there is some evidence to suggest that the experiences of new types of child socialization and affluence are important. Simultaneously, the expanded educational opportunities and experiences of that class have given them the political skills with which to form significant social movements. Finally the most plausible element of Habermas's colonization argument can be brought into play. If affluence, education, socialization and non-productivist employment predispose the new middle classes towards an environmental politics, it is probably also the case that these factors have sensitized them to the pathological consequences of state-delivered welfare, albeit at a lower level of pathological burdens than the poor. Thus the non-environmental political movements of the postwar West have had declining appeal for the new middle class and a political vacuum has emerged. The radical environmental movement has served to combine environmental concerns with defence of the lifeworld, which this class perceives as important.

In this chapter I have emphasized certain elements of Habermas's work and inevitably left other areas unexplored. First, I have emphasized the importance of actual environmental degradation in stimulating environmental movements rather than exploring the political and cultural consequences of unknown and uncertain environmental threats and risks. Second, I have left Habermas's notions of the *critique of growth* and the protest against *excessive system complexity* relatively unexamined. The former is the unifying critical argument of new protest movements against the latter – the ways in which the execution of economic and political power and the pace and form of technological and social change appear to consistently outrun and outflank the cognitive and power capacities of the lifeworld and its normative systems. Both these issues form central themes in the work of Ulrich Beck. In chapter 5, I will explore these issues in connection with his ideas of the *risk society* and *organized irresponsibility*.

Two issues remain which I shall touch on in the conclusion to the book: whether the political forces Habermas describes can generate political movements quickly enough, with sufficient power to arrest the environmental degradation with which we threaten ourselves; and whether they can devise alternative social arrangements able to keep that degradation within tolerable limits, under acceptable political and economic conditions.

5
The Sociology of Risk: Ulrich Beck

Introduction: Ulrich Beck and the Risk Society

One of the most interesting and certainly one of the most idiosyncratic texts written by any social theorist in the last decade has been Ulrich Beck's *Risikogesellschaft*, translated as *Risk Society: Towards a New Modernity*.[1] It is distinguished by two remarkable features. First and foremost, it has sold an enormous number of copies in a relatively short space of time.[2] Second, it is funny. *Risk Society* and his more recent publications, *Ecological Politics in an Age of Risk*, *Reflexive Modernization* and *The Normal Chaos of Love*, are books of monstrous metaphors, testing and probing social conundrums and facing them with a black wit.[3] They are not so much rigorous, analytical accounts of modernity as surveys of the institutional bases of the fears and paradoxes of modern societies – societies that no longer correspond to the classical sociological descriptions or possess cultural resources that allow them to live comfortably with the world.

Beck may be funny, but he is not happy. 'The overwhelming feature of the age is not physical . . . but social: the fundamental and scandalous way in which the institutions, almost without exception, fail it.'[4] It is enough to make anyone angry. What can you do? How can you ride the juggernaut? If modernity is a runaway train, what can the passengers do? Beck cuts things three ways. You can look on the bright side of things. The train will stop. If it doesn't, why worry, the tracks go on for ever. 'One must love a tyrant one cannot overthrow or vote out of office.'[5] Though most of the time you pragmatically assume that the train is not running and it does not matter where it is going or how. In any case, what can you do – nothing. Or, you keep the tracks in focus and assume the worst. Pessimists 'feel the lack of what hardly anyone will admit to missing: braking devices, steering systems . . . They are the ones whose sad, furious, ludicrous gestures at least still remind the travelers of the lack of these elementary requirements.'[6] *Risk Society* and *Ecological Politics* rails against a world in which we must live constantly with the known threat of catastrophes, but are unable to diminish their likelihood; where we know who the perpetrators are, but cannot force them into the open; when we know what the problems are, but proof trickles through our fingertips.

Beck's work has a particular importance for anyone concerned with the response of social theory to environmental degradation and environmental politics. The distinguishing feature of his work is to place the origins and consequences of environmental degradation right at the heart of a theory of modern society, rather than seeing it as a peripheral element or theoretical afterthought. Beck's sociology and the societies it describes are dominated by the existence of environmental threats and the ways we understand and respond to them. Indeed, one could go so far as to argue that the *risk society* is predicated on and defined by the emergence of these distinctively new and distinctively problematic environmental hazards: 'Sociology . . . has not asked what the threat of self-annihilation means to society, yet there would be general agreement that this is what characterizes and distinguishes the latter half of the twentieth century.'[7]

The historical and intellectual origins of Beck's work are not difficult to pin down. First, his own earlier work in industrial sociology and the sociology of the family have informed his later work on risk and insecurity in the economy and private sphere. Second, his own concerns with modernity, its pathologies and its transformation have strong echoes in the work of contemporary German social theory as well as the various three-stage models of sociology (postmodern, postindustrial).[8] Third, Beck's work draws on and reflects an increasing body of work on the sociology of risk and uncertainty in psychology, economics and environmental studies, rooted in rational choice and game theory. This body of work has itself been intimately tied to an ever expanding volume of risk assessment and risk research in public and private bodies (cost–benefit analysis, environmental impact assessments, environmental audits) that draws on and transforms academic study in a truly self-reflexive manner.[9] Fourth, and perhaps most importantly, the politics and concerns of the Federal Republic of Germany and its now unified successor state have clearly made their mark on his work. For it is in the Federal Republic, more than any other Western society, that industrial success has been forced to reveal its catastrophic underside. This is not because the level of ecological degradation in the Federal Republic has been the worst – clearly Eastern Europe and the states of the ex-Soviet Union have paid an altogether heavier ecological price for the benefits of an unrestrained industrialization. If the arguments of chapter 4 were correct, then it is the prosperity and security of the German economy – what Beck calls that temple of high industrialism – that has furnished the psychological and economic room for manoeuvre and allowed such potent critiques to be mounted.

But that security is driven by a radical doubt. For Germans of Beck's generation have already been forced to engage with the underside of

modernity's success, its ruthless efficiency in pursuing the most catastrophic ends. The stakes of environmental catastrophe are high, but I suspect that for the Germans they are higher. Modernity, like nuclear power
stations, was declared safe by public inquiry. It was backed up by regular
inspections, constitutional guarantees, additional safety systems, trip
switches and cut-off mechanisms. But they have already failed once, why
shouldn't they do so again?

While Beck's writings have aroused an enormous amount of interest,
there has as yet been no proper survey of his recent work in English. Nor
have the precise implications of that work for the understanding of environmental degradation and environmental politics been properly
explored. Despite the centrality of environmental issues to his work, others have chosen to focus on and utilize his more general ideas of risk,
reflexivity and reflexive modernization. In part this is because the structure and style of Beck's work do not lend themselves easily to systematic
or analytical examination. Beck's prose is rarely delayed by careful or precise definitions. And he does not shirk from returning again and again to
similar problems, taking them on each time from a new angle. While this
makes for engaging reading, it does not always make for clarity.
However, given the wave of interest that he has generated, and the
absence of any serious attempt to evaluate his work as a whole and any
attempt to test it empirically or historically, there is some need for a systematic exposition and analytical dissection.

In the next section, I analyse the main arguments and theories developed in *Risk Society*, focusing on the distinctive characteristics of contemporary environmental hazards and environmental politics, and how the
same processes of reflexive modernization that created them have also
injected a huge dose of insecurity and change into core institutions of classical industrial society: science, technology, law, families and the labour
market. In the following section, I examine the ways in which these formulations have been developed and expanded on in *Ecological Politics*,
centering on the core notions of *organized irresponsibility, the social explosiveness of hazard* and the *safety state*. *Organized irresponsibility* helps explain
how and why the institutions of modern society must unavoidably
acknowledge the reality of catastrophe while simultaneously denying its
existence, covering its origins and precluding compensation or control.
The social explosiveness of hazard explores the ways in which awareness of
large-scale hazards and catastrophic risk sets off a dynamic of cultural
and political change that undermines state bureaucracies, challenges the
dominance of science and redraws the boundaries and battle lines of contemporary politics. The idea of the *safety state* describes the relationship
between the legitimacy of state institutions and the pledge of political systems to maintain the environmental security of their citizens.

I will then go on to consider briefly Beck's political and normative
response to the dilemmas he has outlined, a response that calls for the
democratization of science, the process of hazard definition and agreed

standards of safety and security. In the final sections of this chapter, I examine how useful and accurate these arguments are. First I ask whether it ultimately makes sense to describe modern societies as risk societies. Then I move from a macro-level assessment of Beck's work to the micro, examining whether his account of environmental politics and policy-making substantiates his claims about the delegitimization of liberal democratic states and scientific discourse. This will allow me to return to one of the major absences in Gorz's account of the political economy of environmental degradation; the capacity of states to deny the existence of environmental threats or their own culpability and responsibilities in creating them. I will return to Beck's political and moral diagnoses of these issues in the conclusion.

Risk Society: the Modernization of Modernity

The main arguments of *Risk Society* can be divided conveniently into three. First, Beck outlines the characteristics and consequences of the threats and dangers generated by the processes of modernization and industrialization, focusing on the ways in which they alter the dynamic and constitution of the classical industrial society that has generated them. In short, the process of *reflexive modernization* – exemplified by the emergence and interpretation of new risks and hazards – is ushering in a *risk society* from the corpse of a decaying industrial society. Second, Beck connects this widening penumbra of risk and insecurity with complementary processes of reflexive modernization, detraditionalization and individualization in the spheres of work, family life and self-identity. Third, he explores the ways in which these two sets of interconnected processes have altered the epistemological and cultural status of the sciences and the conduct and constitution of contemporary politics.

The Characteristics of Modern Risks

While Beck uses the idea of risks and hazards to refer to many areas of social life, it is in the equation of risks and hazards with environmental degradation that these ideas are most closely examined. Of course, dangers and hazards have always threatened human societies. What makes them risks, as Giddens has argued, is that they are dangers and hazards which are known, whose occurrence can be predicted and whose likelihood can be calculated.[10] To be in danger is one thing. To know that one is in danger is quite another. To know that one is in danger and to feel essentially powerless to alter the course of events which generate that danger is another again. Alongside the shift from danger to risk, contemporary environmental problems possess further distinctive characteristics

which elicit and demand very particular patterns of political and psychological response. These demands and responses are of such magnitude
that their emergence can be said to herald the emergence of a distinctive
form of modernity. There are at least three sets of arguments in Beck's
work to suggest that the production and implications of contemporary
risks differ – qualitatively and quantitatively – from earlier forms of risk
and hazard.

First, while the risks that threatened industrial societies were locally significant and often personally devastating, they were ultimately spatially
limited in their effects. They did not threaten entire societies. Neither spatial nor social limitations apply to contemporary hazards. Consider, for
example, the pollution produced by a nineteenth- or mid twentieth-century
steel mill or foundry. The emissions and wastes produced would have had
significant consequences for people who worked within the mill, for the
local community who breathed waste from its stacks, and for those who
drank from the local water supplies it polluted with scrap and solvents.
However, those threats, indeed the sum of the threats generated by all the
steel industries of the industrialized world, did not threaten entire populations, or in fact the planet as a whole. The environmental problems of the
steel industry have not disappeared, although in the West some of its older
manifestations have been mitigated. They have, however, been eclipsed by
new types of environmental degradation from new industrial processes.
The contemporary forms of environmental degradation that Beck focuses
on are not spatially limited in the range of their impact or socially confined
to particular communities. They are potentially global in their reach. The
reasons for this are complex and Beck is less than specific about them,
though he does suggest a number of features of contemporary risk that
account for these qualitative changes. First, the toxicity of contemporary
forms of environmental degradation is quantitatively greater than that of
industrial forms of degradation. Second, the impact of those toxins on
human bodies and the wider ecosystem are irreversible and cumulative in
their effects. Thus the consequences of modern risks outlast their generators. They are risks that accumulate in intensity and complexity across the
generations. In addition to transcending the spatial and social limits of
purely industrial risk, they also exceed their temporal boundaries.

Alongside these threats of increasing toxicity, Beck effectively denotes
a second set of environmental risks which, without hyperbole, can gen-
uinely be described as catastrophic in their potential. The environmental
dangers posed by large-scale nuclear accidents, large-scale chemical
release and by the alteration and manipulation of the genetic make-up of
the planet's flora and fauna actually pose the possibility of self-annihilation. The character of these potential apocalypses is not spelt out in any
great length. It is almost as if Beck assumes that we accept and agree with
his estimations of the dangers we face – a somewhat surprising elision
given Beck's acknowledgement of the relative and contested character of
risk perception and definition.[11]

A third distinctive set of features of modern environmental risks is, according to Beck, that their point of impact is not obviously tied to their point of origin and that their transmission and movements are often invisible and untrackable to everyday perception. This social invisibility means that, unlike many other political issues, environmental risks must first clearly be brought to consciousness, and only then can it be said that they constitute an actual threat, and that involves a process of scientific argument and cultural contestation. Thus the politics of risk is intrinsically a politics of knowledge, expertise and counter-expertise.[12]

The Transition from Industrial Society to Risk Society

In both *Risk Society* and *Ecological Politics* Beck uses this model of risk and hazard to underpin his threefold model of social development, running from preindustrial society to industrial society to risk society. In preindustrial societies, risk takes the form of natural hazards – earthquakes, drought, etc. These are not contingent on decisions made by individuals, thus they cannot be considered voluntary or intentionally created and they are, therefore, effectively unavoidable. The spatial and social range of hazards can be both highly localized and quite extensive, the Black Death, for example, which affected the trajectory of an entire civilization. Preindustrial societies are openly insecure. In cultural terms, the origins of risks are invariably assigned to external, supernatural forces and the help of those same forces must be sought in mitigating or avoiding the worst effects of hazards and contingencies.

With the emergence of classical industrial societies, the origins, consequences and characteristics of risk change. The way in which risks are socially understood and responded to also changes. Risks and accidents become clearly contingent on the actions of both individuals and wider social forces, be they dangers at work from machinery and poisons, or the dangers of unemployment and penury induced by the uncertain dynamics of the business cycle and structural economic change. Given that risks are no longer solely attributable to external agency or individual fecklessness, industrial societies develop institutions and rules for coping with and mitigating the impact of localized risks and dangers. Beck goes so far as to argue that the welfare state can be seen as a collective and institutionalized response to the nature of industrialized risks, based on principles of rule-governed attribution of fault and blame, legally implemented compensation, actuarial insurance principles and collectively shared responsibility. In industrial society, blame or culpability for threats can be confidently asserted and their statistical likelihood calculated. This makes possible the construction of reliable actuarial schedules of the volume and impact of risks against which financially solvent institutions of collective burden-sharing can be maintained. The classic example of this would be the creation of compensation and insurance schemes for accident, injury and unemployment at work.

However, under the impact of modern risks and hazards, these modes of determining and perceiving risk, attributing causality and allocating compensation have irreversibly broken down. In so doing, they have also thrown the functioning and legitimacy of modern bureaucracies, states, economies, and science into question. Risks that were calculable under industrial society become incalculable and unpredictable in the risk society. Compared to the possibility of adjudging blame and cause in classical modernity, risk society possesses no such certainties or guarantees.

We will return to the problems of non-attributability, the limitations of the industrial *safety state* and the collapse of conventional modes of insurance, safety and security in the next section. First we turn to the ways in which the hazards of the risk society transform the conduct and logic of conventional political economy and raise the importance of the politics of knowledge.

The Changing Politics of Risks and Knowledge

Beck examines the changes in political economy by contrasting the logic of wealth creation and distribution with the logic of risk production and avoidance. In sharp contrast to the politics of wealth production that dominated industrial society – the positive logic of distributing wealth and social *goods* – risk society and the politics of socially generated risks are characterized by the negative logic of distributing social and personal *bads*.[13] The main lines of conflict in industrial societies were, according to Beck, conducted over the way in which the 'cake' was divided up between social groups. This kind of situation allows for positive-sum conflict resolutions in which all participants can gain, if in different ways and at different rates. However, if the cake is 'poisoned' then the dynamics of politics change. This in turn can be expressed as a contrast of undersupply and overproduction. In industrial societies, the impact of environmental hazards could be understood in terms of the absence of, or insufficiently high supply of, goods and services to control and mitigate hazards, for example, public health schemes and accessible utilities. By contrast, modern risk production stems inevitably and unavoidably from the very heart of the wealth-creating process, and thus the problem is one of chronic overproduction.

The consequences of these shifts for organized social interests are not dealt with at great length, but Beck touches on them by contrasting class positions and risk positions in industrial society and risk society. Risk positions, in this context, refer to the degrees of exposure of individuals, given their social and geographical locations, to dangers and hazards. The contrast is simple. In industrial society, class positions and risk positions more or less correlate; in risk society they cease to. In industrial society,

the rich live in areas and work under conditions where they are not overt-
ly exposed to danger; the working class and the poor are exposed.
However, once risks and dangers exceed their old spatial and temporal
limitations, wealth, privilege, status and economic power provide no
escape routes. The threat of pesticide poisoning and toxic accumulation in
the food chain affects the suburbs as much as the inner city; nuclear meltdowns are of such scope that rich and poor, North and South, are threatened alike. The position of, and relationship between, classes and other
traditionally defined economic interest groups do not remain unscathed
by the emergence of new risks. While industrial society was organized
along the lines of class and ownership, capital and labour, environmental
degradation threatens capital and labour alike. The new lines of political
and economic conflict cut across the old divide, the sharpest differences
being between sectors of capital and labour whose livelihoods are either
threatened by degradation (as with fishing), need to be actively controlled
to limit risks (as with the car industry) or actively benefit from attempts to
cope with risks (the waste and recycling industries).

If the salience of conventional class-based politics declines in the risk
society, then the importance of the politics of knowledge and the role of
those who produce, disseminate and interpret knowledge – above all
knowledge about risk – are inescapably elevated. Because the existence –
let alone the origins, consequences, scope and scale – of risks must be
deduced by active causal interpretation, they only exist, in the first place,
in so far as there is knowledge of them.[14] They are also open to social definition and construction. At every stage the mobilization of knowledge to
describe and assess risk is central. This is a shift in the centrality of the
politics of knowledge and the status of knowledge professionals that Beck
acknowledges by describing the main lines of conflict and differentiation
in the risk society as the *relations of definition*.[15]

Science and Politics in the Risk Society

Given these arguments, it is not surprising to find that Beck places the discourse and practice of science at the heart of the politics of the risk society.
First, science as applied technology is a cause of modern risks. Second, the
identification and implications of risks must in part be couched in scientific
terms. It is not possible to detect and debate the threats posed by nuclear
power without some kind of scientific knowledge of the processes
involved. Third, in terms of alternative production processes, new products and clean-up technologies, science may provide a source of solutions
to those risks. Fourth, the development of science is a clear example of the
process of reflective modernization. For in industrial society science is
applied to an objective, external, natural world. However, in the risk society, science must confront an external environment that it has profoundly
altered. This reflexivity is taken a stage further when the inherent scepti-

cism and methodological suspiciousness of contemporary science is applied to itself.

One of the axial principles of political life in modern societies is the separation of public and private spheres. The exercise of power in the public sphere has been sharply constrained by the development of the institutions of representative democracy and the entrenched requirements of legality and legitimacy. However, power in the private sphere, above all in the economy and family, have not had the same strictures placed on them. According to Beck, this has hinged ideologically, in the case of the economy, on a basic equation between technical and social progress. The side-effects and social costs of that process have been effectively legitimized and accepted. Meantime, welfare states have picked up the pieces that the side-effects of modernization have thrown up. At an ideological level, 'progress becomes a substitute for questions, a type of consent in advance for goals and consequences that go unnamed and unknown.'[16] However, the twin tracks of the emergent risk society – the scope and scale of material ecological risks and personal insecurity – have undermined the legitimacy of both parts of modern societies and their effective separation. The conventional public sphere of the representative democratic state has become unable to cope adequately with the scale of the risks and uncertainty with which it is faced, while at the same time the welfare state project has exhausted its utopian energies. The private sphere's creation of risks means that it can no longer be considered apolitical, and indeed a whole arena of hybrid *subpolitics* emerges in the previously shielded realms of investment decisions, product development, plant management and scientific research priorities. In this situation the conventional political forces and representatives of industrial society have been sidelined. The attachment of political actors to class positions and interests has been undermined by the emergence of overarching risk positions and interests in security, while their mode of operation, through parliamentary democracy and official bureaucracies, is no longer capable of adequately controlling the forces of an unleashed capitalist dynamic.

In their place, Beck, like many authors, argues that social movements are the leading edge of a new politics in a new type of society. Interestingly, like Giddens, he links the emergence of these movements, and principally of course the environmental movements in the West, to two interconnected sources. First, they are seen as a response to actual and imagined material threats and risks. Second, they appear as a political alternative to the forces of conventional politics whose structures, interests, means and ends no longer correspond with the texture of everyday life transformed out of all proportion: 'on the one hand the new social movements . . . are expressions of the new risk situations in risk societies. On the other, they result from the search for social and personal identities and commitments in a detraditionalized culture.'[17] The form of those everyday destabilizations and insecurities is the second type of reflexive modernization.

Individualization and Detraditionalization in the Risk Society

Alongside the growth and complexity of ecological modernization risks, contemporary societies and individuals must also cope with a second simultaneous wave of personal and biographical risk and insecurity. What links the two processes in Beck's work is the idea of *reflexive modernization*. In the case of ecological threats, modernization, equated with economic growth and technological change, generates the conditions of its own termination. Modernization corrodes the essential structure and principle of modernity. The side-effects of economic growth threaten the possibility of continued economic well-being. The depoliticized character of the private sphere has led it to create risks and dangers of such a scale that its political separation and insulation can no longer be maintained. In the case of personal risks, the process of reflexive modernization dissolves the traditional cultural parameters and institutional social structures of industrial society: class, class consciousness, family structures and gender roles. In this regard, the essential features of the modernization process – the dissolution of tradition and the application of universalistic principles – are applied to what appeared to be essential features of modernity but were actually enclaves of tradition and particularism: rigid economic stratification, clearly demarcated gender roles and the nuclear family. Beck is often imprecise about the weight to be allotted to different elements of the process of reflexive modernization, their historical origins and the ways in which they interact with each other, but there appear to be four elements at work: structural and institutional change; a wave of detraditionalization; a surge of individualization; the simultaneous maintenance of relations of inequality. These interweaving processes of change are best captured in Beck's account of the reflexive modernization of the economy and work and the family and gender roles.

The processes of economic transformation being undergone in Western societies are of such magnitude that 'the principles of the previously existing employment system will be at stake, and not just restratifications in the structure of occupations and qualifications.'[18] Beck is on familiar ground here as he lists the broad shifts that have occurred in the labour markets of Western societies, particularly Western European societies in the last twenty years: the emergence of large-scale, long-term structural unemployment; the transformation of the gender composition of the labour force; the loss of full-time work and the rise of part-time work; the collapse of traditional structures of regular, even lifetime employment; a massive increase in the demand for flexibility, with widespread economic insecurity.[19] This has led to the transformation of class structures and the diminishing importance of work as a source of self-identity, and thus a weakening of the interconnection between social and economic positions and individual interests, identities and consciousness. It has also disrupted all the familiar patterns of personal biography on which industrial society rested for its acceptance and stability. The very meaning and worth of work appears to be collapsing around a rapidly bifurcating labour market permeated at every level by short-termism and insecurity.

The character of gender roles and relations is peculiarly combustible, according to Beck.[20] On the one hand, there has been a seismic and irreversible shift in the conduct of sexual relationships and the discourses of sexuality, as well as more formal changes in the gender dimension of the law, education and the labour market. On the other hand, these changes are most advanced in the realm of consciousness rather than in the behaviour and conditions of men and women, particularly in the labour market and in entitlements to social security: 'This historically created mixture of new consciousness and old conditions is explosive in a double sense.'[21] Women's expectations have unquestionably risen and been accompanied by radical improvements in their performance inside the education system. However, great confidence, expectations, skills and qualifications have not been matched by consummate advances in the labour market and personal economic security, due to the ingrained individual and structural resistance of men and the organizations they continue to dominate. As such, 'the ice of illusion grows thin.'[22]

If the politics of gender are combustible in the work-place, they are perhaps even more so in the family. Industrial society hinged on the existence and acceptance of clearly separate gender roles, which translated into a rigidly demarcated and ideologically policed division between home and work, domestic unpaid labour and child-rearing and paid wage labour, reproduction and production, and feminine and masculine attributes. These were all consolidated in the vision, if not the practice, of the nuclear family. However, reflexive modernization finds this traditionalism and inequality unacceptable in its universalizing frame of reference. 'In the conflicts breaking out today between men and women, therefore, what must be settled are the personalized contradictions of an industrial society that has also destroyed the foundations of their ability to live together through its reflexive modernization and individualization.'[23]

The dissolution of traditional roles and the intensification of individualization have raised the demand for and the emotional stakes of creating sustainable, open relationships. Once traditional roles and the ideological strait-jacket that helped to anchor them have gone, the uncertainties of personal and family life appear to be multiplying – divorce, single parenthood, threats to economic security, conflict over the demands of home and work – at a time when the capacity and intentions of government to provide institutional support – parental leave, conciliatory divorce legislation, affordable child-care – is minimal.

Ecological Politics in an Age of Risk: Organized Irresponsibility and the Social Explosiveness of Hazard

While *Risk Society* cast its sociological net very widely, the substantive focus of its successor, *Ecological Politics in an Age of Risk*, is much narrower. In this book Beck retained most of the conceptual apparatus of *Risk Society*, but chose to focus on the most systemic and encompassing of risks and hazards that modern societies have generated: environmental degradation. The biographical risks and uncertainties of modern families, gender relationships and labour markets are left on one side in *Ecological Politics*, though the implications of those arguments reverberate throughout the text. At the heart of the book are two interconnected ideas; organized irresponsibility and the social explosiveness of hazard. Beck uses that former term to describe the ways in which the political and legal systems of risk societies, intentionally and unintentionally, render the social origins and consequences of large-scale environmental hazards invisible. While the risks and dangers of industrial societies could be adequately captured with the models of social causation and risk available to them, this is no longer possible in risk societies. The industrial fatalism that Beck excoriates describes the dominant response of Western publics to the paradoxical situation: that we must live with the obvious threats of uncontrolled industrial development, but are unable to account for their existence or accurately determine the culpability of either individuals or organizations for those threats. However, such is the magnitude of the risks we face and so lamentable are the ways in which we have politically and institutionally attempted to cope with them that the thin veneer of tranquillity and normality is constantly broken by the harsh overwheening reality of unavoidable dangers and threat. It is this that Beck describes as the *social explosiveness of hazard*. The first casualties of this are conventional, industrial notions of risk perception, safety insurance, and compensation, and with them the legitimacy and utility of the state institutions that have notionally secured, or at the very least convincingly promised, safety and security – what Beck often refers to as the *safety state*. Beck then goes on to examine this social explosiveness in a number of main areas, including the impact of risk on the bureaucracy of the safety state, and the impact on conventional, industrial lines of political conflict and political organization. I examine these in turn below.

Organized Irresponsibility and the Relations of Definition

In chapter 3 I argued that one of the central limitations on Gorz's account of environmental degradation and environmental politics was his failure to examine the ways in which states can and do deny the existence or seriousness of environmental problems or attempt to delegitimize the claims and concerns of those protesting against them. It is this process that is at the heart of Beck's account of contemporary environmental issues. Beck criss-crosses this terrain throughout *Ecological Politics*, in a sustained but unsystematic fashion. Therefore, what follows is a sympathetic reconstruction of what appear to be his core arguments.

Organized irresponsibility denotes a concatenation of cultural and institutional mechanisms by which political and economic elites effectively mask the origins and consequences of the catastrophic risks and dangers of late industrialization. In doing so they limit, deflect and control the protests that these risks engender. 'Thus what is at issue is an elaborate labyrinth designed according to principles, not of non-liability or irresponsibility, but of simultaneous liability and unaccountability: more precisely, liability as unaccountability, or organized irresponsibility.'[24] To put it another way, risk societies are plagued by the paradox of more and more environmental degradation, perceived and possible, and a greater weight of environmental law and regulation. Yet simultaneously, no one individual or institution seems to be held specifically accountable for anything. How can this be? The key to explaining this state of affairs is the mismatch that exists in the risk society between the character of hazards and dangers produced by late industrialism and the prevalent *relations of definition* which date in their construction and content from an earlier and qualitatively different epoch. The relations of definition, as I described them above, are the rules, institutions and capacities that structure the identification and assessment of environmental problems and risks; they are the legal, epistemological and cultural matrix in which environmental politics is conducted.

The relations that Beck focuses on are fourfold. (1) Who is to determine the harmfulness of products or the danger or risks? Is the responsibility on those who generate those risks, those benefiting from them, those affected or potentially affected by them or public agencies? (2) To whom does that proof have to be submitted? Who, after all, are the proper arbiters of risk assessment and who should have to defend or interrogate those claims? (3) What is to count as sufficient proof? In a world in which we necessarily deal with contested knowledge, and probabilities and possibilities, what are the grounds if any for accepting or rejecting different claims about risks and hazards? (4) If there are dangers and damages, who is to decide on compensation for the afflicted and appropriate forms of future control and regulation? If there is to be compensation, who is to be compensated, and by how much relative to others affected?

In relation to each of these questions, risk societies are currently trapped in a vocabulary that befits the risks and hazards interrogated by the relations of definition of industrial societies. They are singularly inappropriate for modern catastrophes. Consequently, we face the paradox that at the very time when threats and hazards seem to become more dangerous and more obvious, they simultaneously slip through the net of proofs, attributions and compensation that the legal and political systems attempt to capture them with.

The responsibility to demonstrate proof, Beck argues, currently lies overwhelmingly with the afflicted rather than potential polluters. The legacy of industrial society's faith in progress is that the legal system assumes that industrial production will be benign unless demonstrated otherwise. Given that companies are the only actors likely to have any sense of the likely risk implications of any given process or product in development, no one else is likely to consider the environmental implications before pollution has begun, and attempts to demonstrate harm will occur only after people have been exposed to the danger. Thus the prevailing relations of definition are weighted towards the polluter. First, because the legal system demands proofs of *post hoc* toxicity rather than *pre hoc* non-toxicity or safety. Second, because those who must prove toxicity are inevitably less endowed with the detailed skills and information necessary to make a convincing case.

The arbitration of such disputes invariably lies with the legal system and courts and judges. However, Beck does not argue that the social origins or political inclinations of the legal system's senior figures can explain the consistent capacity of polluters to be acquitted or treated lightly. Nor does he claim that the quantity of laws and the weight of regulatory agencies are too small. Indeed they have radically increased as levels of pollution and degradation have increased. Rather, it is the qualitative difference between the nineteenth-century relations of definition and twentieth-century risks and hazards that accounts for the problem. Most legal cases attempt to determine whether a single substance is responsible for a particular set of pathological effects. However, we live in world in which there is an enormous number of potentially damaging pollutants, and many of them must have complex interactions with and consequences for human bodies and the wider ecosystem. Further, most cases attempt to determine whether a particular source of a given pollutant is responsible for a particular form of degradation. However, pollutants almost invariably come from many sources. Thus a collective danger from collective origins must be legally pursued through the fiction of the individual legal person or corporation.

The Social Explosiveness of Hazard: Risk and the Safety State

Through the Byzantine labyrinth of organized irresponsibility, protest still breaks out and the claims and legitimacy of the prevailing relations of definition come into question. It is this that Beck describes as the *social explosiveness of hazard*. In short, he sees the existence of large-scale ecological disasters, of which Chernobyl is his favourite example, as the central causal factor in delegitimizing and destabilizing state institutions with responsibilities for pollution control, in particular, and public safety in general. This occurs because the pledges and commitments of modern states to the security of the population are, despite frenzied attempts to patch up the old models of industrial safety and security, overwhelmed by the enormity of contemporary risks. Their models of risk perception and risk insurance are swept away. Governments and bureaucracies, of course, have well-worn routines of denial. Data can be hidden, denied and distorted. Counter-arguments and counter-experts can be mobilized in the face of ecological hazards. Maximum permissible pollution levels can be raised and transformed to accommodate new waves of unexpected pollution. Human error rather than systemic risk can be cast as the villain of the piece. However, states are, according to Beck, fighting a losing battle, for they offer nineteenth-century pledges of security to a world that is unequivocally engaged with risks and hazards of a qualitatively different order.

The key to these arguments is Beck's idea of the safety state, a term derived from the work of François Ewald.[25] Ewald's work, according to Beck, 'allows one to comprehend the production of security as a sociological phenomenon, based upon institutional inventions and arrangements with which industrial society deals with the danger of its own creation.'[26] This is, in effect, a particular take on the construction and origins of welfare states. While the majority of interpretations of welfare states have sought an explanation in terms of class interests, the maintenance of social order or the enhancement of national productivity and military capacity, this argument understands the provision of services (health care), the creation of insurance schemes (pensions and unemployment insurance) and the regulation of the economy and environment (health and safety legislation) in terms of the creation of security. Similarly, it is a model of the modern capitalist state in which its legitimacy and acceptability is interpreted in terms of the maintenance of safety and security pledges, rather than the achievement of economic growth or redistribution, or minimum social conditions and social peace.

What hazards repeatedly demonstrate is that the cultural and institutional legacies of classical industrial society are inadequate to the problems that now face them. We have already seen how the models of causality and attributability of industrial societies have been undermined and replaced by the Kafkaesque construct of organized irresponsibility. Alongside this, industrial society's modes of risk perception and assessment are rendered irrelevant, its systems of risk control and mitigation appear powerless, its models of insurance and compensation are inadequate. The certainties of scientific models are shaken by the occurrence of the worst-case scenario. Simultaneously this demonstrates that societies are locked into a very high-consequence gamble rather than a position of security. Models of insurance and compensation under the industrial safety state were tied to an actuarial and calculable basis. The statistical likelihood of accidents and dangers could be predicted and a schedule of payments from individuals into a collective fund could be calculated. The accumulation of payments could also be predicted in advance and relatively clear rules established as to who would pay, who would be eligible for compensation, and at what rate. All these calculations are rendered meaningless by large-scale hazards. The premise of nuclear power's legitimacy was that it would not go wrong, and that therefore the whole schedule of compensation and insurance was not necessary. However, as Beck argues, Chernobyl rendered the worst-case scenario possible, even probable. The absence of insurance and compensation became more problematic. However, even if there was an admission of danger on the part of the safety state, how could a meaningful insurance scheme for the possibility of very large-scale ecological disruption be calculated, and who would pay for it? 'The shining achievement of nuclear power plants is not only to have made redundant the principle of assurance in the economic sense, but also in its medical, psychological, cultural, and religious senses. Residual risk society is a society without assurance, whose insurance cover paradoxically diminishes in proportion to the scale of the hazard.'[27]

What this adds up to is that some of the basic premises on which the legitimacy and efficacy of the modern capitalist state were established have been cut away. We are faced with a crisis of the safety state.

> With the emergence of hazards for which they assume yet deny responsibility, the institutions enter an unwinnable race against the safety claims that have been exhorted from them. On the one hand, they end up under the perpetual compulsion to render still safer that which is already as safe as it can be; on the other, people's expectations are thus raised, ultimately intensifying awareness to a point where even the merest suspicion of an accident makes the facades of safety crumble.[28]

Risk and Orthodox Politics

In *Ecological Politics* Beck returns to the same lines of argument developed in *Risk Society*. If, as he puts it, the cake is poisoned, then the basic logic of political conflict and economic production is undermined. In contrast to the dominant role of the relations of production in industrial society, where the ownership or non-ownership of capital is the key to explaining political interests and economic power, risk societies are structured by the relations of definition; thus the sites and forms of political conflict change, along with the sources of decisive power and the distribution of interests.

Beck is a little hazy about the precise consequences, but a number of elements of the new politics can be deduced. First, more conflicts will emerge between fractions of capital and their representatives, depending on the degree to which they generate and/or are affected by hazards. Some sectors will be threatened with additional costs, even closure, due to the intensity of the risks they generate. Other sectors will actively benefit from the creation of risks and hazards as new markets for new products in pollution abatement emerge; similarly, for example, as asthma rates rise with increasing urban air pollution, pharmaceutical companies gain.

Other sectors of capital will be directly threatened by environmental degradation if the key resources they use come under threat. The fishing industry is threatened by marine pollution from the chemical industry; the tourism industry is threatened when zealous developers and road-builders destroy prized landscapes and attractions. Alongside these conflicts the significance of the labour–capital conflict is diminished and labour is more likely to fragment along the same sectoral lines as capital – though Beck adds the caveat that the working class is less unfriendly to environmental issues than is sometimes portrayed in the literature. Finally, Beck asserts the increasing significance of regional conflict below the level of the nation-state and international conflicts above the level of the nation-state when transboundary pollution, destruction of the environmental commons and shared resource shortages begin to bite.[29]

Learning to Live with Risk: Ecological Democracy and the Democratization of Science

Scenarios for Future Politics

In *Risk Society* Beck sketches three broad scenarios for the future direction of politics: back to industrial society; the democratization of technological development; the emergence of differential politics. In a rather crude manner they all have their counterparts in contemporary German politics. The first roughly equates with the world-view of the Christian Democratic right in Germany. The second option, which seeks to address the problem of risk from within the institutional framework of industrial society, corresponds to mainstream social democratic thinking. The third option, which calls for new political institutions as well as new rules of political decision-making about risk, corresponds to the politics of the greens, and the broader environmental movement in German civil society.

   The return to industrial society captures the basic political orientation of orthodox politics to the risk society. It remains tied to notions of progress and benign technological change. It believes that the risks we face can still be captured by nineteenth-century, scientific models of hazard assessment and industrial notions of hazard and safety. Simultaneously, the disintegrating institutions of industrial society – nuclear families, stable labour markets, segregated gender roles – can be shored up and buttressed against the waves of reflexive modernization sweeping the West. However, if Beck is right, then this attempt to apply nineteenth-century ideas to the late twentieth century is doomed to failure, for risks and dangers will constantly spill out of the control of bureaucracies, safety pledges will be compromised and the malign face of technology will inevitably be displayed. Similarly, the personal lives of individuals will constantly contradict claims that traditional social roles and institutions retain their efficacy and legitimacy. The consequent irrelevance and delegitimization of orthodox politics could then open up calls for strong leadership and authoritarian political change.[30]

Beck calls the second response to the runaway train of risk society the democratization of techno-economic development. In the same sense that science brought its inherent scepticism to reflexively bear on its epistemological claims, modernity can bring its commitment to self-determination to bear on the consequences of socioeconomic progress and technological development. The institutional model for doing this is varied but rests on bringing the decision-making process in scientific debate and technological research under public scrutiny and parliamentary checks. This would be accompanied by an *ecological variant of the welfare state*. Beck is, once again, rather imprecise as to what this grand term means, but one can assume, I think, that he is describing a project in which the resources of the state and state agencies take responsibility for curtailing environmental degradation, and pick up the pieces – environmentally and socially – once degradation has occurred.

However, both elements of this strategy apply the arguments and deploy the institutional solutions of nineteenth- and early twentieth-century industrial society to late twentieth-century risk societies. In so doing they are inadequate and inappropriate responses – though ones with some mitigating effect – as Beck's third variant of subpolitical activity seeks to demonstrate. Moreover, they bring their own peculiar side-effects and pathologies. They entail an excessive centralization of power in welfare states and parliaments, when the needs of a risk society require the greatest devolution of power and resources to the sites of risk creation and exposure to threats. They entail an excessive bureaucratization. This locates further powers and decision-making capacities in institutions which have hitherto consistently aided and abetted the creation of risks, as well as supervising subsequent public detoxification. Finally, this project does not tackle the displacement of power into the hands of scientific expertise and institutions where actual decisions about safety and permissibility are made. This can only be tackled by a *differential politics*.

The idea of a differential politics turns on Beck's earlier distinction between the conventional politics of parliamentary states and the subpolitics of civil society and democratized para-state institutions.[31] The three key conditions of this politics of control are a strong and independent legal system, a free and critical mass media and what Beck calls the widespread opportunity for self-criticism. 'That means that the preserving, settling, discursive functions of politics – which quietly are already dominant, but remain overshadowed by fictitious power constructions – could become the core of its tasks.'[32] This is a differential politics in that it sees a role for the application of political power in different forms on different institutions. It recognizes a continuing role for state and para-state institutions in democratized forms, and their application to the recognition and mitigation of risk, but it sees them as only a component, and a subsidiary component at that, of a broader programme of political change and democratization. This involves opening up the private sphere of economic decision-making to political debate and control, not merely by the state but by the institutions of civil society.

In *Ecological Politics* Beck returns to the ways in which we might respond to the politics of hazard and how we might learn to live in the risk society. The choices have narrowed to two: *authoritarian technocracy* and *ecological democracy*. Beck expresses the path to authoritarian technocracy:

> Performing on the high-wire act near catastrophes of unimaginable extent, risk societies tend to undergo basic political mood swings, phases of forced normality alternate with dazed states of emergency. Calls for the 'strong hand' [of the state], that is supposed to avert ecological catastrophe, tie in with calls for the 'strong hand' that is supposed to counteract the collapse of state power and rationality.[33]

This line of argument clearly needs expanding on. Beck, it would seem, is arguing that the nature of contemporary threats and hazards leads to occasional crises of insecurity and threat, of which Chernobyl is perhaps the paradigmatic example. These situations appear to demand an intensification of state activity and an expansion of state power to ensure security and guard against threats. That expansion of power and control is all the more necessary, from the perspective of the state at any rate, for its power and legitimacy are constantly threatened by such events. While the relations of definition on proof, attributability and compensation remain unchanged, this expansion of state power will cover both its own legitimation deficits and render external protests absurd due to the lack of proof they can bring to bear as to threats and hazards. This leaves the definitions and control of hazards in the hands of small groups of insulated experts who 'will continue to decide, on everybody's behalf, how safe is safe enough'.[34]

Ecological democracy is, by contrast, the utopia of a responsible modernity. Beck is much more specific about the preconditions of such an arrangement. He can be because the idea of an ecological democracy rests on overturning the relations of definition that Beck has outlined and explored in *Ecological Politics*. First, it envisions a society in which the consequences of technological development and economic change are debated before key decisions are taken. Second, the burden of proof regarding future risks, hazards and current environmental degradation would lie with the perpetrators rather than the injured party: from the polluter *pays* principle to the polluter *proves* principle. Third, there must be established a new body of standards of proof, correctness, truth and agreement in science and law. Beck suggests some lines of attack on the current complacency of the safety state and the system of organized irresponsibility in which the politics of risk is currently mired. He argues for strategies that pursue the *denormalization of acceptance*, in which not only are the limits of probabilistic safety claims and science's own understanding of its limitations ruthlessly probed and turned against them, but in which the very notion of safety is superseded by a baseline commitment to the preservation of life.

Ecological Democracy and the Risk Society

In addition to these formal conditions and political strategies, Beck considers the theories of democratization proposed by two contemporary German sociologists, Claus Offe's critique of majority rule, and Ulrich Preuss's constitution capable of learning – or, as Beck calls it, a reflexive constitution.[35] The limits of majority rule in democracies are twofold. First and most obviously, it is a principle that can easily lead to the abuse of minorities, fermenting rather than resolving social conflicts. Second, and perhaps more significantly in this context, it requires that the complex issues raised by environmental degradation be reduced to yes or no issues on which majoritarian principles can then act. How, for example, can the resolution of environmental problems caused by transport be put to a yes–no vote. Pruess argues that 'the tasks of ecology-orientated constitutional and democratic theory consist in making time, and in keeping the future open to democratic options through the power of a minority veto.'[36] Thus constitutions would no longer be only devices for establishing the institutional framework within which current social conflicts could be mediated, but would provide the means by which institutions and decisions could be reconciled with the absent voices of future generations and future needs.

Environmental Catastrophe and the Risk Society: Evidence For and Against

A critical engagement with the work of Ulrich Beck is necessarily conducted on a number of levels. His writings combine a very broad-brush account of the main lines of structural change and development in modern societies with very detailed accounts of quite narrow areas of social life. The grand sweep of industrial society's reflexive modernization sits side by side with the minutiae of government responses to the paradoxes of pollution legislation. In the next section I will return to some of the minutiae. First and foremost I want to consider the broader picture that Beck describes and the place of environmental degradation and politics within it.

The central issue in assessing Beck's work at this level is whether it is reasonable, plausible and/or useful to describe contemporary Western societies as *risk societies*. On the basis of Beck's characterization of risk societies, there are a number of ways of approaching this question. First, we can ask whether there has been an objective increase in the scope, scale and threat of risks faced by those societies. Second, we can ask whether there has been a decisive increase in the perception of those risks among key social groups and actors and among the population at large. Third, we can ask whether, if there has been a perceptible rise in actual risks and risk perception, this has fundamentally altered the behaviour, beliefs and interests of those groups. Beck's work effectively assumes we can answer all three questions in the affirmative. A similar positive response to these questions is assumed in Giddens's work on risk, although he argues that this shift constitutes the radicalization of modernity rather than a transition to a qualitatively different social order.[37]

In the sphere of gender relations and the transformation of the family, sexuality and identity, Beck has drawn on a broad corpus of empirical research – statistical and interpretive – to back up his arguments.[38] There are good empirical grounds for thinking that in these domains life in the West has become more risky, that people perceive that risk and that they have changed their beliefs and behaviour as a consequence. The rate of divorce and the risks of family break-ups are clearly on the rise. This information is widely known among the general population. This is clearly a contributory factor in changing attitudes to marriage, parenting, etc.

While the significance of these kinds of change cannot be underestimated, the weight of Beck's account of the transformation of industrial into risk societies lies with the newly emerged possibilities of catastrophe, of global annihilation, and thus with the risks of environmental degradation. In this domain, Beck offers some anecdotal evidence but he does not engage with these questions in a sustained empirical fashion and it is difficult to claim that he has decisively sealed the case for his account of a new modernity. Both Beck and Giddens have covered their tracks by suggesting mechanisms and reasons for the avoidance of risk perception. Giddens describes adaptive reactions to a risky environment that filter out its more extreme psychological consequences – *pragmatic acceptance, sustained optimism* and *cynical fatalism*.[39] Beck describes the pervasive influence of an *industrial fatalism* that maintains the fictions of classical industrial society. However, it is simply not acceptable to assume that the empirical case has been made for the widespread existence of the increasing threat of risks and increasing risk perception, or that their combined impact on social behaviour and beliefs is so conclusive that we can properly herald the emergence of a new type of society. The contemporary *relations of definition* in sociology would probably suggest that the onus of proof lies with Beck and Giddens. Before returning to these empirical issues, two theoretical limitations of their work are worth noting.

First, there must be some doubt about the residual psychology of their accounts which assumes that the experience of risk is an essentially negative one. There is certainly a tradition of thinking about risk and uncertainty that extols the exhilaration of the gamble and uncertainty. Moreover, given the pervasiveness of gambling, there is some suggestion that many subscribe to such a philosophy. Within economics particularly, there is an account of economic change and development that is premised on the necessity of risk-taking and innovation. This is not to suggest that these forms of risk-taking do not carry psychological costs, but it is possible that both Giddens and Beck have overestimated the negative and pathological features of living in a world of insecurity and uncertainty.

Secondly, neither of their causal accounts of risk and environmental degradation are very sensitive to historical questions. Why for example, given that modernity harboured these mechanisms of change within it, is it only in the 1980s and 1990s that the related processes of reflexive modernization, individualization and detraditionalization reached such a peak? Why is it only now that the labour market and the family have burst the older structures of biographical and personal security? Why is it only now that expert opinion and the claims of science have been brought to a point of epistemological uncertainty? Why is it only now that environmental hazards have generated such a risky profile?[40] Why is it only now that processes of globalization have reached such epic dimensions? The writings of Beck and Giddens allow us to pose these questions, and indeed they may be the right questions to ask of modern societies, but it is by no means clear that they furnish us with the resources to answer them.

What then is the evidence for the emergence of risk societies? It is probably true to say that the objective existence of environmental risks and their broad subjective perception have increased. Although many forms of contemporary environmental degradation have been going unnoticed for some time, the current profile of environmental danger looks more risky than, say, that of forty years ago: the ozone holes are bigger; the apparent trends of climate change are more ominous; more land is under threat from infrastructures and industrial development or desertification; there are innumerably more nuclear installations dotted across the earth; the state of the world's oceans is declining. Similarly, the level of risk perception has increased. The place of environmental issues in opinion surveys of important political issues has, while varying cyclically, seen a steady overall advance. The number of environmental organizations, their membership and public profile have massively increased. Environmental studies are widespread through the education systems of Western countries. However, what is not clear is whether these changes have resulted in a profound structural reorganization of political, economic and/or cultural behaviour. This is, I believe, the acid test of the arrival of the *risk society* and the decisive transformatory impact of environmental degradation of Western societies.

There are therefore a number of ways of testing and probing Beck's claims. I cannot cover all the possible avenues of investigation that *Risk Society* and *Ecological Politics* throw up. Nor can I claim that investigation of just one aspect of their arguments could constitute a conclusive test of Beck's model of risk society. It may, however, help to swing the balance of evidence for or against. With this proviso, I want to examine an area of Beck's work that is particularly amenable to empirical analysis: his claims regarding the conduct of politics. Beck's account of the changing contours of environmental politics in the risk society makes six broad assertions. First, that the basic logic of contemporary political economy has become the avoidance of bads rather than the distribution of goods. Second, that the universal and unavoidable character of environmental degradation and risk has meant that risk and class positions no longer coincide; class is thus less salient as a feature of political interest formation and organization. Third, that the economic costs and benefits of environmentally problematic economic activities have forced new divisions within old classes and new alliances across old classes. Fourth, that alongside the remnants of older class conflicts, newer conflicts are emerging, internationally and between regions. Fifth, all these conflicts turn more and more on contesting the *relations of definition* rather than the *relations of production*, contesting proofs, grounds of proofs, modes of risk perception assessment and compensation. Sixth, this has led to the politicization of previously private or depoliticized areas of social life, creating a new field of *subpolitics* and bypassing or rendering irrelevant conventional liberal democratic decision-making forums.

Beck is certainly correct in arguing that the locus of political conflict has been moved from the nation-state to the international arena due to the physical characteristics of contemporary environmental risks, though it is not clear that he adds very much to the debate that exists on these issues. In any case, there are good grounds for arguing that the diminishing significance of the nation-state has been brought about by other forms of change. The globalization of the world economy, the transformation of patterns of finance, production and migration have all had a similar impact on the autonomy, sovereignty and relevance of nation-states and national power. The rise of interregional politics below the level of the nation-state is also plausible. There is certainly considerable evidence of increasing friction within Western nation-states (Canada, Spain, UK and Belgium all face serious secessionist movements). However, these regional conflicts are almost invariably rooted in a deeper cultural politics of identity, rather than environmental conflicts or struggles over the distribution of political bads. Beck is also correct to argue that political conflicts are increasingly turning on the possession and articulation of knowledge. Moreover, his assertion that scientific rationality and knowledge has been effectively called into question as science's own scepticism has been turned inwards on its epistemological roots seems plausible. The counterposing of experts and counter-experts has ruthlessly demonstrated to the general public that science's prior claim to clarity and to certainty cannot be accepted in an uncritical fashion, and with this the social authority of science and the automatic equation of science, technology and progress has been brought into question. However, as I argued in chapter 4, anti-technological social movements have a longer history in the West than the last few decades. A suspicion of science and its equation with progress is a deeply rooted Western tradition that is as old as the original enlightenment celebration of science. Judging the relative importance of this strain of thinking in different epochs is exceptionally difficult. Even if there are grounds for claiming that the epistemological and cultural supremacy of science has waned, there is also evidence that scientists' views are being sought ever more assiduously in public debate and that scientists are as important as ever in the decision-making councils and policy communities of Western polities.

As regards the basic logic of political economy in capitalist societies, there is some evidence for a shift from positive to negative logics of distribution. In part this has been accomplished by changes in the economic structure of advanced capitalist economies, rather than by the types of environmental transformation that Beck's risk society and reflexive modernization encompass. Rates of economic growth have been low in the West for nearly twenty years, diminishing the size of the 'cake' available for distribution. Simultaneously, rates of unemployment, official and unofficial, have steadily climbed, as has withdrawal of men from the labour market. Thus economic conflict has become as much about the distribution of employment and unemployment as about overall levels of income for those in employment or about the opposition between capital and labour. This has been particularly sharp in the USA, where wage rates for many in employment have been stagnant or declining. Similarly, rates of expenditure growth in welfare services have been diminishing, or expenditure has declined absolutely, leading to conflicts over the distribution of cuts rather than over shares of a larger public expenditure budget.

The logic of distribution of environmental risks and hazards is more difficult to pin-point. There has certainly been a rise in the number and intensity of protests and conflicts over the siting of toxic facilities, particularly waste depositories, in the West. The siting of nuclear facilities, large-scale infrastructure projects and road-building have all attracted considerable political opposition. The siting of a Nirex nuclear waste depository in the UK was certainly conducted in terms of the distribution of *bads* rather than access to *goods* like local employment. Similarly, road-building in the UK has come to be seen as a local disadvantage rather than as providing access to good transport or boosting a locality's attractiveness to investors. However, it would be much more difficult to assert that the negative logic of distributing bads has come to dominate the conduct of politics in the West. Mainstream political parties of all complexions continue to make their core appeals to the electorate in terms of economic growth, increasing prosperity, more jobs, etc. Government popularity still appears to be closely correlated to economic performance, economic expectations and the economic plausibility of the opposition. Taxation rates and take-home incomes continue to be one of the central issues of public policy.

Thus, while old patterns of class conflict may have diminished in importance as class structures and labour markets have markedly changed in the West, it is not clear that risk issues have come to outweigh production and consumption issues, or that risk positions have become entirely detached from class positions. Beck is right to argue that large-scale catastrophes are so universal and global in their nature that suburb and inner city alike are equally defenceless. Even less threatening risks than nuclear meltdowns, massive climate change or the widespread release of genetically altered and pathogenic organisms are widespread in their effects. Acid rain falls on rich and poor alike. Middle-class children can be affected by polluted city air as much as the poor. However, there are limits to this separation between risk and class positions.

In the first place, the susceptibility of individuals to hazards – for example, asthma in children resulting from local air pollution – is partly shaped by their class position. Almost all Western societies show a clear sliding scale of poor to good health between poor and rich, for children and adults alike. While this does not mean that the children of the wealthy do not get asthma, the children of poorer social classes are less likely to be able to resist the impact of local pollution if their state of health is already worse. In this respect, Beck's work focuses too much on the potentially global catastrophic environmental risks that we face, and insufficiently on those that are currently occurring and impacting on human health. Similarly, the threats posed by local industrial pollution or toxic waste disposal facilities do not fall evenly, but continue to be located in poorer areas. Indeed, in the USA recent research suggests that the inequalities of class exposure to toxic waste are overlain by inequalities of race. African Americans, after allowing for economic differentials, are much more likely to be living in close proximity to toxic facilities than white Americans.[41]

As to the politics of intraclass and cross-class alliance in the new politics of environmental risk, Beck's arguments point to some important shifts, but they are cast at such a high level of generality and with so few empirical examples that a proper evaluation is difficult. He is correct to suggest that environmental problems present conflicts that divide segments of capital and labour. For example, the tourist industry is certainly threatened by the polluting activities of the water and chemical industries. There are real and potential conflicts between organized labour in the car industry and the labour force in the rail industry over the direction of transport policy, and they rotate around the respective environmental merits and costs of different courses of action. It is certainly true that many environmental conflicts are fought out at a sectoral level. However, the main protagonists tend to be the industry or groups of industries involved, specific parts of the broader government machinery and dedicated single-issue protest groups, rather than open conflicts between fragments of organized capital or organized labour. While this kind of conflict lends some support to Beck's claims about the diminishing importance of class conflict, in another sense it restates the significance of class in that capital, if not labour, continues to organize, mobilize and lobby on the basis of specific economic interests. A good example of this is the current conflict over trans-European transport networks. The European Commission has been a prime mover of these plans, seeking to bolster the integrated character of the European single market and acquire greater competencies in the transport and infrastructure fields. The key, if not the only, pressure group lobbying around this programme has been an alliance of European motor manufacturers, road-builders and interests in concrete and minerals. In a word, capital. No sign of organized labour is present either in this group or in the loose alliance of environmentalists opposing the giganticism and car orientation of the proposals.

Finally we come to Beck's claim that the risk society has transformed the subject matter of politics, forcing previously private domains into the public sphere, and in doing so rendering the institutions of accountability and control in classical industrial society irrelevant or inadequate. In this respect, Beck is certainly correct.[42] The environmental consequences of capital expenditure, production process design, technological innovation and methods of waste disposal – previously the hidden prerogatives of private corporations – have become matters of intense public debate. The legal requirements that Western states have begun to impose on corporations, such as environmental audits and environmental impact assessments, are the limited if practical consequences of this politicization. Whether this constitutes, as yet, a profound structural shift in the character of the political in Western societies is more open to question. In many ways the basic thrust of political economy in the last decade has been the diminishing capacity and inclination of states to intervene in the external or internal regulation of firms. Moreover, while pressure groups, consumer associations and local environmental associations have been important actors in forcing open the internal activities of corporations (a form of Beck's subpolitics or differential politics), they have not done so in isolation from, or without some kind of support from, the actors and institutions of mainstream politics. Therefore, it is difficult to argue that the evidence unambiguously supports the emergence of a radically different type of politics and polity in Western societies that would truly herald the emergence of a risk society. Granted, there are shifts of emphasis that do appear uniquely new, but they do not add up to the kind of epochal transformation that Beck seems to be pointing to.

Environmental Politics in the Risk Society: the Rise and Fall of the Safety State?

The core of Beck's account of environmental politics in the risk society is, first, that capitalist states have pledged themselves to ensuring the economic and environmental security and safety of their citizens. Second, they have done so, hitherto, with the legal institutions and conceptual instruments of classical industrial society. Third, those institutions and instruments are inappropriate for dealing with contemporary environmental risk – indeed they act so as to obscure the origins and consequences of environmental degradation. This is what Beck calls *organized irresponsibility*. Fourth, this has generated a radical delegitimization of the *safety state*. States may try and cover their tracks and repledge themselves to safety and security, but they are unable to do so. In this vacuum a range of new political forms and protests are emerging: a transformation of the logic of class politics, the elevation of the politics of knowledge and a short-circuiting of conventional politics and parliamentary institutions. In this section I will examine the theoretical coherence and historical evidence in support of each of these claims.

The Idea of the Safety State

Much of Beck's account of the character and consequences of contemporary environmental politics turns on the accuracy and usefulness of the idea of the *safety state*. It is worth recalling precisely the claims that he seems to be making in using this term. First, states in the late nineteenth and early twentieth century are seen as having secured their legitimacy by making a pledge of security and safety to their citizens in the face of the characteristic risks and hazards of classical industrial society. Second, when faced with the radically new forms of risk and hazard of the late twentieth century, the institutional machinery and cultural perspectives of the safety state have become antiquated: security cannot be guaranteed, risks cannot be calculated, insurance and compensation cannot be offered and the perpetrators of environmental degradation cannot be legally announced, proved and prosecuted. This constitutes an important set of arguments for a number of reasons. It is valuable because it brings together into the same historical narrative the politics of individual and collective security and insecurity. It combines an explanation of the interlinking politics of economic change and insecurity and environmental degradation and protection. In addition, it attempts to address the broader long-term implications of persistent environmental degradation and environmental insecurity on states and political systems. Although we explored in chapter 3 Gorz's account of the structural economic implications of environmental degradation on capitalist states (exacerbating the fiscal crisis of the state, slowing processes of capital accumulation), we have not so far addressed the structural political implications of environmental degradation. Beck, by focusing on legitimacy, allows us to do so. The questions remains, however, whether the idea of the safety state can be accurately applied to the modern state or aspects of its operations, and how accurate a picture of the subsequent development of modern states Beck gives.

Perhaps the central problem with Beck's idea of the safety state is that it is explicitly and implicitly a description and explanation of one aspect of one particular type of modern capitalist state. Although it appears to be used in a universal manner, the idea of the safety state is much more closely correlated with the institutions and procedures of continental Western European states than either the states of Anglo-American capitalism or the social democratic states of Scandinavia. Three things mark out the idea of the safety state as a particular type of state: its use of insurance as the main principle of social compensation; the centrality of the law as an instrument of environmental protection and control; the essentially regulatory and conflictual stance of state institutions towards pollution.

The creation of insurance schemes financed and regulated by the state to cover the economic risks of unemployment or the environmental risks of work-place injury are primarily the creation of Western European conservative welfare states. Bismarck's social legislation of the 1880s and 1890s is probably the paradigmatic example and provided the institutional template for similar schemes in France, the Low Countries and Italy. However, this is not the only model that exists for collective provision in the face of individual risks. In some societies, state involvement has been much more minimal and actuarial principles of insurance and compensation have been highly restricted: private schemes and the provision of flat-rate minimum benefits have been the norm. In other countries, insurance schemes, with the inequalities of coverage and compensation that they entail, have been abandoned and replaced with more comprehensive and generous security systems. In these states, payments and entitlements are rooted in ideas of equal and universal citizenship rather than individual risk exposure and compensation. The social democratic welfare systems of Scandinavia most closely correspond to this model.[43]

A similar variation in the role of law and the legal system can be detected in different capitalist states. The Federal Republic has been an exemplar of the idea of a *Rechtstaat*, in which the distribution of power, the responsibilities of institutions and those of individuals within public organizations are carefully and copiously codified. Social conflicts are necessarily channelled in these contexts through the medium of the law and legal institutions. While most Western states possess a considerable quantity of environmental legislation, it is not clear that the legal system plays the same qualitative and quantitative role in all polities. Once again Beck's implicit model of the Federal Republic falls between two alternatives. In the USA, environmental politics is probably more focused on legal proceedings and legal interactions than anywhere else. For both cultural and institutional reasons the legal system has formed a much more central component of politics in the USA than it has in Europe, and this is reflected in environmental politics, with a much greater number of cases, proportionately, coming before the courts. Not only government agencies but individuals, pressure groups and corporations will begin and carry through legal actions in defence or prosecution of their environmental interests. Regulatory agencies are generally weaker in the US given the fractured quality of the federal government and the enormous variation in laws and regulations across the states. Thus bureaucratic or administrative control is often an inadequate source of regulation and decision-making.

By contrast, in the UK the legal system is less used for environmental regulation than in either Germany or the USA. In part, this is because a different kind of relationship has been established between polluters and regulatory agencies. The latter do not see themselves primarily as prosecuters and investigators of pollution and polluters. Rather they have traditionally sought to regulate by consensus, giving advice and encouraging technical improvements and local adaptation. In addition, the legal avenues of individual and class actions in pursuit of environmental issues have been more limited in the UK than elsewhere. Environmentalists have sought to press their case outside the legal system through parliamentary lobbying, pressure on the executive (where most power actually resides) and direct action.[44]

If there is some doubt as to the conceptual accuracy of Beck's model of the safety state, it is no surprise that it should prove a problematic tool for historical investigation. It is not, however, a concept without any validity. It is fair to say that the modern welfare state did emerge in some nations as a response to risks and insecurities. In Sweden, for example, the welfare state came to be known as the *Folkhus* or people's home, a term which was resonant of the security and safety of the private sphere, of home and hearth. However, it is not clear that either the language of risk and insurance or the desire to deal with risk and hazard have been the sole or the central motivating forces in the creation and expansion of welfare states and the institutions of collective security. First, as is well documented, the well-being of soldiers, the needs of industrialized military institutions and questions of national security have always figured prominently in the declared and undeclared intentions of policy-makers in welfare states. Second, equally powerful arguments and forces at work in the creation of welfare institutions have been attempts to maintain and improve national economic productivity and the national fertility rate. Third, the place of what we might now term environmental issues in the creation of welfare states alongside insurance and protection from the vissicitudes of economic and life-cycle risk is probably less significant than Beck seems to be suggesting. Health and safety at work have on occasion been important issues in developing welfare states. However, they have usually taken second place to proposals and plans for pensions, social security and education, health care and housing. Early social reforms and programmes of the late nineteenth and early twentieth centuries addressed some of the worst excesses of urban pollution and dangerous work-places, and instituted some programmes of preventative health care – particularly immunization programmes – but these kinds of regulations were not so prominent in the large-scale postwar expansion of welfare states. Environmental legislation to control the emission of pollutants within and outside of the work-place was on a relatively small scale until the explosion of environmental politics in the 1960s.

Organized Irresponsibility and the Politics of Environmental Law

In placing the character and functioning of environmental law at the heart of his account of contemporary environmental politics, Beck has undoubtedly enriched our understanding of the issue. Social theory in general and the sociology of environmental politics in particular have been curiously reluctant to engage with what is probably the central institutional battleground of environmental politics. Moreover, as Beck himself argues, we need to try and explain why, given the massive expansion of environmental legislation and accompanying regulatory institutions, as well as public and political concern, the level of environmental degradation does not seem to be subsiding and the prospect of dangers we face does not seem to be receding. In this respect his contrast of nineteenth-century relations of definition and risk perception with contemporary risks and hazards is a powerful analytical and political argument.

The focus of Beck's account of organized legal irresponsibility has been on the processes by which environmental threats are registered, their precise impact calibrated, the origins uncovered and either control extended or compensation extracted. While this model captures some aspects of environmental legal processes, and in some cases accurately traces the character of the conflict, it does not do so for all forms of environmental politics. First and foremost, Beck's model of environmental law and conflict is focused on pollution problems, primarily those that have an impact on human health. However, as I argued in chapter 1 and chapter 4, there are a number of other issues that motivate and generate environmental protests. These include objections to transformations in the landscape, the ecological disruption of the countryside, cruelty to animals and the preservation of species, and the degradation of the urban environment. Beck's model of organized irresponsibility does not sit easily with conflicts over road-building, large-scale infrastructure projects, protests over factory farming methods or the disappearance of wilderness and aesthetically valued landscapes. In these cases it is not the threat but the actuality of environmental degradation that is at stake. In addition, the perpetrators of environmental degradation are usually pretty obvious. No recourse to the complex epistemology of proofs is required to establish who is going to build a road or who is conducting battery farming of hens or who is chopping down ancient woodlands. Similarly, the idea of risk is somewhat inappropriate here. No one is at risk from factory farming methods in so far as one's objection is cruelty to poultry rather than eating the hormone-ridden products of the farms. Similarly, no one is actively endangered by the loss of hedgerows or migratory birds, though one's quality of life may be radically diminished and one's moral sensibilities outraged.

With regard to more conventional problems of pollution, Beck does acknowledge the variability of the relations of definition that exist in different polities, and he contrasts the organized irresponsibility of the Federal Republic with the more proactive stance of the law in both California and Japan, where the obligation to demonstrate non-toxicity falls more heavily on the polluter than the proof of toxicity falls on the afflicted.[45] However, there are more variations than this in the construction and character of pollution legislation and thus more variability than Beck asserts in the conduct of environmental legal conflicts. Beck's model of environmental law is very closely correlated with the processes that occur when a new risk or problem is perceived and there is considerable uncertainty about whether a given pollutant causes a given environmental problem. Yet in may cases there is very little dispute as to the toxicity of a pollutant, or indeed its sources. In the case of acid rain there is a very broad consensus across environmental organizations, scientists and governments that the emission of sulphur and nitrogen oxides in the atmosphere from the burning of fuel in power stations and motor vehicles causes the problem and that its consequences fall on forest, freshwater flora and fauna, buildings and human respiratory systems. There is, admittedly, a degree of uncertainty as to how many of which respiratory diseases can be allocated to acid rain and to what extent it interacts with other forms of air pollution. However, the main conflicts that have occurred legally and otherwise have been over the precise character of the regulations that should govern sources of sulphur oxide emission, how fast pollution reduction should occur, to what level and who pays. Beck's model of organized irresponsibility captures none of these processes very effectively.

Similarly he takes no account of the different regulatory strategies and philosophies that legal systems have established. His only example is that of maximum permissible levels, a concept that sees pollution regulation as a device for constraining emissions at a given level and no more. However, this is, like his model of the safety state, tied too closely to German practice, where pollution was regulated on the basis of one medium of pollution at a time and maximum permissible levels consistent with acceptable environmental quality.[46] In the Netherlands and Sweden, by contrast, pollution control is conducted on a multimedia or integrated basis. So, for example, pollution control from a power plant is not conducted on the basis of separate targets for emission into the air, water and soil, but overall emissions. Nor are maximum permissible levels of emission set, but an overall level of environmental degradation is established. In so doing, different combinations of pollution control and technical change can be devised and weighed against each other, allowing different economic costs and benefits of process and product change to be taken into account. The German system of pollution control allowed none of these. It is for this reason, in part, that pollution may appear to evade pollution control and environmental law in Germany. One might lift overall levels of air pollution by fixing filters, but then one generates more unregulated pollution when trying to dispose of the residues that the filters collect.

In either case, be it integrated or unitary pollution regulation, the failures of environmental law show up less at the legal stage and more at the implementation stage – a process that Beck seems far less concerned with. Once one moves from the courtroom and debates over toxicity and permissibility to the actual world of pollution regulation, the reason why legislation and environmental agencies have not translated into considerably lower levels of pollution is less difficult to see and less arcane in its origins than the model of organized irresponsibility would suggest. First, almost no environmental regulatory agency has the funding or staffing to properly carry out its remit. They are usually unable to visit the premises of polluters with any frequency, if at all. They are often unable to take regular measurements of pollution emissions or to conduct detailed environmental impact assessments or risk assessments. Nor are they usually able to obtain the necessary information to form any kind of judgement without the co-operation of the company concerned. Second, where multiple agencies of environmental regulation are involved (as they were in the Federal Republic), administrative confusion, overlap and failures of co-ordination provide the administrative spaces through which corporations and their pollution can slip. Third, while legislation may not take account of the economic costs and benefits of pollution regulation, these factors do come into play at the actual regulatory end of the process. Companies are obviously concerned and environmental agencies and officers must inevitably balance the economic costs of pollution regulation with environmental benefits. In the UK this has actually been codified in the somewhat clumsy notion of *best environmental practicable option not entailing excessive cost*.

A final limitation of Beck's model arises when the culprits are not producers or corporations but consumers. Over 20 per cent of UK greenhouse emissions and a good percentage of its acid rain emission arise from the use of private cars. It is eminently clear that – whatever the structural role that has been played by industry and government – consumers or motorists are highly culpable in creating this pollution. There is little debate as to whether car emissions are toxic or environmentally degrading. Indeed there is a strong consensus that cars are environmentally problematic. Admittedly Beck's model is right in suggesting that the prosecution of motorists is problematic: it is usual to sue an individual or corporation for degradation, so that the multiplicity of polluters – individual or corporate – makes the law an inappropriate device for achieving redress. However, equally important is the fact that the vast majority of motorists are simply not prepared to give up their cars or pay the real social and environmental costs of their extraordinarily anti-social mode of transport, and as yet politicians have found neither the devices nor the political will to force them to do so. The law may help corporate polluters to escape compensation and regulation. Liberal democracy and competitive party politics help individual consumers and polluters to do the same.

A Crisis of the Safety State?

The two most important claims of Beck's in describing the crisis of the safety state are his account of the social explosiveness of hazard, and the limitations of the safety state's security pledges, with its belated attempts to cover the tracks of inadmissible environmental danger. These arguments parallel a number of arguments I made in earlier chapters. In particular, in chapter 4 I argued that no account of environmental politics can be given without attending to the impact of actual and perceived environmental degradation on political mobilization and conflict. Similarly, in chapter 3 I argued that if and when environmental risks are threatened or environmental damage occurs there is no guarantee that governments and states will admit its existence, acknowledge its origins, award compensation or arrest the processes that cause it. Indeed, they have a multiplicity of resources and strategies for avoiding doing so. How much further do Beck's arguments take us in investigating these phenomena?

Beck's idea of the social explosiveness of hazard covers more ground than my own assessment of the political impact of environmental degradation. He argues that the eruption of catastrophe or large-scale environmental degradation does much more than stimulate and shape the level and character of environmental protest. Rather, in demonstrating that the 'worst-case scenario is possible', hazards at a stroke undercut the legitimacy of state institutions and the claims and rationality of state bureaucracies, and demand a furious (and ultimately inadequate) response from politicians and political institutions. Establishing what actually constitutes legitimacy, as opposed to mere acquiescence or indifference, is a difficult theoretical task and an even more complex empirical project.[47] At best we can infer some idea of the problem from indirect evidence.

There is some evidence to suggest that trust in politicians, political parties and political systems is declining across the West. Measured by voting rates, stability of party identification and party voting, and public opinion surveys on the trustworthiness of state institutions and state personnel, then the legitimacy of Western states is probably on the decline – though such a judgement would also require us to establish a reliable historical picture of past legitimacy. In addition, the rise of protest parties, extremist right-wing parties and regional and secessionist parties in many Western countries suggests that mainstream politics has become less capable of commanding allegiance. However, whether this decline can be accounted for in terms of the state's decreasing capacity to meet safety and security pledges in the face of new risks and hazards is less certain. One could probably make a more convincing case for attributing the decline in legitimacy to the failure of governments in the West to arrest the rise in structural unemployment, and to the accompanying process of social and geographical polarization. A cursory examination of the three polities of developed countries where government and the governing classes have fallen lowest in the estimation of their publics – the USA, Japan and Italy – suggests other mechanisms at work. In Italy and Japan the revelation and open acknowledgement of pervasive and intrinsic corruption and malpractice in the postwar era has been the central reason for declining political legitimacy. In the USA the structurally determined gridlock of a divided polity in both policy-making and implementation has done the same. In none of these cases can environmental questions be allocated anything other than a peripheral role. Thus the central role of Western governments' simultaneous failure to protect their citizens from environmental hazards is difficult to sustain. However, this is in part due to the fact the Western publics and Western governments are still responding more urgently to environmental degradation that is currently having a substantial impact rather than to future or potential risks and hazards, however catastrophic.

It is difficult to come to an overall conclusion about Ulrich Beck's work. It is designed to be provocative rather than comprehensive, stimulating rather than strictly analytical. It is clear enough that many of his arguments are less tempered than the available historical and contemporary empirical evidence suggests they should be and that we should pause before accepting the existence of risk societies and the passing of classical modernity or industrialism. But to condemn his work on these grounds is, in part, to miss the point. These texts are the *furious, ludicrous* gestures of which Beck speaks: the warnings that modernity is off the rails and all the safety checks and assurances are worthless. His accounts of the politics of pollution and the bizarreness of the legal system are sharp and often funny reminders that modern societies have equipped themselves with control mechanisms that are wholly inappropriate to the dangers that they face. Moreover, the basic thrust of Beck's response to this – that the relations of definition must undergo an epistemological and democratic revolution – are clearly an important component of a thoroughgoing reform of the mechanisms of pollution control, prevention and regulation. Whether this on its own will be enough to counteract and control the catastrophes that await us is less certain. In order to examine that, I want to return to questions I began with: how can we control the dynamic of economic and political power that generates environmental hazard, and what, if anything, is the role of the socialist political tradition in doing so.

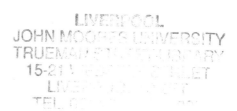

Conclusion:
Social Theory, Socialism and the Environment

In this book I have sought to examine two sets of interconnected issues: the origins and consequences of environmental degradation and the dual role of culture and politics in facilitating and controlling that process; and the conditions under which an environmentally orientated politics is mobilized, the causal role of ideals and interests in that mobilization, the constraints under which that politics operates and thus some of the conditions of its success and failure. In both these areas, contemporary social theory has proved to be a useful resource. On the basis of my critical investigations of Giddens, Gorz, Habermas and Beck, I have drawn a number of conclusions.

First, contemporary forms of environmental degradation are generated by the interaction of economic, demographic, cultural and political causes. Second, the dynamics of economic power are the most significant and those dynamics are best captured through the model of capitalist rather than industrial economies. Third, any account of the rise of environmental politics must begin with historically specific, actual and perceived transformations of the environment. This is the material substrate on which any account of the emergence of environmental movements must be raised. Fourth, those transformations evoke and help shape a redefinition of both material interests and moral ideals. Under conditions of material prosperity above a certain level, these can form the basis for a widespread if unarticulated and unorganized environmental protest. Fifth, the structural impediments to the political success of such a movement are manifold. The same material prosperity that generates the possibility of contemporary forms of environmental politics is paradoxically its greatest opponent. The kinds of changes in consumption and definition of well-being required to bring Western societies within the orbit of sustainability are both extensive in their coverage and intensive in their consequence. Everyone will be affected in such a transition. Negotiated social change of this form is an enormous political task. At the same time, the political and legal systems of capitalist societies are not neutral but structurally biased in their allocation of power to environmentally problematic interests. If, as I argued in chapter 3, the balance of rationality lies with the precautionary principle, then environmental politics must act against the clock.

I have, however, hardly touched on the most important condition of the success of an environmentally orientated politics: the plausibility and political appeal of the practical institutional alternatives and innovations that it proposes. Here, classical social theory has left a limited bequest. In formal and abstract terms, classical social theory correctly identified, in its discussions of socialism, the necessity of bringing culture and morality to bear on the dynamic of economic and political interests. In my studies of Giddens, Gorz, Habermas and Beck I have highlighted the extent to which the dynamic of economic and political interests generates environmental degradation and the extent to which a successful environmental politics is mobilized by enlightened self-interest and normative argument. Thus classical social theory's conception of socialism retains a vital intellectual relevance to contemporary environmentalism. But beyond this the intellectual incoherence of those conceptions of socialism and the passage of time have rendered them effectively irrelevant. Has contemporary social theory moved on? The central task of this conclusion will be to consider the light which is thrown on the prospects for environmental politics by the ways in which Giddens, Gorz, Habermas and Beck have analysed the contemporary value of the socialist tradition. I will explore the strengths and weaknesses of their accounts in relation to two aspects of environmental politics: the creation of institutional alternatives to contemporary capitalism; and the role of democratic theory and democratic institutions in creating a more environmentally sustainable society.

Habermas on Socialism and the Environment

It is not a promising historical moment at which to conduct such an exercise. Irrespective of its environmental dimensions, the sociological and intellectual resources of socialism are more fragile than at any point in the twentieth century. The historical trajectory of capitalist development has failed to yield the socializable economy which Marx predicted. The twentieth-century mutations of the capitalist mode of production do not, even on the most sympathetic reading, lay themselves open to collective appropriation and control. The core forces of socialist politics in the West, the organized working classes, have become demographically diminished and structurally fragmented. The central institutional project of socialist politics, the state-planned economy, has in its communist variant been discredited beyond all redemption, while the social democratic welfare states of the OECD continue to groan beneath the dual pressures of international competitiveness and domestic spending commitments. Finally, the notion of equality, always the moral nerve centre of socialist politics, has, as a normative ideal, declining purchase on substantial parts of increasingly affluent and individualized Western electorates.

This conjuncture has been registered to differing degrees by Gorz, Giddens and Habermas.[1] It is in Habermas's work that the limits to the classical socialist project have been most sharply drawn and yet its continuing relevance to the problems of environmental degradation and politics most clearly stated. Habermas traces the weakness of the original Marxist socialist project to a number of significant theoretical limitations: its productivist paradigm; a holistic conception of society that radically underestimated the schism of system and lifeworld; a fundamental miscalculation of the relationship between social stratification and political agency; a woefully inadequate theory of the modern state, and correspondingly a fatal underestimation of the importance of democracy in complex societies; and, finally, an evolutionary model of history underscored by unacceptable normative presuppositions that cleared the way for unprincipled vanguardism.

These theoretical limits have had baleful consequences for both the general success of a Marxist-inspired politics, and more specifically for its continuing relevance to environmental questions. The dominance of productivism in socialist thinking refers to both the centrality of economic power and economic issues in socialist political theory and practice, and a model of economics that asserts the overwhelming value of increasing levels of production and productivity to human well-being. This has left little space for a critique of economic rationality that acknowledges the environmental degradation that accompanies both capitalist and socialist modes of production, or for explanations of environmental degradation other than the dynamics of capitalism. Nor has it generated the intellectual resources for exploring the environmental consequences of consumption. The mirage of an unproblematic abundance weighs heavily against socialism's environmental imagination. The holism of socialist thinking stands in contradiction to Habermas's bi-level model of society, of systems and lifeworlds. Because socialist thought has failed to distinguish between these radically different domains of modern societies, it has maintained the illusion that the enormous complexity and differentiation of modern economies can be brought, *in toto*, under the sway of public control and be consciously orientated towards the common good. However, as the Soviet experience testifies, the attempt to marry centralized control with modern economics results in both a gross inefficiency and a failure to impose adequate moral or ecological constraints on economic power. This has, of course, been exacerbated by the intellectual vacuum between socialism's minimal theoretical engagement with democracy and the public protestations of its importance.

Social democracy, as the great historical alternative to these traditions, disengaged itself from 'a holistic conception of society and embarrassment at the autonomous dynamic of a market system; from a dogmatic view of class structure and the class struggle; from a false evaluation of the normative content of constitutional democracy; and from latent, evolutionist presuppositions'.[2] Moreover, whatever the limitations of social democracy in practice, its core component – the reformist control and limitation of the dynamic of capital accumulation – is of central relevance to the problems posed by environmental degradation. In this respect Habermas's argument tallies with my own, describing capitalism as the key if not sole cause of environmental degradation: 'The social and ecological *curbing* of the market economy is the international formula into which the social-democratic aims of the social curbing of capitalism were bound to be generalised.'[3]

However, social democracy has bought its success at a price sufficiently high to question its coherence as a political force and its continuing relevance to environmental problems. These costs are twofold: first, social democracy 'learns to live with the normatively undesirable consequences of capitalist economic growth', which welfare states can ameliorate but not eradicate; second, it has had to do without radical forms of democracy in its accommodation of the powerful interests inside and outside a decidedly non-neutral state apparatus.[4] It has also generated social pathologies and political blockages that have undermined its postwar European successes: the pathologies of the state and the interconnected problems of political demoralization and social polarization. We have already rehearsed the former in relation to the colonization thesis and explored the culpability of the social democratic welfare state in chapter 4.

The problems of polarization and demoralization are of more immediate relevance to the problems of environmental politics, and they connect us back to the work of Gorz and Giddens. By demoralization, Habermas means that the only issues that have any purchase on the political agendas of modern societies are those that threaten the reproduction and stability of the political and economic subsystems that have been shorn off from the lifeworld.[5] Habermas argues that 'the absorption of political parties by the state is accompanied by the displacement of the democratic formation of political will into a largely self-programming political system.'[6] This has been the fate of a reformist social democracy which has curbed the market through the occupation of an unreformed state and the abandonment of a more radical democratic politics.[7]

By 'polarization' Habermas is referring to the transformation of social cleavages in contemporary capitalist societies. The capital–labour relationship has been replaced as the sharpest political division by the relationship between net contributors to and recipients of the welfare state: those in secure employment and those on the fringes of a fragmented labour market or dependent on welfare payments respectively. This polarization of Western societies has occurred under the aegis of the social democratic welfare state, though the restructuring of the global economy should be accorded more causal weight than Habermas has so far allowed.[8] The connection between demoralization, polarization and the environment turns on the argument that 'problems of this nature do not . . . have enough driving force to be adopted as a topic of broad and effective public debate. A dynamic of self-correction cannot be set in motion without introducing morality into the debate, without universalising interests from a normative point of view.'[9] To put this another way, the polarization of capitalist societies is replicated at a global and environmental level between North and South. In both cases the power available to the weak is structurally insufficient to force the issues of catastrophic environmental degradation on to the political agenda, let alone effect a fundamental shift in the direction of economic and political policy, for the fortunes of the strong are so closely bound to the continuing misfortune of the powerless.

The polarization of global capitalism and the subsequent demoralization of public debate cannot be corrected unless the normative force of moral argument can cancel the dynamic of interests. Thus, in addition to the inherent weaknesses of social democracy as an environmentally sustainable politics identified in Gorz's work, we can add its current inability to actualize a level of normative force sufficient to remoralize public debate and transcend the balance of forces that capitalist societies produce.[10] The abandonment of a radical vision of democracy by social democrats is the key reason for this. According to Habermas the level of moral articulation and power required to place the real implications, costs and consequences of environmental degradation on the political agenda can only be actualized by participatory debate at the widest level: 'These problems can only be brought to a head by rethinking topics morally, by universalising interests in a more or less discursive manner in the forums of liberal political cultures which have not been stripped of all their powers.'[11] Thus Habermas argues that it is not democracy in general that is a necessary precondition of a successful environmental politics, but, by the current standards of Western polities, a very much more radical form.

Giddens and Beck on Socialism and the Environment

Giddens, in his most recent work, has generated an even more wide-ranging critique of the relevance of socialism to contemporary politics and proposed an alternative radicalism that diverges even more sharply than does Habermas from classical socialist arguments. Beck has not engaged with the fate of socialism in the same detail as Giddens, but given the similarities of their recent work, many of Beck's arguments reinforce Giddens's position. In the wake of the collapse of the Soviet Union and its Eastern European satellites, Giddens argues that we must face a political paradox that has been evident for some time. Radical socialism has become conservative. Conservatism has become radical.[12] Socialism, whatever else it may have been in its multiple variants, was progressive. Descending from enlightenment conceptions of the relationship between theory and practice, knowledge and control, socialists believed that an interpretation of the past and the present would yield sufficient understanding of the trajectory of social change for us to be able to intervene actively and consciously in its course. The present could be grasped, the future actively shaped. However, alongside its contemporary economic limitations and declining political fortunes, socialism has lost that self-confidence, and for good reason. Late modernity does not admit of such a simple relationship between cognitive capacity and political potential. More information does not mean more knowledge. More knowledge does not mean more control. Indeed more knowledge in the form of science is a cause of environmental degradation. Such a cognitive retreat is reflected in political practice: calls for revolution and proposals for the transcendence of capitalism by socialism have become rather thin on the ground. Socialists have reverted in practical terms to the defence of existing welfare states as their central *raison d'être*. By contrast conservatism and conservative political movements which have been traditionally tied to notions of continuity and a resistance to change have become radical. Hitched to the economic and political dictats of neoliberalism, conservatism as a political movement has helped to accelerate the pace of social change and institutional fragmentation. Letting the market and market rationality loose into increasingly wide areas of social life has led to the destruction of older embedded institutions and social practices: families, work patterns and labour markets, welfare states, sovereign national governments.

The collapse of socialism's progressivism is closely tied to a reworked version of Giddens's model of late modernity. In this formulation modern societies are being transformed by the intersection of globalization, detraditionalization and manufactured uncertainty or risk, which combined together create a process of *reflexive modernization*.[13] The parallels with Beck are obvious here. Socialism's attempts to control complex capitalist economies through planning and intervention have been undermined by the increasing globalization and reflexiveness of modern life. Too many decisions about economic rationality have to be made by reflexive agents on the ground, on the basis of tacit practical knowledge, to make the transfer of decision-making powers to the centre effective. No state, however flexible, can gather enough information, process it quickly enough or embody the essentially local knowledge and skills required in a rapidly changing economy. In periods of low reflexivity, where economic development could be based on the simple expansion of capital and labour inputs, such control was minimally successful. This is no longer the case. In addition, the globalization of economic activity makes the models of communist and social democratic economic policy based on the nation-state increasingly redundant as control of capital, labour, technology and trade consistently evades the limits of national boundaries.

As if this were not enough, the welfare state that remains the central moral and practical purpose of contemporary socialism is also undermined by the advance of reflexive modernization. Giddens advances a range of arguments to suggest that the old model of welfare states in the West is incapable of renewal.[14] Global economic change has rendered the maintenance of national productivity more structurally significant than the maintenance of high social benefits. Demographic change, the rise of structural unemployment, the changing balance of class and political power between taxpayers and welfare recipients have made the compromise and consensus on which the welfare state rested difficult to sustain. Older traditional structures and institutions on which welfare states rested – particularly traditional families, gender roles and gendered divisions of labour – have been detraditionalized and increasingly forced into question. In practical terms, the welfare state has failed to deliver significant redistribution, it has rested on an untenable notion of economic citizenship and it has created, according to Giddens, forms of welfare dependency and exclusion. Finally, the overemphasis of the welfare state on economic and emancipatory issues has left a massive agenda of moral, cultural and emotional politics outside the orbit of socialism. It is hardly surprising, given this position, that Giddens sees no future for socialism as a coherent political force on environmental issues, or any other for that matter. In any case, he argues that socialism has carried implicitly with it an instrumental model of the natural world that makes it an inappropriate political tradition from which to craft a response to environmental catastrophe.

Yet craft a response we must, for, according to Giddens, environmental problems are at the very centre of contemporary politics. Curiously, his study yields almost no considered discussion of precisely what we might do to diminish environmental threats or to stop generating them in the first place. His model of a post-scarcity society touches on the form an alternative welfare state might take and suggests a reordering of economic priorities, but it offers almost no institutional alternatives or practical measures of environmental control beyond a general and bland call for the diminishing of risks, a more open and democratic assessment of science and technology and better educational programmes.[15]

He does, however, offer a broad framework for an alternative radical politics, drawing on elements of both socialism and conservatism, from which some aspects of a political response to environmental degradation might be drawn.[16] First, he asserts that radical politics is now about the repair of damaged solidarities rather than the encouragement and control of obsessive change. Rather than seeking to continually direct the pace and trajectory of history, radical politics must attend to the defence and repair of the institutions and relationships that the unstoppable juggernaut of modernity continually tramples on. In so doing it should seek to generate a form of social solidarity that combines both autonomy and interdependence. Second, the centrepiece of a radical political agenda should shift from the emancipatory politics of classical modernity to life politics. The central concern of radicalism should cease to be the distribution and redistribution of life chances and become the development of particular lifestyles which confront and tackle the central moral and emotional issues of contemporary life. Third, in place of an older emancipatory economistic politics, radicalism should be based on a generative politics in which the state and the welfare state attempt to act as facilitators and catalysts of social self-organization and development, rather than as service providers and overall planners. Radicalism must also confront in a much more systematic fashion the pervasiveness of violence in human social life, from interstate warfare to the hidden violence of the family.

The key principle on which all these social changes should be devised and implemented is dialogic democracy, in which proposals for social change and the implementation of moral positions are achieved by consensual agreement rather than the use or threat of extraneous force. Finally, Giddens acknowledges that there is no privileged single social actor or class that can deliver such a programme, or whose economic interests correspond with the greater good. Defining and implementing the good life and the good society can only be achieved by a multiplicity of negotiated and carefully built projects, alliances and consensuses. There is no guarantee of success.

Gorz on Socialism and the Environment

Of all the social theorists I have considered, Gorz is probably the one who has remained closest to socialist arguments, though he could hardly be considered an uncritical supporter. In some ways Gorz had broken from many of the positions and arguments of classical socialism and Marxism long before Habermas and Giddens. In the wake of 1989, it is possible that he has felt less reason to move as far as the others. Gorz is unambiguous about the nature of socialism, its continuing relevance to contemporary radical politics and the connection of both to environmental questions. Socialism should not be understood as a social system totally different from capitalism or as a ready-made set of institutional alternatives. As Gorz puts it: 'The socialist movement grew out of the struggle carried on by individuals united in solidarity to impose new social restrictions, based on ethical demands, on the sphere in which economic rationality can operate.'[17] In an passage that draws explicitly on the model of modernity developed by Habermas, Gorz goes on to argue that 'socialism, in my opinion, does not aim to abolish the economic and administrative systems, but only to limit and bind them into the lifeworld, so that a synergy with self-determined social and individual forms of living results.'[18] To recall the arguments of chapter 3, Gorz interprets the origins of environmental degradation in terms of the unrestrained logic of capital accumulation and economic rationality that pursues the maximization of rates of return over and above short-term and long-term ecological damage and social costs. There is, however, no alternative to the prevailing economic rationality of capitalism. As such, the socialist project becomes tied to restricting the operation of that logic to as narrow a sphere of life as possible and, where it is allowed to continue, hedging its operation with ecological and social restrictions.

However, much of the baggage of classical socialism must be shed if we are to successfully pursue this goal. The definitions of wealth and well-being characterizing old socialism must be dropped. Instead of defining self-worth in terms of stable employment, and self-satisfaction in terms of uninhibited consumption, Gorz argues for a political and economic system in which a multitude of social situations and processes of self-definition create self-identity. Similarly he argues for a political economy in which the equation between 'more' and 'better' is broken, in favour of a society in which we 'consume less but consume better'. Both of these projects will be facilitated by the liberation of time: by a massive reduction in working hours, by increased flexibility and control over time; by the expansion of free time unhindered and unfettered by the logic of economic rationality. These processes of change will be facilitated and supported by radicalized trade unions, but the classical models of working-class mobilization and political action are redundant. Gorz describes the new configuration of social conflict, writing, 'There is a central conflict and a central stake, but there is no longer a central front. The reappropriation struggle is essentially a struggle to withdraw and shield from . . . the apparatus spaces which a growing productivity makes potentially available.'[19]

Institutional Alternatives

Across all four social theorists studied in this book there are central areas of agreement on the contemporary state of socialism. Its models of historical change and evolution are unacceptable. Its programmes for economic reform or revolution unfeasible. Its political theory, although notionally democratic, is too timid in its models of democratization. Its historic agents of change are sociologically diminished. Its great historical success – the welfare state – has become socially pathological and politically and economically unsustainable. Its productivism, assumptions of abundance and its models of well-being – of the good life and the good society – make it unsuited for the tasks presented to it by contemporary environmental degradation. The questions remain as to whether anything of relevance is left from the socialist tradition in facing environmental threats, and whether the alternative proposals yielded by the work of these theorists are in any sense an improvement.

All four social theorists have drawn on the legacy of classical social theory in establishing what an alternative and environmentally benign modernity would look like. From Marx and classical socialism, they have argued for the normative-cultural control of political economy – albeit cast in a reformulated theoretical language. However, none of them accept the economic models of socialism which have descended from the Marxist or reformist social democratic traditions. In rejecting the command and control models of state-directed socialist economies, they have drawn on liberal critiques of its economic efficiency.[20] But they have also denounced this model on the basis of a particular reading of modernity. In so doing, all these theorists have explicitly or implicitly drawn the distinction made by Durkheim between communism and socialism. Communism, according to Durkheim, was a premodern model of society in which social differentiation and the separation of different domains and institutions of social life were brought back together in a harmonious self-regulating whole. Socialism, by contrast, was a uniquely modern form of society in which social and institutional differentiation would be retained, but some form of centralized economic and moral regulation would be deployed on otherwise autonomous subsystems of action. Durkheim argued that the normatively objectionable consequences of the abnormal division of labour could be solved by recourse to a state-directed moral education in social solidarity. The inevitable co-operation that springs from the interdependencies of a complex division of labour combined with a corporatist, occupation-based democracy would supersede the temporary structural divisions of modern capitalism.

At a theoretical and empirical level, the effortless emergence of secular solidarity and moral education from these institutional structures now appears rather hopeful. The structural divisions and rapacious rationality of capitalist economies have remained with us. Education has proved no gurantee of enlightenment. In proposing related but different diagnoses of modernity, contemporary social theory has sought different diagnoses of the pathologies of differentiation and different responses to them than Durkheim did.

As we know from chapter 4, in Habermas's work this argument takes the form of a call for the defence of systemically threatened lifeworlds. Modernization takes the form of simultaneous and interconnected processes of social and cultural rationalization. The rationalization of the lifeworld and the generation of modern constitutional and commercial law enable the transfer of economic and political action into separated subsystems of instrumental and strategic action. In the course of this, the rational potential of communicative action bound up in the lifeworld is released. Economic and political development is accompanied by the release of the democratic and critical potential at the heart of a modernized culture. Once this has happened it is no longer possible to return either economy or polity to an integrated society subsumed by the lifeworld, or it can be done only at the cost of a return to the irrationalities and inequalities of premodern societies. What can be averted are the *contingent* pathologies of the colonization of the lifeworld. Those domains of life which should be organized according to the normative principles of social solidarity and cultural integrity, including the environmental or

organic foundations of the lifeworld, must be protected from the dynamic
of interests let loose by the separation of economy and polity from the
lifeworld. Gorz argued in his early work that the sphere of economic
autonomy must be expanded in order to bypass the sphere of economic
heteronomy. The rationality of capitalist economies must be disengaged
from environmentally benign patterns of self-production and collective
consumption. In his later work, in explicitly Habermasian terms, he has
called for the sphere of economic rationality to be narrowed and curtailed,
confined to as small an area of life as possible so that the unmonetariz-
able, unquantifiable activities of the lifeworld can be pursued.

Neither Giddens nor Beck confronts the dynamics of capital as clearly
as Habermas and Gorz, though they do address themselves to the environmental degradation generated more explicitly. Their arguments are
couched in terms of a broader set of social irrationalities – risk, catastrophe and uncertainty – and a different model of rationalization: reflexive
modernization. Giddens has argued for the remoralization of the abstract
systems of social organization on which modernity is founded. Beck has
called for the prevention, minimization and control of risk and uncertainty.
Both Giddens and Beck argue that the manufactured uncertainties and
catastrophic risk that modern economies and modern science have generated cannot be undone. We must, instead, find ways in which the worst of
their effects can be mitigated.

Thus where these social theorists have successfully departed from classical socialism is in their belief that the differences between these domains
of modern life – system and lifeworld, spheres of autonomy and heteronomy, abstract systems and the reflexive self – cannot be eradicated or
abandoned altogether. In each case, *the political project advocated has become
one of limitation and control*. In this respect they are all closer to the legacy
of Weber than of Marx or Durkheim. However, where they differ from
Weber is that they deny the inevitability of bureaucratization and cultural
disintegration, nor are they prepared to trust the defence of the lifeworld
to plebiscitary democracies and charismatic leaders. Thus Giddens's
utopian realism resigns itself to the realities of power without abandoning
moral demands. Gorz argues for the subversion and circumvention of the
market and wealth in exchange for free time, rather than for the eradication of the market. Habermas argues for the evacuation of systemic
imperatives from the lifeworld, without calling for the reabsorption of
economy and polity back into the lifeworld. Beck has called for an epistemological and institutional revolution which puts the onus of proof and
safety on to corporate and public polluters and regulators, rather than
more rigid political and legal regulation. For Habermas and Gorz the
weight of danger comes from the existence of an unbridled capitalism,
and thus the project of limitation and control can still be said to fall within
the broader socialist project. Giddens and Beck, while acknowledging the
role of markets and economic power, have cast the origins of environmental threats in such broad terms (reflexivity, globalization, detraditionaliza-

tion, etc.) that they consider their political project to be quite separate from that of socialism.

The central conclusion that emerges from this many-headed debate is a conception of the socialist project stripped down to its bare essentials. In a differentiated society neither economy nor polity can be reincorporated into the morally suffused domains of lifeworld or everyday life. We must learn to live with this irrevocable separation. But there are sufficient moral and political resources available to us to check, control and limit the environmentally and socially pathological dynamic of economic and political power that modernity has unleashed. Therefore, it seems to me that, *in so far as we identify capitalism and capitalist economic rationality as the mainspring of the environmental dynamic, and oppose it in the name of a broader human solidarity, we remain within the socialist tradition.*

If the arguments of chapters 1–3 in this book are correct, then for both Giddens and Beck their rather minimal engagement with capitalism and their separation from the socialist tradition are premature. Globalization may alter the spatial and temporal experience of environmental degradation. Reflexivity and detraditionalization may alter the perception and phenomenology of environmental damage. But they do not, in and of themselves, explain the scope and scale of environmental degradation. Environmental degradation is caused by the interaction of economic, political and cultural power with demographic change. The driving force of that process in capitalist societies, which are now approaching something like universality, are economic forces, institutions and actions. No social theory of the environment and environmental degradation can adequately capture the origins of that degradation or provide a basis for considering its control without attending to the dynamics of capitalist production and consumption. Acknowledging that other forces are at work, or that traditional socialist economic alternatives and assumptions are flawed, does not diminish the need to critically engage with those dynamics. In the rush to bury socialism, Giddens, in particular, has abandoned some of its most important theoretical facets. This has important practical consequences as well. As I argued in chapter 3, the social democratic tradition may remain tied to unsustainable forms of consumption, well-being and working patterns, but it does retain some of the key ideas, dispositions and mechanisms for countering aspects of environmental degradation: taxing environmental bads, regulating corporate capital, intervening in markets, directing research, investment and technological development, providing appropriate infrastructure.[21]

Capitalism: can't live with it, can't live without it. That is the shape of the problem. If contemporary social theory has clarified this dilemma, then the substantive critique of these social theorists has left us with precious little content; the economic and institutional implications of their work for an environmentally sustainable politics are not clear. Giddens has argued for the humanization of technology and socialized production in a post-scarcity order, but he has been less than explicit about what this would actually entail.[22] Beck and Habermas have yet to venture on to the terrain of economics at all. Gorz's proposals are the most developed institutionally, yet even he has baulked at finding a way in which the global control of capital might be managed.[23] One lesson of this survey is that social theory, for all its strengths, is not an idiom or discipline that is well suited to the elaboration or discussion of this kind of political problem. It requires closer attention to the minutiae of social institutions and their operation than the overarching structural themes that are social theory's speciality. It also requires a degree of institutional imagination and innovation that the discipline seems ill at ease with. Above all, it requires that theorists engage with the economics and economic institutions of contemporary capitalism in more detail than hitherto.

Democratic Arguments

If these social theorists have yet to describe a plausible set of alternative economic arrangements, they have made some advance on the classical socialist tradition by giving more attention to the democratization of state power and civil society. Indeed for all of them the reassertion of political power over economic power and ethical and cultural norms over systemic imperatives must be conducted on a democratic basis. Moreover, if not in the works of these writers, a body of contemporary literature has begun to investigate some of the institutional parameters of this radical democratization.[24]

Giddens initially suggested that new forms of local, national and international democracy may emerge and will form an essential component of any politics that seeks to transcend the risks and threats of high modernity.[25] This argument has been given more weight and more detail in his most recent work, *Beyond Left and Right*, where dialogic democracy serves as the normative touchstone of social organization and personal relationships in a renovated radical politics. However, the increasing importance of dialogic and participatory democracy is not clearly related to environmental threats. Tangentially, he has called, following David Held's work, for the extension of the democratic community to a transnational and global level. Clearly, given the global character of environmental degradation and the irrelevance of national responses to many environmental problems, this is important.

Habermas, while clearly acknowledging the limited degree to which modern state power can be democratized, has argued for its limitation and the recreation and defence of a public sphere in which a rational, democratic discourse can occur. It is only on the basis of such a discourse that a successful normative resistance to the pathological consequences in general, and the environmental consequences in particular, of the formal economy and polity can be mounted. Beck has argued for a *differential politics* and an *ecological democracy* as the central political response to the dangers of the risk society. Previously depoliticized areas of decision-making'that profoundly affect the environment must be opened to public scrutiny and debate. Corporate economic decisions, scientific research agendas, plans for the development and deployment of new technologies must all be opened up to a generalized process of discussion, and a legal and institutional framework for their democratic control must be elaborated. Moreover, the terms of that democratic engagement must be shifted so that the onus of proof lies with polluters rather than the afflicted.

In these respects the work of these social theorists has moved significantly on from the classical socialist tradition, placing democratic theory and democratic concerns at the heart of their work rather than making them an under-theorized addition. Moreover, they all make the case, in one way or another, that more democracy and more radical democracy are an essential precondition of creating environmental sustainability. How plausible is this argument? They expose three key elements of contemporary liberal democracies as ill-suited to the control of environmental degradation. Beck is certainly correct to argue for the opening up of previously depoliticized realms of decision-making to democratic scrutiny. Moreover, the enormous strength of his work is to recognize the ways in which contemporary debates of this sort – by which the nuclear and biotechnology industries, for example, have been forced to justify and defend their activities in the public domain – are constrained by the epistemological and legal systems within which they are conducted. Therefore democratic institutions and democratic spaces are an insufficiently radical mode of environmental control unless the terms on which those debates are conducted are changed. Habermas, in particular, has demonstrated that the predominantly representative rather than participatory character of liberal democracy ensures that the existing inequalities of economic and political power, as well as environmental exposure, are replicated in the construction of political agendas. Finally, Giddens's call for a cosmopolitan and global political discourse carries weight by exposing the limits of representative democracy at the purely national level.

A number of points can be made about this linkage between democratic politics and environmental sustainability. First, while the limits of representative democracy have been usefully exposed by these social theorists, its necessary strengths have been insufficiently emphasized. If, as the drift of all of their arguments would suggest, we cannot incorporate the polity *in toto* back into the lifeworld or everyday life, then we shall continue to have to live with the dynamic of political power unhinged from everyday life. Moreover, we shall have to continue living with the state – not least because the control, regulation and limitation of the dynamic of economic power cannot be mounted from within the lifeworld or civil society alone. In this respect, although representation may be an insufficient form of democracy, plagued by a range of deficiencies, it remains a necessary component of a democratic polity in a differentiated world. There is considerable scope for investigating the conditions under which representation itself might be made more effective and more open to environmental concerns. Indeed, given the urgency of the tasks facing us, and the enormity of social and economic change it seems to imply, we would do well to think about how state power can be usefully and immediately deployed.

Second, if we are to envisage greater participation in decision-making then it would be wise to try and elaborate what the forums for that decision-making are, what powers might be allocated to them and how that power would be executed. In the absence of such proposals, calls for democratization remain remarkably vacuous. Neither Habermas's reconstituted public sphere nor Beck's even vaguer ecological democracy are a sufficient basis for the design of practical institutions of democratic participation. Who will participate? Who will decide what powers are available to the participators? Who will provide the resources and logistics for conducting these debates? These kinds of problems are particularly acute when calls for participation – which already look problematic at the level of large and complex societies – are coupled with calls for transnational, cosmopolitan and global democratic institutions. Third, no participatory democracy is likely to meet the kind of normative criteria established by Giddens and Habermas in the absence of a substantial reduction of inequalities in other spheres of life. Once again, we are back to the reordering, control and regulation of capitalism among other social institutions that generate radical inequalities.

Even where social and political theorists have become more confident in advocating the formal apparatus by which morally informed environmental control can be enacted over economy and polity, it remains to be seen whether the force of moral argument can be deployed within this framework. *Democracy may be a necessary condition of making the case for environmental sustainability heard, but it does not guarantee that its arguments will be accepted.* As Giddens suggested in his earlier work, socialism is still in need of moral justification.[26] In Habermas's terms, the success of the environmental movement rests on the peculiar force of better argument. These social theorists, and indeed contemporary environmental movements, have yet to find the public idiom and institutional format in which that argument, in the face of structural resistance and public apathy, becomes utterly compelling. Habermas's intuition is that given sufficient time and openness our collective fate and shared self-interests will be disclosed and a consensus on an equitable and lasting response to environmental degradation will be established. I hope he is right. I am less certain that we have enough time available to us to talk everyone round. We know that environmental degradation is dangerous. We know that we cannot go on as before. But how to go on, how to live individually and collectively, how to make the transition soon and how to persuade the intransigent, the selfish, the powerful and the uninterested? These are the questions that neither classical socialism nor contemporary social theory have provided sufficient intellectual or moral resources to answer. We shall have to equip ourselves.

Abbreviations

The following abbreviations are used in the notes for the main works of Giddens, Gorz, Beck and Habermas. Full details are in the bibliography.

Ulrich Beck

EPAR	*Ecological Politics in an Age of Risk*
RS	*Risk Society*

Anthony Giddens

BLR	*Beyond Left and Right*
CCHM	*A Contemporary Critique of Historical Materialism*
CMST	*Capitalism and Modern Social Theory*
COM	*The Consequences of Modernity*
CPST	*Central Problems in Social Theory*
CS	*The Constitution of Society*
CSAS	*The Class Structure of the Advanced Societies*
MSI	*Modernity and Self-Identity*
NRSM	*New Rules of Sociological Method*
NSV	*The Nation-State and Violence*
PCST	*Profiles and Critiques in Social Theory*
SSPT	*Studies in Social and Political Theory*
STMS	*Social Theory and Modern Sociology*

André Gorz

CER	*Critique of Economic Reason*
CSE	*Capitalism, Socialism, Ecology*
EP	*Ecology as Politics*
FWC	*Farewell to the Working Class*
PTP	*Paths to Paradise: On the Liberation from Work*

Jürgen Habermas

CES	*Communication and the Evolution of Society*
KHI	*Knowledge and Human Interests*
LC	*Legitimation Crisis*
PDM	*The Philosophical Discourse of Modernity*
STPS	*The Structural Transformation of the Public Sphere*
TCA1	*The Theory of Communicative Action, Volume 1: Reason and the Rationalization of Society*
TCA2	*The Theory of Communicative Action, Volume 2: Lifeworld and System: A Critique of Functionalist Reason.*
TP	*Theory and Practice*
WDSMT	'What Does Socialism Mean Today?'

Notes

Introduction: Social Theory, Environmental Degradation and Environmental Politics

1   See the discussions on the limitations of sociology and social theory when confronted by the natural world and human societies' relationship to it, in Dickens, *Society and Nature*; Benton, 'Biology and Social Theory'; Redclift and Benton, 'Sociology and the Environment'.
2   Benton, 'Biology and Social Theory', p. 29.
3   Spencer, *On Social Evolution*.
4   Malthus, *Essay on the Principle of Population*; Ricardo, *On the Principles of Political Economy*; Mill, *Principles of Political Economy*.
5   Weber, *Ancient Judaism*, pp. 5–10.
6   Weber, *Agrarian Sociology of Ancient Civilizations*.
7   Weber, *The Religion of India* and *The Religion of China*.
8   Weber, *Economy and Society*, vol. 1, p. 8.
9   Durkheim, *Division of Labour*, pp. 201–17.
10   It is for similar reasons that I have chosen not to focus on the work of the Frankfurt School, which remains one of the few bodies of work in social theory to have considered the relationship between human societies and nature. The arguments and concerns of the school's key text on this subject, *Dialectic of Enlightenment*, fall outside my areas of concern for the following additional reasons. First, the central relationship between nature and society that the book explores is cognitive rather than material. Theodor Adorno and Max Horkheimer are concerned with the way in which the natural world is perceived rather than physically transformed. Second, the roots of that perception and subsequent domination are primarily located in the development of modern reason. While this kind of cultural argument is important, my central concern is to relate the transformation of the natural world to changing economic and political institutions. See Adorno and Horkheimer, *Dialectic of Enlightenment*.
11   Weber, *Economy and Society*, vol. 1, pp. 63–8, 71–4.
12   Tönnies, *Community and Association*.
13   Durkheim, *Division of Labour*, pp. 291–328.

14 Engels, *Condition of the Working Class*. For Marx's collected reflections on environmental problems, see Parsons (ed.), *Marx and Engels on Ecology*. See also Benton, 'Marxism and Natural Limits'; Grundmann, 'The Ecological Challenge to Marxism'; Schmidt, *The Concept of Nature in Marx*.

15 Sartre, *Critique of Dialectical Reason I*.

16 Wittfogel, *Oriental Despotism*.

17 See, for example, Parsons, *The Structure of Social Action*.

18 For surveys of the field, see White, 'American Environmental History', pp. 297–335; D. Worster, 'The Vulnerable Earth, Towards a Planetary History', in Worster (ed.), *The Ends of the Earth*.

19 For example, the work of Foucault, see *Madness and Civilisation; Discipline and Punish; The History of Sexuality*, vol. 1.

20 Key anthropological texts which have illuminated the relationship between societies and their environments with an important emphasis on cultural perceptions of the environment include Rappaport, *Pigs for the Ancestors*; Douglas, *Purity and Danger*.

21 For an overview of the historical development of ecological ideas, see Worster, *Nature's Economy*.

22 For good discussions of these methodological issues, see Rackham, *The History of the Countryside*, ch. 2, and Cronon, *Changes in the Land*, ch. 1.

23 For an excellent methodological discussion, see Skocpol (ed.), *Vision and Method*.

24 See, for example, Mann, *The Sources of Social Power*, vol. 1; McNeil, *The Human Condition*.

25 It is because of his failure to do precisely this that I chose not to examine the works of Rudolph Bahro, see Bahro, *Socialism and Survival* and *From Red to Green*. While Bahro has been a politically significant figure on the radical wing of the German environmental movement, his published work does not really contain a consistent and fully formed position on the social origins of environmental degradation. There are only scattered explanations and undeveloped positions that can be gleaned from his work. The work of Niklas Luhmann on this subject is more difficult to exclude on these grounds. He has developed some ideas on this topic through his particular brand of functionalist sociology in Luhmann, *Ecological Communication*. However, Giddens's focus on the relationship between, and combined consequences of, industrialism, capitalism and the modern state, and Gorz's explicit use of political economy provide more promising points of departure.

26 Possible candidates for study would have included Claus Offe and Alberto Melucci. See Offe, 'Challenging the Boundaries of the Political', and Melucci, *Nomads of the Present*. Outside of social theoretical perspectives, there is also a huge literature on social movements. I have tried to draw on some of this literature in my assessment of Habermas's work, including rational choice theory and resource mobilization theory. However, none of those theories place the rise of social movements in general or environmental movements in particular within a broad historical framework. Habermas's work, as I hope chapter 4 will demonstrate, attempts to do so, if not always successfully.

Chapter 1   Capitalism, Industrialism and the Transformation of Nature

1   See Held and Thompson (eds), *Social Theory of Modern Societies*; Cohen, *Structuration Theory*; Bryant and Jary (eds), *Giddens' Theory of Structuration*; Craib, *Anthony Giddens*.
2   Giddens, *Capitalism and Modern Social Theory* (1971), henceforth *CMST*.
3   *CMST*, pp. 234–7.
4   Giddens, *The Class Structure of the Advanced Societies*, 2nd edn (1981), henceforth *CSAS*.
5   This break with historical materialism turns on a reassessment of the sources of social power in different historical epochs. Only in capitalist societies is the control of allocative resources of prime importance. *CSAS*, pp. 82–4.
6   Giddens, *New Rules of Sociological Method: a Positive Critique of Interpretative Sociologies* (1976), henceforth *NRSM*. The theory of structuration was subsequently refined, see particularly Giddens, *The Constitution of Society: Outline of a Theory of Structuration* (1984), henceforth *CS*.
7   Giddens, *Profiles and Critiques in Social Theory* (1982), henceforth *PCST*; Giddens, *Central Problems in Social Theory: Action, Structure and Contradiction in Social Analysis* (1979), henceforth *CPST*. See also the chapter 'Positivism and its Critics', in Giddens, *Studies in Social and Political Theory* (1977), henceforth *SSPT*.
8   For a fuller account of the theory of structuration and some sharp criticisms, see J. B. Thompson, 'The Theory of Structuration', in Held and Thompson (eds), *Social Theory of Modern Societies*.
9   Giddens's key statements on this matter are *NRSM*, concluding chapter; chapter 7 of *A Contemporary Critique of Historical Materialism*, vol. 1: *Power, Property and the State* (1981), henceforth *CCHM*; and the opening chapters of *CS*.
10 *CCHM* and Giddens, *The Nation-State and Violence*, vol. 2 of *A Contemporary Critique of Historical Materialism* (1985), henceforth *NSV*.
11 *CCHM*, ch. 3.
12 *CCHM*, pp. 164–9.
13 On space and time, see *CCHM*, ch. 1; on the city, see ch. 6 and *NSV*, ch. 8; on the nation-state, see *CCHM*, chs 7–9, and *NSV*, chs 4 and 6; on military power, see *NSV*, ch. 9.
14 Giddens, *The Consequences of Modernity* (1990); *Modernity and Self-Identity: Self and Society in the Late Modern Age* (1991); *The Transformation of Intimacy* (1993); *Beyond Left and Right* (1994), henceforth *COM*, *MSI*, *TI* and *BLR*.
15 'In class-divided societies, production does not greatly transform nature, even where, for example, major schemes of irrigation exist . . . The advent of industrial capitalism alters all this.' *NSV*, p. 146.
16 *NSV*, pp. 122–3.
17 *NSV*, p. 122.
18 *NSV*, p. 122.
19 *NSV*, p. 141.
20 'The labour contract is the focal element of Marx's analysis here, demonstrating how distinct capitalism is from all previous systems of

the exploitation of labour.' *NSV*, p. 131, see also *CCHM*, pp. 117–21.

21 *NSV*, pp. 133–4.
22 *NSV*, p. 135.
23 *NSV*, p. 136.
24 *NSV*, p. 136.
25 *NSV*, pp. 136–7.
26 *SSPT*, pp. 15–18; *CSAS*, pp. 139–43.
27 *NSV*, p. 137.
28 *NSV*, p. 138.
29 A machine for these purposes being defined as 'an artefact that accomplishes certain set tasks through the regularised application of inanimate power resources'. *NSV*, p. 138.
30 *NSV*, p. 139.
31 When 'industrialism [is] considered alone, such a source of dynamism – one of the main features of the discontinuity of modernity – is lacking'. *NSV*, p. 140.
32 *NSV*, p. 141.
33 *NSV*, pp. 141–2.
34 *NSV*, pp. 143–5.
35 *NSV*, p. 145.
36 *NSV*, p. 146.
37 *NSV*, p. 311.
38 *NSV*, p. 312, emphasis added.
39 See the discussion in *NSV*, pp. 323–4; see also the comments in *CSAS*, pp. 152–4.
40 Contrast *COM*, p. 59, with *NSV*, p. 311.
41 *COM*, p. 110, emphasis added.
42 *NSV*, p. 313.
43 *COM*, p. 127.
44 For an interesting discussion of this dilemma, see D. Worster, 'Doing Environmental History', in Worster (ed.), *The Ends of the Earth*.
45 Cronon, *Changes in the Land*.
46 Things are, of course, rarely this simple. Population change can have more complex impacts, stimulating trade, new technologies, warfare, etc. See Boserup, *The Conditions of Agricultural Growth*. Conversely, the role of food supplies in determining demographic change has been substantially qualified, see Livvi-Bacci, *Population and Nutrition*.
47 Warfare has produced important environmental impacts. See, for example, Panos, *Greenwar*; Dejene, *Environment, Famine and Politics in Ethiopia*.
48 See the review of evidence in G. Utterstrom, 'Climatic Fluctuations and Population Problems in Early Modern History', in Worster (ed.), *The Ends of the Earth*.
49 On the impact of the horse, see Goody, *Technology, Tradition and the State in Africa*. Similarly dramatic was the conquistadors' gift of disease bacteria and viruses to South American Indians, see Crosby, *The Columbian Exchange*, or the coming of the potato to Ireland, see Salaman, *History and Social Influence of the Potato*.
50 See Goudie, *The Human Impact*, ch. 4. An interesting case study of soil change is C. Earle, 'The Myth of the Southern Soil Miner', in Worster (ed.), *The Ends of the Earth*.

51 Goudie, *The Human Impact*, chs 5 and 7.
52 Giddens's structuration theory, with its emphasis on participant knowledge, suggests this course of investigation, though he has not pursued it.
53 Dunlap, *DDT: Scientists, Citizens, and Public Policy*.
54 For a similar though less encompassing notion of pollution as opposed to environmental degradation, see Weale, *The New Politics of Pollution*, p. 3.
55 Wrigley, *Continuity, Chance and Change: the Character of the Industrial Revolution, in England* and *Cities, Wealth and People*.
56 Wrigley, *Continuity, Chance and Change*, pp. 14–17.
57 Ibid., pp. 35–6.
58 On raw materials in general, see Wrigley, 'Supply of Raw Materials'. On the importance and limitations of water and wind energy in the advanced organic economy, see de Zeeuw, 'Peat and the Dutch Golden Age', and the critique in Unger, 'Energy Sources for the Dutch Golden Age'.
59 Wrigley, 'Supply of Raw Materials'.
60 For the role of the railways in getting carcasses to urban markets, see Schorger, *The Passenger Pigeon*.
61 See Martin, *Treasure of the Land of Darkness*; Fisher, *The Russian Fur Trade, 1550–1700*, ch. 6.
62 Cronon, *Changes in the Land*, ch. 5, and Silver, *A New Face on the Countryside*.
63 Busch, *The War Against the Seals*.
64 Worster, *Dust Bowl*.
65 See the discussions of these issues in D. North, 'Institutions, Transaction Costs, and the Rise of Merchant Empires', and J. Price 'Transaction Costs: a Note on Merchant Credit and the Organisation of Private Trade', in Tracy (ed.), *Political Economy of Merchant Empires*.
66 See for example the historical discussion in Cronon, *Changes in the Land*, pp. 75–9.
67 For an overview of these issues from the perspective of environmental economics, see Pearce and Turner, *Economics of Natural Resources*.
68 On the rise of modern consumption patterns, see McKendrick et al., *Birth of a Consumer Society*. For a provocative reinterpretation of the origins of the modern propensity to consume, see Campbell, *Romantic Ethic*.
69 Wrigley, *Continuity, Chance and Change*, pp. 57–60. It is important to note that the decline of the Dutch Republic has been overestimated. See the reassessment in Riley, 'The Dutch Economy after 1650'.
70 Unger, 'Energy Sources for the Dutch Golden Age', for the limitations on non-fossil fuels in the preindustrial economy.
71 Coal, of course, is organic in origin, but for the purposes of resource use it can be considered inorganic given the time-scale required to produce coal naturally from vegetable matter.
72 On Chinese technology, see Needham, *Science and Civilisation in China*.
73 See Landes, *The Unbound Prometheus*.
74 Lilley, 'Technological Progress'.
75 See the argument in Aron, *Eighteen Lectures on Industrial Society*, esp. ch. 5.

76 See Rostow, *The Stages of Economic Growth*.
77 For British growth rates, see Deane and Cole, *British Economic Growth, 1688–1959*.
78 See Minchinton, 'Patterns of Demand'; von Tunzelmann, 'Trends in Real Wages'.
79 The classic statements of this position in recent years have been Meadows et al., *Limits to Growth*, and The Ecologist, 'Blueprint For Survival'.
80 See chapter 1 of Ekins (ed.), *The Living Economy*.
81 For a summary of this sort of analysis, see O'Riordan, *Environmentalism*, pp. 64–81.
82 For an argument along these lines, see the introduction to Pearce et al., *Blueprint for a Green Economy*.
83 The question for contemporary political analysis remains whether a form of environmentally sustainable growth is possible.
84 I shall deal with the question of urban sprawl in more detail in chapter 2, while the economic and political decision-making behind infrastructure projects will be considered in chapter 3.
85 Richards, 'Global Patterns of Land Conversion'. Richards estimates that from 1860 to 1920, 432 million hectares of land were converted to regular cropping and another 419 million from 1920 to 1978.
86 The Soviet Union has been particularly active in this form of environmental transformation, with its penchant for the especially large-scale and disastrous infrastructure projects, see Micklin, 'The Falling Level of the Caspian Sea'.
87 For the British experience, see Rackham, *The History of the Countryside*.
88 See L. R. Brown and J. E. Young, 'Feeding the World in the Nineties', in Brown et al., *State of the World 1990*.
89 Mahar, *Government Policies and Deforestation in Brazil's Amazon Region*.
90 See Cipolla, *Economic History of World Population*. On this topic in particular this analysis has paid the price of not incorporating a more international dimension, for the majority of population growth has occurred outside of the West.
91 For a further discussion of the differences between monetary costs and environmental impacts of environmental degradation, see chapter 3.
92 The classic technical statement on the matter is Pigou, *Wealth and Welfare*.
93 See my discussion of technological development, capital investment and environmental degradation, in chapter 3 below.
94 Giddens has attempted to account for the emergence of pluralist polities in the modern world through the notion of polyarchy, see *NSV*, pp. 198–209. He has not, however, complemented it with a study of the implications of representative democracies. He has focused on the capacity of the modern state to collect and deploy information in the pursuit of political control, and on the emergence of citizenship. See *CCHM*, pp. 220–9.
95 Cronon, *Changes in the Land*.
96 See the discussion of just this problem, from the perspective of distributive justice, in Walzer, *Spheres of Justice*.
97 Cronon, *Nature's Metropolis*, ch. 3.

98   An interesting example of an argument on similar lines is that of Karl Polanyi, *The Great Transformation*, in which the political struggle required to create markets and wage labour is given a causal prominence unusual for economic history.

99   This is broadly the line of argument pursued by Marxist writers, with particular reference to the implications of welfare spending. See O'Connor, *Fiscal Crisis of the State*; Gough, *Political Economy of the Welfare State*; Offe, *Contradictions of the Welfare State*.

100 The classic statement of this position is Miliband, *The State in Capitalist Society*.

101 See the discussion of this problem in Przeworski, *Capitalism and Social Democracy*.

102 It is more surprising given his familiarity with Weber's classic work on this subject. See Giddens, *Politics and Sociology in the Thought of Max Weber*.

103 See the discussion of technology in Goody, *Technology, Tradition and the State in Africa*.

104 It is worth noting that Wrigley has emphasized the contingent rather than necessary character of the development of industrialism, arguing that a technically perfect capitalism is conceivable in the absence of industrialization. The latter was a result not merely of the factors listed but the chance existence of accessible coal reserves and a water transport system to move them, without which the industrialization of England and thus elsewhere was impossible. See Wrigley, 'The Process of Modernisation'.

105 With regard to Giddens's analytical definition of industrialism, the impact of the centralized work-place and industrial dominance have yet to be discussed. I will analyse the impact of the centralized work-place in connection with Giddens's discussion of urbanism. As for the dominance of industrial production, it is only a relative factor depending on the impact of industrialism's other component parts.

106 A critique of science and positivism along these lines has recently been advanced by Deep Ecologists. See, for example, Fox, *Towards a Transpersonal Ecology*.

107 This is the thrust of the opening chapters of Thomas, *Man and the Natural World*.

108 Ibid., particularly the argument deployed in the closing chapters.

109 Scientists have been in the forefront of campaigns against nuclear power and nuclear weapons, and for the protection of landscapes, the restriction of pesticide use, etc. They have of course been instrumental in actually alerting the rest of the public to otherwise unperceived environmental problems: global warming, ozone depletion, etc.

110 For accounts of environmental degradation in the Soviet Union and Eastern Europe, see Goldman, *The Spoils of Progress*; Volgyes (ed.), *Environmental Deterioration in the Soviet Union and Eastern Europe*; Singleton (ed.), *Environmental Misuse in the Soviet Union*; Volf'son, *The Destruction of Nature in the Soviet Union*; Pryde, *Environmental Management in the Soviet Union*.

111 This is not entirely true for parts of the Soviet Union and the westernmost states of Eastern Europe. None the less, the overwhelming majori-

ty of industrialization in these areas was conducted under the auspices of state-socialist regimes.

112 See Nove, *Economics of a Feasible Socialism* and Nove, *Economic History of the USSR*.

113 On the success of Soviet economic growth, see Nove, *Economics of a Feasible Socialism*, pp. 106–7.

114 On production bonuses, see ibid., pp. 73–5.

115 Goldman, *The Spoils of Progress*, pp. 48–52.

116 Pryde, *Environmental Management in the Soviet Union*, ch. 7.

117 On Soviet environmental legislation, see Goldman, *The Spoils of Progress*, ch. 1, and Pryde, *Environmental Management in the Soviet Union*, ch. 1.

118 On the differentials between fines and bonuses, see, L. S. Taga, 'Externalities in a Command Economy', in Singleton (ed.), *Environmental Misuse in the Soviet Union*.

119 On this issue see ibid., pp. 60–1; Pryde, *Environmental Management in the Soviet Union*, ch. 2.

120 On the problem of bureaucratic planning, see Nove, *Economics of a Feasible Socialism*, pp. 68–70, 75–81; Goldman, *The Spoils of Progress*, pp. 38–9.

121 Weiner, *Models of Nature*.

Chapter 2   Urbanism, Globalization and Environmental Politics

1 *CPST*, ch. 6. For overviews of Giddens's work on space, see Gregory, 'Presences and Absences', and Saunders, 'Space, Urbanism and the Created Environment'.

2 'An essential thesis of this book is that the city cannot be regarded as merely incidental to social theory but belongs at its very core. Similarly, "urban sociology" is more than just one branch of sociology among others – it stands at the heart of some of the most fundamental problems of general sociological interest.' *CCHM*, p. 140.

3 *CCHM*, pp. 157–61.

4 *CCHM*, pp. 93–4, see also *NSV*, pp. 195–6, and *CPST*, pp. 216–22.

5 *CCHM*, pp. 150–6.

6 *CCHM*, pp. 142–3.

7 *CCHM*, pp. 145–6.

8 *CCHM*, p. 147.

9 *CCHM*, pp. 148–50.

10 *CCHM*, p. 148.

11 *CCHM*, p. 149.

12 See Saunders, *Social Theory and the Urban Question*, ch. 3. In urban sociology this has been strikingly expressed by Louis Wirth, see for example, 'Urbanism as a Way of Life'.

13 *CCHM*, p. 151.

14 *NSV*, p. 146, emphasis added.

15 *COM*, p. 60, original emphasis.

16 In *COM* Giddens offers a renewed investigation of the dissolution of tradition, the reflexivity of knowledge and the nature of insecurity in mod-

ern societies (pp. 38–43, 100–11), but the central role of a commodified created environment appears to have receded into the background. This argument has been taken a stage further in *BLR*, in which Giddens argues for the continuing importance of the security and certainty that tradition provides in an otherwise risky world.

17 See a similar argument pursued from a different angle in Saunders, *Social Theory and the Urban Question*.
18 We should note that Giddens had made allowance for this criticism in considering the question of regionalization in *NSV*, pp. 192–4, but the focus is on the idea of sequestration and cultural concealment, see pp. 194–6.
19 Giddens does mention the importance of concentrations of population, see *NSV*, p. 194, but this rather cursory reference has not been followed up.
20 A historical perspective illustrates that the modern world has no monopoly on urban environmental problems, see Melosi, *Garbage in the Cities*, and the early sections of Savas, *Organisation and Efficiency of Solid Waste Collection*; Mumford, *The City in History*.
21 Wrigley and Schofield, *The Population History of England*.
22 On medieval urban pollution, see Savas, *Organisation and Efficiency of Solid Waste Collection*, pp. 14–15; Mumford, *The City in History*, pp. 290–2.
23 de Vries, 'Decline and Rise of the Dutch Economy'.
24 TeBrake, 'Air Pollution and Fuel Crises'.
25 Ibid.
26 Wohl, *Endangered Lives*, p. 212.
27 For the German experience see Evans, *Death In Hamburg*, pp. 111, 129–30, 147–9.
28 For calculations on this difficult topic, see Thompson, 'Nineteenth-Century Horse Sense'.
29 See the discussion of housing conditions in nineteenth-century Britain in Wohl, *Endangered Lives*, ch. 11; Wohl, *The External Slum*.
30 Evans, *Death in Hamburg*, pp. 144–51; Wohl, *Endangered Lives*, ch. 9.
31 Melosi, *Garbage in the Cities*, ch. 6 on this problem. On refuse pollution and municipal reform in general, see Melosi (ed.), *Pollution and Reform*.
32 The classic statement on public goods is Samuelson, 'The Pure Theory of Public Expenditures'.
33 Wohl, *Endangered Lives*, pp. 264–79.
34 On the politics of planning in the nineteenth century, see Cherry, *Cities and Plans*.
35 For local studies, see Colten, 'Industrial Wastes'; Tarr, 'Historical Perspectives on Hazardous Wastes'.
36 Wohl, *Endangered Lives*, pp. 233–42.
37 See the discussions in Clarke, *Water*, ch. 7; Carrol (ed.), *International Environmental Diplomacy*.
38 *CCHM*, p. 168.
39 *CCHM*, p. 198.
40 *NSV*, ch. 10, and *COM*, pp. 63–78.
41 *NSV*, p. 289.
42 *COM*, p. 64.
43 *COM*, p. 76.

44 *COM*, pp. 76–7.
45 *NSV*, p. 267.
46 On the diffusion of industrial technology, see Headrick, *The Tentacles of Progress*.
47 See Gilpin, *Political Economy of International Relations*, ch. 6; Fröbel, Heinrichs and Kreye, *New International Division of Labour*.
48 On the political dynamics of these changes, see Wohl, *Endangered Lives*, pp. 220–32 on the Alkali Acts, pp. 242–56 on control of water pollution. For the United States, see Grinder, 'The Battle for Clean Air'. For Germany, see Evans, *Death In Hamburg*, pp. 126–44.
49 'Ecological threats are the outcome of socially organised knowledge, mediated by the impact of industrialism, upon the material environment.' *COM*, p. 110.
50 See, for example, Abercrombie, 'Writings on Smoke'.
51 *NSV*, pp. 310–25.
52 *NSV*, pp. 315–16.
53 Thomas, *Man and the Natural World*.
54 Giddens has acknowledged this point to a certain extent, see *NSV*, p. 194, and more so in *COM*, pp. 161–2.
55 See particularly the critique by Saunders, 'Space, Urbanism and the Created Environment'.
56 *COM*, ch. 3. *MSI*, chs 2 and 7.
57 *COM*, pp. 120–31.
58 *COM*, p. 161.
59 *MSI*, p. 214.
60 *MSI*, pp. 223–6. This focus on the remoralization of abstract social systems and its connections to environmental politics is also taken up by Jürgen Habermas. See the account of his model of social movement mobilization in chapter 4 below.
61 *COM*, p. 221.

Chapter 3 The Political Ecology of Capitalism

1 Gorz's main works include *Ecology as Politics*, henceforth *EP*; *Farewell to the Working Class: an Essay on Post-Industrial Socialism*, henceforth *FWC*; *Paths to Paradise: On the Liberation from Work*, henceforth *PTP*; *Capitalism, Socialism, Ecology*, henceforth *CSE*.
2 For Gorz's place in the development of environmental thought, see Paehlke, *Environmentalism*.
3 In economics he has drawn on the work of the 'limits to growth' school, see Meadows, *Limits to Growth*; The Ecologist, 'Blueprint for Survival'; Hirsch, *Social Limits to Growth*; Mishan, *The Costs of Economic Growth*; Schumacher, *Small is Beautiful*. Politically and sociologically he has drawn on the anarchist critique of technology in Illich's work, see Illich, *Deschooling Society* and *Tools for Conviviality*.
4 For the connections between these different aspects of the green/environmentalist political position, see Pepper, *The Roots of Modern Environmentalism*, pp. 27–30, and Dobson, *Green Politics*.
5 See, for example, Robertson, *Future Wealth*.

6   Bookchin, Review of A. Gorz, *Ecology as Politics*, *Telos* 46 (1980); A. Giddens, 'The Perils of Punditry: Gorz and the End of the Working Class', in *STMS*; J. Keane, 'Work and the Civilising Process', in Keane, *Democracy and Civil Society*.

7   See Badham, 'Sociology of Industrial and Post-industrial Societies'; Frankel, *The Post-industrial Utopians*. K. Kumar's classic study of postindustrial thought hardly pays any attention to Gorz's work, see Kumar, *Prophecy and Progress*.

8   Ryle, *Ecology and Socialism*.

9   Gorz, *Strategy for Labour: a Radical Proposal*.

10 For the political shifts in the French intelligentsia during this period, see Anderson, *In the Tracks of Historical Materialism*; Dews, *Logics of Disintegration*.

11 See, for example, the arguments in Gorz, *Strategy for Labour*. See also the arguments in his introduction, in Gorz (ed.), *The Division of Labour*.

12 On co-operation see, for example, the third appendix in *PTP*.

13 It would seem that *Farewell to the Working Class* was the work where this term first received prominence.

14 For an excellent summary of these issues, see Allen 'Post-industrialism and Post-Fordism'.

15 Rowthorn and Wells, *De-industrialisation and Foreign Trade*, ch. 1.

16 Gill, *Work, Unemployment and the New Technology*, chs 1–4.

17 See Therborn, *Why Are Some People More Unemployed than Other People?*

18 Leadbetter and Lloyd, *In Search Of Work*, chs 7–8.

19 See for example, Lash and Urry *The End of Organised Capitalism*. On the Fordism to neo-Fordism transition see Lipietz, *Mirages and Miracles*; Aglietta, *A Theory of Capitalist Regulation*; Piore and Sabel, *The Second Industrial Divide*.

20 Badham, 'Sociology of Industrial and Post-industrial Societies'.

21 See Toffler, *Future Shock; The Third Wave; Previews and Premises*; Bell, *The Coming of Post-industrial Society*. See also Gorz's review of Toffler in *PTP*, pp. 81–91.

22 Consider, for example, Illich's remarks on the problems of collective ownership of technology in *Tools for Conviviality*.

23 See, for example, section 3 in Gorz, *Critique of Economic Reason*, henceforth *CER*.

24 *EP*, pp. 3–11.

25 See in particular section 3 of *EP*, 'The Logic of Tools', pp. 99–148.

26 *EP*, pp. 6–7, pp. 20–8.

27 *FWC*, ch. 3.

28 *FWC*, ch. 2.

29 *FWC*, chs 6 and 7.

30 *PTP*, pp. 13–17, 29–32.

31 *PTP*, pp. 6–8, 34–5.

32 *PTP*, pp. 40–79, but see the similar earlier attempts on this issue in *EP*, 'A Possible Utopia', pp. 42–54; *FWC*, pp. 90–119. See also Gorz 'The New Agenda'.

33 See, for example, *EP*, p. 22.

34 See my discussion in chapter 1, pp. 46–7.

35 *EP*, p. 13.

36   *EP*, pp. 32–3.
37   For an argument suggesting that the market can recognize and adequately account for the costs of environmental degradation, see Pearce, *Blueprint for a Green Economy*; Barde and Pearce (eds), *Valuing the Environment*. For a variety of arguments against, see Sagoff, *The Economy of the Earth*.
38   See the reflections of Saunders on the importance of consumption to social theory, in Saunders, *Social Theory and the Urban Question*.
39   *EP*, pp. 29–31.
40   *EP*, pp. 35–6; *PTP*, pp. 24–8.
41   See *EP*, pp. 23–7; *CER*, pp. 224–5.
42   See, particularly, 'Twelve Billion People', in *EP*, pp. 91–7, and 'Their Famine, our Food', in *PTP*, pp. 91–100.
43   *EP*, pp. 18–19.
44   'Societal choices are continually imposed on us under the guise of technical choices.' *EP*, p. 19.
45   *EP*, p. 19.
46   See, particularly, the essays 'Nuclear Energy: a Preeminently Political Choice' and 'From Nuclear Electricity to Electric Fascism' in *EP*. See also Ince, 'Secrecy, Policy-Making and the Nuclear State'.
47   *EP*, p. 20.
48   *EP*, p. 21.
49   *EP*, p. 21.
50   *EP*, pp. 23–4.
51   *PTP*, pp. 8–12.
52   *EP*, pp. 24–5.
53   *EP*, p. 25.
54   *EP*, pp. 26–7.
55   *PTP*, p. 14.
56   *PTP*, p. 16, emphasis in the original.
57   *PTP*, pp. 16–18.
58   *PTP*, pp. 29–30.
59   *PTP*, p. 29, emphasis in the original.
60   *PTP*, pp. 24–5.
61   *PTP*, pp. 36–7.
62   *PTP*, p. 39, emphasis in the original.
63   *PTP*, pp. 35–67.
64   Keane, *Democracy and Civil Society*.
65   See A. Giddens 'The Perils of Punditry', in *STMS*.
66   See, for example, the second appendix to *PTP*.
67   On the impact of globalization on the nation-state, see Held, 'Democracy, the Nation-State and the Global System'.
68   For an overview of the globalization of the capitalist economies, see Dicken, *Global Shift*.
69   See the account of the economic fortunes of the French Socialists in Hall, 'Evolution of Economic Policy under Mitterrand'.
70   This draws on the account of the impact of global capital mobility on different economic strategies in Friedan, 'Invested Interests'. On the Mundell–Flemming approach to monetary policy and capital mobility, see Mundell, 'Capital Mobility and Stabilisation Policy'.

71 On the growth of international environmental law and regimes, see Carrol, *International Environmental Diplomacy*, and Hurrel and Kingsbury (eds), *International Politics of the Environment*.

72 For the impact of EC environmental policies on the UK, see Haigh, *EEC Environmental Policy and Britain*.

73 See the discussion in Salamon, 'What is Technology?'

74 On the sociology of technology, see Bijker et al., *Social Construction of Technological Systems*. Giddens has addressed, at least in passing, the appropriate political response to the dilemmas posed by unrestrained technological development. See *COM*, pp. 163–73.

75 El-Hinnawi (ed.), *Nuclear Energy and the Environment*.

76 Erskine and Webber, 'Accidents, Risks and Consequences'.

77 On the development of radio technology and the way in which commercial and non-commercial interests shaped its progress, see the discussion in Williams, *Towards 2000*.

78 Social democratic governments have found it hard enough to keep capital investment at home, let alone reorder its priorities in socially useful directions.

79 On the appalling record of that bastion of socialism, the Central Electricity Generating Board, see Hall, *Nuclear Politics*. On a similar note, see the record of the water industry in Britain, Pearce, *Watershed*.

80 Plowden, *The Motor Car and Politics*.

81 On the shifting balance between infrastructural investment in road and non-road transport, see Wistrich, *The Politics of Transport*, ch. 1. On the active dismemberment of the American urban public transport networks, see Ponting, *Green History of the World*, pp. 312–13; on tax relief for commercial motoring, see TEST, *The Company Car Factor*; on the experience of the cyclist and pedestrian, see Hillman, *Walking is Transport*.

82 See the classic study of the British road lobby in action, Hamer, *Wheels within Wheels*.

83 Cockburn and Hecht, *Fate of the Forest*.

84 Caldwell, *Between Two Worlds*.

85 See, for example, Falkingham, 'Britain's Aging Population'.

86 Brittan, *The Economic Consequences of Democracy*.

87 All four strategies have been pursued by nuclear authorities over the link between radiation and ill-health, see Hall, *Nuclear Politics*, ch. 9. For an excellent typology of the ways in which democratic governments can pursue policies contrary to the interests and demands of social groups, see Nordlinger, *On the Autonomy of the Democratic State*.

88 See above, pp. 83–5.

89 For an overview of this area from a methodological viewpoint, see Hill and Ham, *Policy Process*, and from a comparative viewpoint, Castles (ed.), *Comparative History of Public Policy*.

90 On the construction of the environmental policy agenda, see Solesbury, 'The Environmental Agenda'.

91 Even in his most recent book, *Capitalism, Socialism, Ecology*, there are only scattered references to the greens and no systematic engagement with their origins or potential, see *CSE*, pp. 6–7, 112, for example.

92 See, for example, Cranston, *Law, Government and Public Policy*, ch. 5.

93   The importance of political opportunity structures in the relative suc-
     cess of environmental movements has been demonstrated in Kitschelt,
     'Political Opportunity Structures'.

94   On the factors that facilitate the success of environmental campaigns,
     see the concluding survey in Richardson and Kimber (eds), *Campaigning
     for the Environment.*

95   Evidence that electorates do not vote on the basis of economic self-inter-
     est alone but respond to more general understandings of the general
     good is summarized in Lewin, *Self-Interest and Public Interest.*

96   Rawls, *A Theory of Justice*, p. 5. 'Justice is the first virtue of social institu-
     tions, as truth is of systems of thought. A theory however elegant and
     economical must be rejected or revised if it is untrue; likewise laws and
     institutions no matter how efficient and well-arranged must be
     reformed or abolished if they are unjust.' Why this should be consid-
     ered the moral common sense of Western societies is an issue I shall
     explore in connection with Habermas's provocative 'rationalization of
     the lifeworld' argument. This suggests that the rationalization of the
     lifeworld generates a culture that can only accept as legitimate social
     institutions those that are both just and democratic.

97   See, for example, Passmore, *Man's Responsibility For Nature*; B. Barry,
     'Justice between Generations' and 'The Ethics of Resource Depletion', in
     Barry, *Liberty and Justice.*

98   There have been occasions on which industries have had to absorb
     directly the costs of their own pollution, but they are more likely to
     move or arrange for pollutants to be dispersed. A good example of the
     former are the problems encountered by the industrial complex on Lake
     Baikal in Siberia, see Pryde, *Environmental Management in the Soviet
     Union.*

99   See, for example, the range of measures adopted described in Opschoor
     and Vos, *Application of Economic Instruments.* See also Le Grand and
     Robinson, *The Economics of Social Problems*; Pearce, *Blueprint for a Green
     Economy.*

100 See chapter 1, pp. 45–6, and chapter 2, p. 62.

101 Consider, for example, the travesty of the Sizewell inquiry, see Hall,
     Nuclear Politics, ch. 10.

102 For an informed critique of cost–benefit analysis, see Plowden, *Transport
     Reform*, pp. 235–47.

103 On the differential capacity of lobbying groups, see Richardson and
     Kimber (eds), *Campaigning for the Environment.* On the relative strengths
     of the agricultural and conservation lobbies in Britain, see Lowe et al.,
     Countryside Conflicts, chs 4 and 5.

104 See, in general, *COM*, pp. 36–44. Giddens writes (p. 40), 'In the social
     sciences, to the unsettled character of all empirically based knowledge
     we have to add the "subversion" which comes from the reentry of
     social scientific knowledge into the contexts it analyses.' Furthermore,
     'the social sciences are . . . deeply implicated in modernity . . . since the
     chronic revision of social practices in the light of knowledge about those
     practices is part of the very tissue of modern institutions.'

105 See the argument in favour of extending intergenerational questions
     this far in Passmore, *Man's Responsibility for Nature.*

106 See, for example, Department of the Environment, *Possible Impacts of Climatic Change*.
107 See the research in Le Grand, *The Strategy of Equality*.
108 On the problems of social democratic reflation strategies, see Armstrong et al., *Capitalism since World War II*, ch. 19.
109 See, for example, the essays in Hobsbawm (ed.), *Forward March of Labour Halted?*
110 This is not to suggest that green parties and the environmental movement have not won political representation, or that they have not significantly altered the political agenda of capitalist societies. Rather it is to suggest that, as yet, they have not translated their small bases of support into a credible challenge for forming majority governments or a leading element in a national coalition.
111 For a compelling description of how these sorts of environmental problems can be controlled, from a social democratic framework, see Jacobs, *The Green Economy*.
112 On the ethical dimension to this question, see the excellent essay 'Humanity and Justice in Global Perspective', in Barry, *Liberty and Justice*.
113 Precisely such an economic scenario has been traced in Rowthorn and Wells, *Deindustrialisation and Foreign Trade*.
114 On the informal economy, see Offe and Heinze, *Beyond Employment*.

Chapter 4   Social and Cultural Origins of Environmental Movements

1 See chapter 2, pp. 69–71.
2 Habermas, *The Theory of Communicative Action, Volume 1: Reason and the Rationalization of Society*, and *The Theory of Communicative Action, Volume 2: Lifeworld and System: A Critique of Functionalist Reason*, henceforth *TCA1* and *TCA2*.
3 Habermas 'Life-Forms, Morality and the Tasks of the Philosopher', in P. Dews (ed.), *Autonomy and Solidarity*, emphasis added.
4 See J. B. Thompson, 'Rationality and Social Rationalisation: an Assessment of Habermas' Theory of Communicative Action', in Thompson, *Studies in the Theory of Ideology*. From a feminist perspective, see the perceptive essay by N. Fraser, 'What's Critical about Critical Theory? The Case of Habermas and Gender', in Fraser, *Unruly Practices*. Also see Bernstein (ed.), *Habermas and Modernity*; Baxter, 'System and Lifeworld'; A. Giddens, 'Reason without Revolution? Habermas' *Theorie des kommunikativen Handelns*', in *PCST*; Honneth and Joas (eds), *Communicative Action*.
5 For surveys of *TCA* and its relation to Habermas's earlier work, see White, *The Recent Work of Jürgen Habermas*; Ingram, *Habermas and the Dialectic of Reason*; Rasmussen, *Reading Habermas*; Roderick, *Habermas and the Foundations of Critical Theory*.
6 Habermas, *The Philosophical Discourse of Modernity: Twelve Lectures*, henceforth *PDM*.
7 Habermas, *Legitimation Crisis* and *Communication and the Evolution of*

Society, henceforth *LC* and *CES* respectively.

8 For the central account of this argument, see Habermas, *Knowledge and Human Interests*, henceforth *KHI*. For stiff criticisms, see McCarthy, *The Critical Theory of Jürgen Habermas*.

9 Habermas has questioned whether his work constitutes an ethical foundationalism. See discussion in White, *The Recent Work of Jürgen Habermas*, pp. 129–36.

10 On their development, Thompson, *Critical Hermeneutics*; also 'Universal Pragmatics?', in Thompson, *Studies in the Theory of Ideology*.

11 For a discussion and defence of the process of rational reconstruction, see the postscript to *KHI*.

12 Habermas has not pursued this question at the level of philosophy alone, but has also sought to elaborate the conditions under which the ideal speech situation might be institutionalized as a public sphere. See Habermas, *The Structural Transformation of the Public Sphere*, henceforth *STPS*.

13 *TCA1*, pp. 82–4.

14 *TCA1*, pp. 279–86.

15 *PDM*, p. 200.

16 See the discussion in *PDM*, chapter 11.

17 Habermas took up the rationality problematic a decade beforehand. See his discussion of Marcuse in Habermas, *Toward a Rational Society*.

18 *TCA1*, pp. 143–5.

19 On the loss of meaning, *TCA1*, pp. 241–2; on the loss of freedom, pp. 243–54.

20 See the essays, Habermas, 'Theory and Evolution'; Habermas, 'Towards the Reconstruction of Historical Materialism', in *CES*.

21 Habermas, 'Labour and Interaction: Remarks on Hegel's Jena Philosophy of Mind', in Habermas, *Theory and Practice*, henceforth *TP*.

22 See Habermas, 'Historical Materialism and the Development of Normative Structures', in *CES*. The criteria of the moral advance remained somewhat problematic, but Habermas has suggested that the developmental psychology of Piaget and Kohlberg is illuminating, see 'Moral Development and Ego Identity', in *CES*.

23 See the discussion in *TCA2*, p. 114.

24 *TCA2*, p. 115, emphasis in the original.

25 *TCA2*, p. 116.

26 *TCA2*, p. 117, emphasis added.

27 The notion of the lifeworld is conceptualized as the milieu of everyday life, the taken-for-granted structures, beliefs and arguments which form the basic backdrop to action. *TCA2*, pp. 119–35.

28 *TCA2*, pp. 119–26.

29 *TCA2*, pp. 140–4.

30 *TCA2*, p. 137.

31 For Habermas wishes to argue that 'the structures of historical lifeworlds vary within the scope defined by the structural constraints of communicative action not accidentally but directionally, that is, in dependence on learning processes'. *TCA2*, p. 145.

32 *TCA2*, p. 145, emphasis in the original.

33 *TCA2*, p. 173.

34 This is, in essence, a Parsonian position, *TCA2*, pp. 235–40, 286–9.
35 This is what Habermas refers to as the technization of the lifeworld, which should be differentiated in his work from the colonization of the lifeworld. *TCA2*, p. 183.
36 *TCA2*, pp. 175–9.
37 See McCarthy, *The Critical Theory of Jürgen Habermas*, ch. 4; D. Held, 'Legitimation Problems and Crisis Tendencies', in Held, *Political Theory and the Modern State*.
38 *LC*, part 2, ch. 1.
39 *LC*, pp. 68–75.
40 *TCA2*, p. 343.
41 *TCA2*, pp. 318–23.
42 Recalling *Legitimation Crisis*, Habermas argues, 'economically conditioned crisis tendencies are not only administratively processed, flattened out, and intercepted, but are inadvertently displaced into the administrative system.' *TCA2*, p. 344.
43 *TCA2*, p. 345.
44 *TCA2*, p. 346.
45 *TCA2*, pp. 346–7.
46 *TCA2*, pp. 349–50.
47 Habermas goes to considerable lengths to substantiate this argument. He argues that Parsons's description of culture as an action system organized by steering media rests on a fundamental misunderstanding of the necessary features of steering media, features which culture and language do not possess. *TCA2*, pp. 256–83.
48 *TCA2*, p. 356.
49 *TCA2*, p. 365.
50 *TCA2*, p. 367.
51 Social problems are presented as legal entitlements: 'The situation to be regulated is embedded in the context of a life-history and of a concrete form of life; it has to be subjected to violent abstraction, not merely because it has to be subsumed under the law, but so that it can be dealt with administratively.' *TCA2*, p. 363.
52 *TCA2*, p. 367.
53 *TCA2*, p. 368.
54 'The compulsion toward litigation-proof certainty of grades and the over-regulation of the curriculum lead to such phenomena as depersonalization, inhibition of innovation, breakdown of responsibility . . .' *TCA2*, p. 371.
55 *TCA2*, pp. 384–5.
56 See the somewhat obscure arguments in *TCA2*, p. 353.
57 *TCA2*, p. 355.
58 *TCA1*, p. 237.
59 *TCA1*, pp. 238–9.
60 *TCA1*, p. 240.
61 *TCA1*, pp. 240–1.
62 *TCA2*, p. 392, emphasis added.
63 *TCA2*, pp. 393–4. Habermas appears to be arguing that the feminist movement has been orientated primarily towards the achievement of equality between genders in the formal domain of the economy and

polity. However, there is a good case to be made which argues that the feminist movement has engaged with *the grammer of forms of life* and the basic texture, quality and conduct of interpersonal relations, the construction of cultural meanings and the formation of social roles which characterize the Habermasian lifeworld.

64 *TCA2*, p. 394.
65 *TCA2*, p. 393.
66 *TCA2*, p. 394.
67 *TCA2*, p. 394.
68 *TCA2*, p. 395.
69 In Habermas's own words,

> 'In terms of social statistics, the "old politics" is more strongly support-ed by employers, workers and middle-class tradesmen, whereas *the new politics finds stronger support in the new middle classes, among the younger generation, and in groups with more formal education.* These phenomena tally with my thesis regarding internal colonization. If we take the view that the growth of the economic-administrative complex sets off processes of erosion of the lifeworld, then we would expect old con-flicts to be overlaid with new ones. A line of conflict forms between . . . a centre composed of strata directly involved in the production process and interested in maintaining capitalist growth as the basis of the wel-fare-state compromise, and . . . a periphery composed of a variegated array of groups . . . Among the latter are those groups that are further removed from "the productivist core of performance" . . . *that have been most strongly sensitized to the self-destructive consequences of the growth in complexity or have been more strongly affected by them'*. (*TCA2*, p. 392, emphasis added)

Habermas notes the work of Inglehart, Dalton, Hildebrandt, Barnes and Kaase.

70 For assessments of Habermas's work on new social movements, see Scott, *Ideology and the New Social Movements*; Cohen, 'Strategy or Identity'. On the women's movement, Fraser, *Unruly Practices*.
71 Smelser, *Theories of Collective Behaviour*.
72 Castells, *The Urban Question*. Castells has shifted his position on the importance of class, see Castells, *The City and the Grassroots*.
73 A more satisfactory method, building on rational choice theory, is resource mobilization theory. RMT focuses on the organizational infra-structure of movements, the importance of charismatic leadership and bureaucratization, see Oberschall, *Social Conflict and Social Movements*; Zald and McCarthy (eds), *Social Movements in an Organizational Society*.
74 *TCA2*, p. 394, emphasis added.
75 Pryde, *Environmental Management in the Soviet Union*, pp. 254–64.
76 See chapter 2, pp. 63–5.
77 See thesis 8 in the summary of Habermas above, and also my discussion on pp. 140–4 above.
78 For critical assessments of the model of social evolution, see Scott, *Ideology and New Social Movements*, pp. 78–9, and Thompson, *Studies in the Theory of Ideology*, pp. 297–9.
79 The model has, however, come under concerted attack for supposing

the possibility of aesthetic learning and for excluding certain forms of knowledge from the realm of the rationalizable. See T. McCarthy 'Reflections on Rationalisation in the *Theory of Communicative Action*', in Bernstein (ed.), *Habermas on Modernity*, pp. 188–9; White, *The Recent Work of Jürgen Habermas*, p. 94; Ingram, *Habermas and the Dialectic of Reason*, pp. 57–8.

80 See chapter 2, p. 68.

81 See the survey of this problem in Lewin, *Self-Interest and Public Interest*. See also the discussion of the problematic notion of true or real interests in Geuss, *The Idea of a Critical Theory*.

82 In addition to this more conventional understanding of interests, he has attempted to construct a stronger normative notion of interests, for example, the semi-transcendental, knowledge-constitutive emancipatory interest of *Knowledge and Human Interests*, and the notion of generalizable interests in *Legitimation Crisis*. Indeed, the normative claims of the ideal speech situation rest on the possibility of participants, in an open and equal dialogue, generating common interests to which all can freely and willingly assent.

83 Quoted in *TCA1*, p. 119.

84 On problems of definition, see Kaase, 'Social Movements and Political Innovation'.

85 For reviews of the movement's internal complexity, see McCormick, *British Politics and the Environment*; Lowe and Goyder, *Environmental Groups in Politics*.

86 Klandemans (ed.), *Organising for Change*. On the problems this poses for political parties, see Kitschelt, *The Logic of Party Formation*.

87 For a focus on the expressive elements of participation, see Muller and Opp, 'Rational Choice', Mitchell, 'National Environment Lobbies'.

88 See Melucci, 'Symbolic Challenge'; Offe, 'Challenging the Boundaries'.

89 Dunlap and van Liere, 'The New Environmental Paradigm'; Cotgrove, *Catastrophe or Cornucopia*.

90 See the experience of Friends of the Earth, in Weston, *The FOE Experience*.

91 See Dalton et al., 'Challenge of New Social Movements'.

92 See the excellent study, Wilson, 'Neo-corporatism and New Social Movements'.

93 On the emergence of environmental movements outside of the West, see Ekins, *A New World Order*.

94 On the prewar history of peace movements in the West, see Hinton, *Protests and Visions*; Brock, *Twentieth Century Pacifism*.

95 On Britain, Hardy, *Alternative Communities*; on cultural revolt in America, see Jackson Lears, *No Place of Grace*.

96 Brand, 'Cyclical Aspects'.

97 Ibid., p. 37.

98 Ibid., p. 29.

99 See Habermas's discussion of the different ways in which different intellectual traditions have approached the normative paradox of modernity in *PDM*, chs 3 and 4.

100 See the emphases suggested in Lowe and Rudig, 'Withered Greening of British Politics'; Baker, 'Evolution of the Irish Ecology Movement'; Desales Affigne, 'Environmental Crisis, Green Party Power'.

101 See chapter 1.
102 On this dilemma in sociological theory, see Winch, *The Idea of a Social Science*, and the sharp criticism of Winch's position which suggests that actors' accounts are not sufficient, Thompson, *Critical Hermeneutics*, chs 4–6.
103 On the cultural importance of the countryside, see Williams, *The Country and the City*; Nash, *Wilderness and the American Mind*.
104 For general surveys of these issues, see Hays, *Beauty, Health and Permanence*, ch. 6; Paehlke, *Environmentalism*, ch. 2.
105 The important role of the media in covering these events is dealt with in Lowe and Morrison, 'Bad News or Good News'.
106 On changing popular conceptions of health, see Coward, *The Whole Truth*; Hays, *Beauty, Health and Permanence*, pp. 260–1.
107 On the garden city and urban reform movements, see Cherry, *Cities and Plans*, ch. 3.
108 Aldous, *Battle for the Environment*; Richardson and Kimber (eds), *Campaigning for the Environment*.
109 For the British experience, see Evans, *History of Nature Conservation*.
110 See the account in Newby, *Green and Pleasant Land*.
111 For an account of the American experience, see Hays, *Beauty, Health and Permanence*, chs 4 and 5.
112 On the transformation of the British countryside under multiple pressures, see Rose and Pye-Smith, *Crisis and Conservation*.
113 Witness the growth in the membership and public profile of these movements, see Porrit and Winner, *The Coming of the Greens*.
114 Dasmann, 'Towards a Biosphere Consciousness'.
115 Nancy Fraser has pointed to the model's incompatibility with Western domestic life. She argues that the private sphere cannot be so sharply separated from economic and political systems. For the family and gender relations are not only involved in social reproduction, and marked by the presence of communicative rationality, but are equally implicated in material reproduction, and are structured by domination and strategic action. Conversely, systems are not pure, formally organized, norm-free spheres, but rely on networks of solidarity and shared cultural identity. Fraser, *Unruly Practices*.
116 See, for example, Willis, *Learning to Labour*.
117 Dahrendorf, 'The Erosion of Citizenship'.
118 For international comparisons on this issue, see Goodin and Le Grand, *Not Only the Poor*.
119 Le Grand, *The Strategy of Equality*, pp. 60–1.
120 Ibid., pp. 90–4, 107–20.
121 Berger, 'Worldview of the New Class'.
122 J. Habermas, 'The New Obscurity: the Crisis of the Welfare State and the Exhaustion of Utopian Energies', in Habermas, *The New Conservatism*.
123 Bell, 'The New Class'.
124 Inglehart's work in this area was first set down in his 'The Silent Revolution in Europe: Inter-generational Change in Post-industrial Societies', and given its seminal expression in *The Silent Revolution: Changing Values and Political Styles among Western Publics*.
125 Inglehart, *The Silent Revolution*, pp. 116–48. Inglehart is highly reliant on

the psychological work of Abraham Maslow, see Maslow, *Toward a Psychology of Being* and *Motivation and Personality*.

126 Inglehart, *The Silent Revolution*, pp. 96–8.

127 Ibid., pp. 263–7.

128 Ibid., pp. 72–8.

129 See Inglehart, 'Post-materialism in an Environment of Insecurity'; Muller-Rommel, 'Social Movements and the Greens'.

130 See the argument on this point in Paehlke, *Environmentalism*, ch. 1.

131 Cotgrove and Duff, 'Environmentalism, Middle Class Radicalism and Politics' and 'Environmentalism, Values and Social Change'.

132 'The goal of environmentalists is to realise a society in which alternative values and institutions can take root. Post-material values are the values which they want to see made real in some future utopia. Thus it is . . . not their conditions of social existence . . . but what they would like to see as their conditions of existence.' Cotgrove and Duff, 'Environmentalism, Values and Social Change', p. 99.

133 Ibid., p. 102.

134 Ibid., p. 106. See also Flacks, 'Revolt of the Young Intelligentsia'.

Chapter 5 The Sociology of Risk

1 Beck, *Risikogesellschaft: Auf dem Weg in eine andere Moderne* (1986); *Risk Society: Towards a New Modernity* (1991), henceforth *RS*.

2 From 1986 to 1991 the German edition alone sold over 60,000 copies, while reviews, debates and borrowings from the book found themselves the currency of the German media and political debate.

3 Beck, *Ecological Politics in an Age of Risk* (1995), henceforth *EPAR*; Beck, Giddens and Lash, *Reflexive Modernization: Politics, Tradition and Aesthetics in the Modern Social Order* (1994); Beck and Beck-Gernsheim, *The Normal Chaos of Love* (1995).

4 *EPAR*, p. 69.

5 *EPAR*, p. 65.

6 *EPAR*, p. 66.

7 *EPAR*, p. 125.

8 For example, Habermas's work discussed in chapter 4 has obvious parallels in its engagement with modernization and rationalization. Luhmann has written specifically on the subjects of risk and its psychological antidotes, love and trust. Luhmann, *Trust and Power*. Beck's work also relies on the kinds of empirical and theoretical investigations of delegitimized Western states and segmented labour markets that characterize the work of Offe, see *Disorganized Capitalism*.

9 See, for example, O'Riordan, 'Cognitive and Political Dimension of Risk Analysis'; Short, 'The Social Fabric of Risk'; Fischhoff et al., *Acceptable Risk*.

10 Extensive use of Beck's work has been made by Giddens, see esp. *The Consequences of Modernity* and *Beyond Left and Right*. See also Lash and Urry, *Economies of Signs and Space*.

11 See the discussions in *RS*, pp. 27–8, 31–2.

12 See my discussion of this point in chapter 4, p.140.

13 *RS*, pp. 19–21.
14 See my distinction between environmental impacts and social costs, and the transition from one to the other, in chapter 4 above.
15 *RS*, pp. 26–34.
16 *RS*, p. 184.
17 *RS*, p. 90. Compare with my discussion of Giddens's model of environmental politics in *COM*, see chapter 2.
18 *RS*, p. 140.
19 *RS*, pp. 139–49.
20 The arguments of *Risk Society* on these issues have been greatly extended and further explored in Beck and Beck-Gernsheim, *The Normal Chaos of Love*.
21 *RS*, p. 103.
22 *RS*, p. 104.
23 *RS*, p. 105.
24 *EPAR*, p. 61.
25 Ewald, *L'État de providence*.
26 *EPAR*, p. 107.
27 *EPAR*, p. 85.
28 *EPAR*, p. 80.
29 *EPAR*, pp. 152–7.
30 *RS*, pp. 223–35.
31 Beck pursues a similar set of arguments under the heading of subpolitics, see Beck, Giddens and Lash, *Reflexive Modernisation*, pp. 13–23.
32 *RS*, p. 235.
33 *EPAR*, p. 168.
34 *EPAR*, p. 167.
35 *EPAR*, pp. 180–3.
36 *EPAR*, pp. 181–2.
37 See *COM*, ch. 5.
38 See Beck and Beck-Gernsheim, *The Normal Chaos of Love*.
39 *COM*, pp. 134–7.
40 Cf. my explanation of this problem in chapter 4, pp. 132–3, and a similar set of criticisms of Habermas's model of modernity.
41 Mohoi and Bryant (eds), *Race and the Incidence of Environmental Hazards: a Time for Discourse*.
42 Similarly, the transformation of the relationship between the genders and the possibilities of technological intervention in the reproduction process previously cosseted within the private sphere of the family have continually spilt over into the public domain. The last decade has seen an explosion of debate, legislation and state intervention regarding the regulation of reproductive technologies, equal opportunities and affirmative action in the work-place, the status of women in social security, taxation, pension and property law, shifts in divorce law, children's law and legal parenting obligations. However, in the case of familial and gender politics it would be wrong to account for this politicization in terms of changes in risk exposure and perception alone. Alongside the new situations presented by new reproductive technologies and changing family structures, there has been a decisive role for the emerging arguments and organizations of contemporary feminism, which has presented its case as much in

terms of older conceptions of equality as protection from new risks.

43 On different types of welfare state and the differing use of insurance models, see Esping-Andersen, *Three Worlds of Welfare Capitalism*.

44 For an excellent study contrasting different modes and forms of regulation, see Vogel, *National Styles of Regulation*.

45 *EPAR*, pp. 136–7.

46 For international comparative studies which illuminate the diversity of policy models and regulatory strategies, see Downing and Hanf (eds), *International Comparisons*; Haigh and Irwin (eds), *Integrated Pollution Control*.

47 For a good discussion of both these aspects of the legitimacy problem, see D. Held, 'Legitimation Problems and Crisis Tendencies', in Held, *Political Theory and the Modern State*.

Conclusion: Social Theory, Socialism and the Environment

1 Habermas's most important recent statement on these issues is 'What Does Socialism Mean Today?', henceforth WDSMT. See also the interview 'Conservative Politics, Work, Socialism and Utopia Today', in Dews (ed.), *Autonomy and Solidarity*, and the essay 'The New Obscurity: the Crisis of the Welfare State and the Exhaustion of Utopian Energies', in Habermas, *The New Conservatism*. Giddens's most relevant earlier writings can be found in *CCHM*, pp. 248–52, *COM*, pp. 154–73, *MSI*, ch. 7. In *Beyond Left and Right* he has developed his critique of socialism in far greater detail and in profoundly changed historical circumstances. For Gorz's arguments see chapter 3 above and the essays in his recent *Capitalism, Socialism, Ecology*.

2 WDSMT, p. 36.

3 WDSMT, p. 41, see my argument in chapter 3.

4 WDSMT, p. 36.

5 WDSMT, pp. 42–3.

6 WDSMT, p. 36

7 While Habermas has argued that the demand for remoralization has its origins in the intuitive moral order of a rationalized lifeworld, Giddens has located its origins in the reflexive project of self that the institutions of modernity create, see *MSI*, pp. 214–23. Exploring and clarifying the differences between these perspectives would greatly illuminate the conditions under which those 'latent' moral positions could be converted into effective public argument.

8 See Gorz's remarks on this subject which inform his rejection of classical socialist goals and strategy, Gorz, 'The New Agenda', pp. 292–4.

9 WDSMT, p. 43.

10 See chapter 3, final section.

11 WDSMT, p. 44.

12 *BLR*, pp. 8–11.

13 *BLR*, pp. 80–7, 92–103.

14 *BLR*, pp. 69–73, 135–50.

15 *BLR*, pp. 223–7.

16 *BLR*, pp. 12–20.

17   *CSE*, p. 39.
18   *CSE*, p. 41.
19   *CSE*, p. 21.
20   Giddens has been most explicit about this, see *BLR*, pp. 66–7. Both Gorz
     and Habermas have explicitly argued that capitalist economic rationality,
     on its own terms, is the most rational and efficient economic system avail-
     able.
21   See chapter 3, final section.
22   *COM*, pp. 163–70.
23   See my discussion in chapter 3, final section.
24   See Held, *Models of Democracy*; Held (ed.), *Prospects for Democracy*; Keane,
     Democracy and Civil Society.
25   *COM*, pp. 167–8.
26   *CCHM*, p. 249.

Bibliography

Abercrombie, P., 'Writings on Smoke', in H. Bradby (ed.), *Dirty Words: Writings on the History and Culture of Pollution*, Earthscan, London, 1990.

Adorno, T. W. and Horkheimer, M., *Dialectic of Enlightenment*, trans. J. Cummings, Herder and Herder, New York, 1972.

Aglietta, M., *A Theory of Capitalist Regulation: the US Experience*, trans. D. Fernbach, New Left Books, London, 1979.

Aldous, T., *Battle for the Environment*, Fontana, London, 1972.

Allen, J., 'Post-industrialism and Post-Fordism', in S. Hall, D. Held and T. McGrew (eds), *Modernity and its Futures*, Polity, Cambridge, 1992.

Anderson, P., *In the Tracks of Historical Materialism*, Verso, London, 1986.

Armstrong, P., Glyn, A. and Harrison, J., *Capitalism since World War II: the Making and Breakup of the Great Boom*, Fontana, London, 1984.

Aron, R., *Eighteen Lectures on Industrial Society*, Weidenfeld and Nicolson, London, 1967.

Aya, R. and Miller, N. (eds), *The New American Revolution*, Macmillan, London 1971.

Badham, R., 'The Sociology of Industrial and Post-industrial Societies', *Current Sociology* 32 (1984).

Bahro, R., *Socialism and Survival*, Heretic Books, London, 1982.

—— *From Red to Green: Interviews with New Left Review*, trans. G. Fagan and R. Hurts, Verso, London, 1984.

Baker, S., 'The Evolution of the Irish Ecology Movement', *Green Politics* 1 (1990).

Barde, J. -P. and Pearce, D. (eds), *Valuing the Environment*, Earthscan, London, 1991.

Barry, B., *Liberty and Justice: Essays in Political Theory 2*, Oxford University Press, Oxford, 1991.

Baxter, H., 'System and Lifeworld in Habermas's Theory of Communicative Action', *Theory and Society* 16 (1987).

Beck, U., *Risk Society: Towards a New Modernity*, trans. M. Ritter, Sage, London, 1991; originally *Risikogesellschaft: Auf dem Weg in eine andere Moderne*, Suhrkamp, Frankfurt, 1986.

—— *Ecological Politics in an Age of Risk*, trans. Amos Oz, Polity, Cambridge, 1995.

Beck, U. and Beck-Gernsheim, E., *The Normal Chaos of Love*, trans. Mark Ritter and Jane Wiebel, Polity, Cambridge, 1995.

Beck, U., Giddens, A. and Lash, S., *Reflexive Modernisation: Politics, Tradition and Aesthetics in the Modern Social Order*, Polity, Cambridge, 1994.

Bell, D., *The Coming of Post-Industrial Society*, Penguin, London, 1973.

—— 'The New Class: a Muddled Concept', in B. Bruce-Briggs (ed.), *The New Class?* Transaction Books, New Brunswick, 1979.

Benton, T., 'Marxism and Natural Limits: an Ecological Critique and Reconstruction', *New Left Review* 178 (1989).

—— 'Biology and Social Theory in the Environment Debate', in M. Redclift and T. Benton (eds), *Social Theory and the Global Environment*, Routledge, London, 1994.

Berger, P. L., 'The Worldview of the New Class: Secularity and its Discontents', in B. Bruce-Briggs (ed.), *The New Class?* Transaction Books, New Brunswick, 1979.

Bernstein, R. (ed.), *Habermas and Modernity*, Polity, Cambridge, 1985.

Bijker, W., Hughes, T. and Pinch, T., *The Social Construction of Technological Systems*, Harvard University Press, Cambridge, 1987.

Blackburn, R. (ed.), *After the Fall: the Failure of Communism and the Future of Socialism*, Verso, London, 1991.

Bookchin, M., Review of A. Gorz, *Ecology as Politics, Telos* 46 (Winter 1980–1).

Boserup, E., *The Conditions of Agricultural Growth: the Economics of Agrarian Change under Population Pressure*, Aldine, Chicago, 1965.

Bradby, H. (ed.), *Dirty Words: Writings on the History and Culture of Pollution*, Earthscan, London, 1990.

Brand, K. -W., 'Cyclical Aspects of New Social Movements', in R. Dalton and M. Keuchler (eds), *Challenging the Political Order*, Polity, Cambridge, 1990.

Brittan, S., *The Economic Consequences of Democracy*, Temple Smith, London, 1977.

Brock, P., *Twentieth Century Pacifism*, Van Nostrand, New York, 1970.

Brown, L. R. et al., *State of the World 1990*, WWI, Washington, 1990.

Bruce-Briggs, B. (ed.), *The New Class?* Transaction Books, New Brunswick, 1979.

Bryant, C. G. A. and Jary, D. (eds), *Giddens' Theory of Structuration: a Critical Appreciation*, Routledge, London, 1991.

Busch, B. C., *The War Against the Seals: a History of the North American Seal Fishery*, McGill–Queen's University Press, Montreal, 1985.

Caldwell, L. K., *Between Two Worlds: Science, the Environmental Movement and Policy Choice*, Cambridge University Press, Cambridge, 1990.

Campbell, C., *The Romantic Ethic and the Spirit of Modern Consumerism*, Blackwell, Oxford, 1987.

Carrol, J. (ed.), *International Environmental Diplomacy: the Management and Resolution of Transfrontier Environmental Problems*, Cambridge University Press, Cambridge, 1988.

Castells, M., *The Urban Question*, trans. A. Sheridan, Edward Arnold, London, 1977.

—— *The City and the Grassroots*, Edward Arnold, London, 1983.

Castles, F. (ed.), *The Comparative History of Public Policy*, Polity, Cambridge, 1989.

Cherry, G., *Cities and Plans: the Shaping of Urban Britain in the Nineteenth and Twentieth Century*, Edward Arnold, London, 1988.

Cipolla, C. M., *The Economic History of World Population*, Harvester, Brighton, 1978.

—— (ed.), *The Fontana Economic History of Europe*, vol. 3, Fontana, London, 1973.

Clarke, R., *Water: the International Crisis*, Earthscan, London, 1991.

Cockburn, A. and Hecht, S., *Fate of the Forest*, Verso, London, 1989.

Cohen, I., *Structuration Theory*, Macmillan, London, 1989.

Cohen, J., 'Strategy or Identity: New Theoretical Paradigms and Contemporary Social Movements', *Social Research* 52 (1985).

Colten, C., 'Industrial Wastes in South East Chicago: Production and Disposal 1870–1970', *Environmental Review* (Summer 1986).

Cotgrove, S., *Catastrophe or Cornucopia*, Wiley, Chichester, 1982.

Cotgrove, S. and Duff, A., 'Environmentalism, Middle Class Radicalism and Politics', *Sociological Review* 28 (1980).

—— 'Environmentalism, Values and Social Change', *British Journal of Sociology* 32 (1981).

Coward, R., *The Whole Truth*, Faber, London, 1989.

Craib, I., *Anthony Giddens*, Routledge, London, 1992.

Cranston, R., *Law, Government and Public Policy*, Oxford University Press, Oxford, 1987.

Cronon, W., *Changes in the Land: Indians, Colonists and the Ecology of New England*, Hill and Wang, New York, 1983.

—— *Nature's Metropolis: Chicago and the Great West*, Norton, New York, 1991.

Crosby, A. J., *The Columbian Exchange: Biological and Cultural Consequences of 1492*, Greenwood, Westport, 1972.

Dahrendorf, R., 'The Erosion of Citizenship', *New Statesman*, 12 June 1987.

Dalton, R. and Kuechler, M. (eds), *Challenging the Political Order: New Social and Political Movements in Western Democracies*, Polity, Cambridge, 1990.

Dalton, R., Kuechler, M. and Burklin, W., 'The Challenge of New Social Movements', in R. Dalton and M. Kuechler (eds), *Challenging the Political Order*, Polity, Cambridge, 1990.

Dasmann, R., 'Towards a Biosphere Consciousness', in D. Worster (ed.), *The Ends of the Earth*, Cambridge University Press, Cambridge, 1988.

Deane, P. and Cole, W. A., *British Economic Growth, 1688–1959: Trends and Structure*, Cambridge University Press, Cambridge, 1962.

Dejene, A., *Environment, Famine and Politics in Ethiopia*, Eurospan, London, 1991.

Desales Affigne, A., 'Environmental Crisis, Green Party Power: Chernobyl and the Swedish Greens', *Green Politics* 1 (1990).

Department of the Environment, *Possible Impacts of Climatic Change on the Natural Environment in the United Kingdom*, HMSO, London, 1988.

de Vries, J., 'The Decline and Rise of the Dutch Economy 1675–1900', *Research in Economic History*, suppl. 3 (1984).

Dews, P., *Logics of Disintegration*, Verso, London, 1987.

—— (ed.), *Autonomy and Solidarity: Interviews with Jürgen Habermas*, Verso, London, 1986.

de Zeeuw, J. W., 'Peat and the Dutch Golden Age: the Historical Meaning of Energy Attainability', *A. A. G. Bijdragen* 21 (1978).

Dicken, P., *Global Shift: the Internationalisation of Economic Activity*, Paul Chapman, London, 1992.

Dickens, P., *Society and Nature: Towards a Green Social Theory*, Harvester Wheatsheaf, Hemel Hempstead, 1992.

Djilas, M., *The New Class: an Analysis of the Communist System*, Thames and Hudson, London, 1957.

Dobson, A., *Green Politics*, Unwin Hyman, London, 1990.

Douglas, M., *Purity and Danger: an Analysis of Concepts of Pollution and Taboo*, Routledge, London, 1966.

Downing, P. and Hanf, K. (eds), *International Comparisons in Implementing Pollution Laws*, Kluwer-Nijhoff, The Hague, 1983.

Dunlap, R. and van Liere, K., 'The New Environmental Paradigm', *Journal of Environmental Education* 9 (1978).

Dunlap, T., *DDT: Scientists, Citizens and Public Policy*, Princeton University Press, Princeton, 1981.

Durkheim, E., *The Division of Labour in Society*, trans. W. D. Halls, Macmillan, London, 1984.

The Ecologist, 'Blueprint for Survival', *The Ecologist* 2 (1972).

Ekins, P., *A New World Order: Grassroots Movements for Global Change*, Routledge, London, 1991.

—— (ed.), *The Living Economy: a New Economy in the Making*, Routledge, London, 1986.

El-Hinnawi, E. E. (ed.), *Nuclear Energy and the Environment*, Oxford University Press, Oxford, 1982.

Engels, F., *The Condition of the Working Class in England*, Oxford University Press, Oxford, 1968.

Erskine, R. and Webber, R., 'Accidents, Risks and Consequences', in L. Mackay and M. Thompson (eds), *Something in the Wind*, Pluto, London, 1988.

Esping-Andersen, G., *Three Worlds of Welfare Capitalism*, Polity, Cambridge, 1990.

Evans, D., *A History of Nature Conservation in Britain*, Routledge, London, 1991.

Evans, R. J., *Death in Hamburg: Society and Politics in the Cholera Years 1830–1910*, Oxford University Press, Oxford, 1987.

Ewald, F., *L'État de providence*, Grasset, Paris, 1986.

Falkingham, J., 'Britain's Ageing Population: the Engine behind Increasing Dependency?', Welfare State Programme Discussion Paper, London School of Economics, London, 1987.

Fischhoff, B. et al., *Acceptable Risk*, Cambridge University Press, Cambridge, 1981.

Fisher, R. H., *The Russian Fur Trade, 1550–1700*, University of California Press, Berkeley, 1963.

Flacks, R., 'The Revolt of the Young Intelligentsia: Revolutionary Class-Consciousness in Post-Scarcity America', in R. Aya and N. Miller (eds), *The New American Revolution*, Macmillan, London, 1971.

Foucault, M., *Madness and Civilisation*, trans. R. Howard, Pantheon, New York, 1965.

—— *Discipline and Punish*, trans. A. Sheridan, Pantheon, New York, 1977.

—— *The History of Sexuality*, vol. 1, trans. R. Hurley, Penguin, Harmondsworth, 1981.

Fox, W., *Towards a Transpersonal Ecology*, Shambhala, London, 1990.

Frankel, B., *The Post-industrial Utopians*, Polity, Cambridge, 1987.

Fraser, N., *Unruly Practices: Power, Discourse and Gender in Contemporary Social*

Theory, Polity, Cambridge, 1989.

Friedan, J., 'Invested Interests: the Politics of National Economic Policies in a World of Global Finance', *International Organisation* 45.4 (1991).

Fröbel, F., Heinrichs J. and Kreye, O., *The New International Division of Labour*, trans. P. Burgess, Cambridge University Press, Cambridge, 1981.

Geuss, R., *The Idea of a Critical Theory*, Cambridge University Press, Cambridge, 1981.

Giddens, A., *Capitalism and Modern Social Theory*, Cambridge University Press, Cambridge, 1971.

—— *Politics and Sociology in the Thought of Max Weber*, Macmillan, London, 1972.

—— *New Rules of Sociological Method: a Positive Critique of Interpretative Sociologies*, Hutchinson, London, 1976.

—— *Studies in Social and Political Theory*, Hutchinson, London, 1977.

—— *Central Problems in Social Theory: Action, Structure and Contradiction in Social Analysis*, Macmillan, London, 1979.

—— *The Class Structure of the Advanced Societies*, 2nd edn, Hutchinson, London, 1981.

—— *A Contemporary Critique of Historical Materialism*, vol. 1: *Power, Property and the State*, Macmillan, London, 1981.

—— *Profiles and Critiques in Social Theory*, Macmillan, London, 1982.

—— *The Constitution of Society: Outline of a Theory of Structuration*, Polity, Cambridge, 1984.

—— *The Nation-State and Violence*, vol. 2 of *A Contemporary Critique of Historical Materialism*, Polity, Cambridge, 1985.

—— *Social Theory and Modern Sociology*, Polity, Cambridge, 1987.

—— *The Consequences of Modernity*, Polity, Cambridge, 1990.

—— *Modernity and Self-Identity: Self and Society in the Late Modern Age*, Polity, Cambridge, 1991.

—— *The Transformation of Intimacy*, Polity, Cambridge, 1993.

—— *Beyond Left and Right*, Polity, Cambridge, 1994.

Gill, C., *Work, Unemployment and the New Technology*, Polity, Cambridge, 1985.

Gilpin, R., *The Political Economy of International Relations*, Princeton University Press, Princeton, 1987.

Goldman, M., *The Spoils of Progress*, MIT Press, Cambridge, 1972.

Goodin, R. E. and Le Grand, J., *Not Only the Poor: the Middle Classes and the Welfare State*, Allen and Unwin, London, 1987.

Goody, J., *Technology, Tradition and the State in Africa*, Hutchinson, London, 1971.

Gorz, A., *Strategy for Labour: a Radical Proposal*, trans. T. Martin and V. Oritz, Beacon Press, Boston, 1964.

—— *Ecology as Politics*, trans. J. Cloud and P. Vigderman, Pluto, London, 1980.

—— *Farewell to the Working Class: an Essay on Post-industrial Socialism*, trans. M. Sonenscher, Pluto, London, 1981.

—— *Paths to Paradise: On the Liberation from Work*, trans. M. Imrie, Pluto, London, 1985.

—— *Critique of Economic Reason*, trans. G. Handside and C. Turner, Verso, London, 1989.

—— 'The New Agenda', in R. Blackburn (ed.), *After the Fall*, Verso, London, 1991.

—— *Capitalism, Socialism, Ecology*, trans. C. Turner, Verso, London, 1994.

—— (ed.), *The Division of Labour: the Labour Process and Class Struggle in Modern Capitalism*, Harvester, Brighton, 1976.

Goudie, A., *The Human Impact: Man's Role in Environmental Change*, Oxford University Press, Oxford, 1981.

Gough, I., *The Political Economy of the Welfare State*, Macmillan, London, 1979.

Gregory, D., 'Presences and Absences: Time-Space Relations and Structuration Theory', in D. Held and J. B. Thompson (eds), *The Social Theory of Modern Societies*, Cambridge University Press, Cambridge, 1989.

Grinder, R. D., 'The Battle for Clean Air: the Smoke Problem in Post–Civil War America', in M. Melosi (ed.), *Pollution and Reform*, University of Texas Press, Austin, 1985.

Grundmann, R., 'The Ecological Challenge to Marxism', *New Left Review* 188 (1991).

Habermas, J., *Toward a Rational Society*, trans. J. Shapiro, Beacon Press, Boston, 1970; Polity, Cambridge, 1986.

—— *Knowledge and Human Interests*, trans. J. Shapiro, Beacon Press, Boston, 1972; Polity, Cambridge, 1986.

—— *Legitimation Crisis*, trans. T. McCarthy, HEB, London, 1973; Polity, Cambridge, 1988.

—— *Theory and Practice*, trans. J. Viertel, Heinemann, London, 1974; Polity, Cambridge, 1986.

—— *Communication and the Evolution of Society*, trans. T. McCarthy, HEB, London, 1976; Polity, Cambridge, 1991.

—— 'Theory and Evolution', *Telos* 39 (1979).

—— *The Theory of Communicative Action, Volume 1: Reason and the Rationalization of Society*, trans. T. McCarthy, Polity, Cambridge, 1987.

—— *The Theory of Communicative Action, Volume 2: Lifeword and System: A Critique of Functionalist Reason*, trans. T. McCarthy, Polity, Cambridge, 1987.

—— *The New Conservatism: Cultural Criticism and the Historians' Debate*, trans. S. Weber Nicholsen and R. Wolin, Polity, Cambridge, 1989.

—— *The Structural Transformation of the Public Sphere*, trans. T. Berger and F. Lawrence, Polity, Cambridge, 1989.

—— *The Philosophical Discourse of Modernity: Twelve Lectures*, trans. F. Lawrence, Polity, Cambridge, 1990.

—— 'What Does Socialism Mean Today?', in R. Blackburn (ed.), *After the Fall*, Verso, London, 1991.

Haigh, N., *EEC Environmental Policy and Britain*, Longman, London, 1990.

Haigh, N. and Irwin, F. (eds), *Integrated Pollution Control in Europe and North America*, Conservation Foundation, Washington D. C., 1990.

Hall, P. 'The Evolution of Economic Policy under Mitterrand', in G. Ross, S. Hoffman and S. Malzacher (eds), *The Mitterrand Experiment*, Polity, Cambridge, 1987.

Hall, S., Held, D. and McGrew. T. (eds), *Modernity and its Futures*, Polity, Cambridge, 1992.

Hall, T., *Nuclear Politics*, Penguin, Harmondsworth, 1986.

Hamer, M., *Wheels within Wheels: a Study of the Road Lobby*, Routledge, London, 1987.

Hardy, D., *Alternative Communities in Nineteenth Century England*, Longman, London, 1979.

Hays, S., *Beauty, Health and Permanence: Environmental Politics in the United States, 1955–1985*, Cambridge University Press, Cambridge, 1987.

Headrick, D., *The Tentacles of Progress: Technology Transfer in the Age of Imperialism, 1850–1940*, Oxford University Press, Oxford, 1988.

Held, D., *Models of Democracy*, Polity, Cambridge, 1987.

—— *Political Theory and the Modern State*, Polity, Cambridge, 1989.

—— 'Democracy, the Nation-State and the Global System', in D. Held (ed.), *Political Theory Today*, Polity, Cambridge, 1991.

—— *Prospects for Democracy: North, South, East, West*, Polity, Cambridge, 1994.

Held, D. and Thompson, J. B. (eds), *The Social Theory of Modern Societies: Anthony Giddens and his Critics*, Cambridge University Press, Cambridge, 1989.

Hill, M. and Ham, C., *The Policy Process in the Modern Capitalist State*, Wheatsheaf, Brighton, 1985.

Hillman, M., *Walking is Transport*, PSI, London, 1979.

Hinton, J., *Protests and Visions*, Hutchinson, London, 1989.

Hirsch, F., *Social Limits to Growth*, Routledge, London, 1976.

Hobsbawm, E. (ed.), *The Forward March of Labour Halted?* New Left Books, London, 1981.

Honneth, A. and Joas, H. (eds), *Communicative Action: Essays on Jürgen Habermas's 'The Theory of Communicative Action'*, trans. J. Gaines and D. L. Jones, Polity, Cambridge, 1991.

Hurrel, A. and Kingsbury, B. (eds), *The International Politics of the Environment*, Oxford University Press, Oxford, 1992.

Illich, I., *Deschooling Society*, Harper and Row, New York, 1971.

—— *Tools for Conviviality*, Harper and Row, New York, 1973.

Ince, M., 'Secrecy, Policy-Making and the Nuclear State', in L. Mackay and M. Thompson (eds), *Something in the Wind*, Pluto, London, 1988.

Inglehart, R., 'The Silent Revolution in Europe: Inter-generational Change in Post-industrial Societies', *American Political Science Review* 65 (1971).

—— *The Silent Revolution: Changing Values and Political Styles among Western Publics*, Princeton University Press, Princeton, 1977.

—— 'Post-materialism in an Environment of Insecurity', *American Political Science Review* 75 (1981).

Ingram, D., *Habermas and the Dialectic of Reason*, Yale University Press, New Haven, 1987.

Jackson Lears, T., *No Place of Grace: Antimodernism and the Transformation of American Culture 1880–1920*, Pantheon, New York, 1981.

Jacobs, M., *The Green Economy*, Pluto, London, 1991.

Kaase, M., 'Social Movements and Political Innovation', in R. Dalton and M. Kuechler (eds), *Challenging the Political Order*, Polity, Cambridge, 1990.

Keane, J., *Democracy and Civil Society*, Verso, London, 1988.

Kitschelt, H., 'Political Opportunity Structures and Political Protest: Anti-Nuclear Movements in Four Democracies', *British Journal of Political Science* 14.1 (1986).

—— *The Logic of Party Formation: Structure and Strategy of Belgian and West German Ecology Parties*, Cornell University Press, Ithaca, 1989.

Klandemans, B. (ed.), *Organising for Change: Social Movement Organisation across Cultures*, JAI Press, Greenwich, 1989.

Kumar, K., *Prophecy and Progress*, Penguin, London, 1978.

Landes, D. S., *The Unbound Prometheus: Technological Change and Industrial Development in Western Europe from 1750 to the Present*, Cambridge University Press, Cambridge, 1969.

Lash, S. and Urry, J., *The End of Organised Capitalism*, Polity, Cambridge, 1988.

—— *Economies of Signs and Space*, Sage, London, 1993.

Leadbetter, C. and Lloyd, J., *In Search of Work*, Penguin, London, 1986.

Le Grand, J., *The Strategy of Equality*, Allen and Unwin, London, 1982.

Le Grand, J. and Robinson, R., *The Economics of Social Problems*, Macmillan, London, 1976.

Lewin, L., *Self-Interest and Public Interest in Western Politics*, Oxford University Press, Oxford, 1991.

Lilley, S., 'Technological Progress and the Industrial Revolution 1700–1914', in C. M. Cipolla (ed.), *The Fontana Economic History of Europe*, vol. 3, Fontana, London, 1973.

Lipietz, A., *Mirages and Miracles: the Crises of Global Fordism*, trans. D. Macey, Verso, London, 1985.

Livvi-Bacci, M., *Population and Nutrition: an Essay on European Demographic History*, Cambridge University Press, Cambridge, 1990.

Lowe, P. and Goyder, J., *Environmental Groups in Politics*, Allen and Unwin, London, 1983.

Lowe, P. and Morrison, D., 'Bad News or Good News: Environmental Politics and the Mass Media', *Sociological Review* 32 (1984).

Lowe, P. and Rudig, W., 'The Withered Greening of British Politics', *Political Studies* 34 (1986).

Lowe, P. et al., *Countryside Conflicts*, Temple Smith, London, 1986.

Luhmann, N., *Trust and Power*, trans. H. Davies, J. Raffan and K. Rooney, Wiley, Chichester, 1979.

—— *Ecological Communication*, trans. J. Bernadez Jr, Polity, Cambridge, 1988.

McCarthy, T., *The Critical Theory of Jürgen Habermas*, Polity, Cambridge, 1984.

McCormick, J., *British Politics and the Environment*, Earthscan, London, 1991.

Mackay, L. and Thompson, M. (eds), *Something in the Wind: Politics after Chernobyl*, Pluto, London, 1988.

McKendrick, N., Brewer, J. and Plumb, J. H., *The Birth of a Consumer Society: the Commercialisation of Eighteenth Century England*, Hutchinson, London, 1982.

McNeil, W. H., *The Human Condition: an Ecological Perspective*, Princeton University Press, Princeton, 1980.

Mahar, D., *Government Policies and Deforestation in Brazil's Amazon Region*, World Bank, Washington, 1990.

Malthus, T., *An Essay on the Principle of Population*, 7th edn, Dent, London, 1872.

Mann, M., *The Sources of Social Power*, vol. 1, Cambridge University Press, Cambridge, 1986.

Martin, J., *The Treasure of the Land of Darkness: the Fur Trade and its Significance in Medieval Russia*, Cambridge University Press, Cambridge, 1986.

Maslow, A., *Toward a Psychology of Being*, Van Nostrand, Englewood-Cliffs, 1962.

—— *Motivation and Personality*, 2nd edn, Harper and Row, New York, 1970.

Meadows, D. et al., *Limits to Growth*, Earth Island, London, 1972.

Melucci, A., 'The Symbolic Challenge of Social Movements', *Social Research* 52 (1985).

—— *Nomads of the Present*, ed. and trans. J. Keane and P. Mier, Hutchinson, London, 1989.

Melosi, M., *Garbage in the Cities: Refuse, Reform and the Environment*, Texas University Press, Austin, 1981.

—— (ed.), *Pollution and Reform in American Cities, 1870–1930*, University of Texas Press, Austin, 1985.

Micklin, P., 'The Falling Level of the Caspian Sea', in I. Volgyes (ed.), *Environmental Deterioration in the Soviet Union and Eastern Europe*, Praeger, New York, 1974.

Miliband, R., *The State in Capitalist Society: an Analysis of the Western System of Power*, Quartet, London, 1969.

Mill, J. S., *Principles of Political Economy with Some of their Applications to Social Philosophy*, ed. D. Winch, Penguin, Harmondsworth, 1970.

Minchinton, W., 'Patterns of Demand', in C. M. Cipolla (ed.), *The Fontana Economic History of Europe*, vol. 3, Fontana, London, 1973.

Mishan, E. J., *The Costs of Economic Growth*, Staples, London, 1967.

Mitchell, R., 'National Environment Lobbies and the Apparent Illogic of Collective Action', in C. Russel (ed.), *Collective Decision Making*, Johns Hopkins University Press, Baltimore, 1979.

Mohoi, P. and Bryant, B. (eds), *Race and the Incidence of Environmental Hazards: a Time for Discourse*, Westview, Boulder, Colo., 1992.

Muller, E. and Opp, K. -D., 'Rational Choice and Rebellious Collective Action', *American Political Science Review* 80 (1986).

Muller-Rommel, F., 'Social Movements and the Greens: New Internal Politics in Germany', *European Journal of Political Research* 13 (1985).

Mumford, L., *The City in History: Its Origins, its Transformations, its Prospects*, Harcourt, Brace and World, New York, 1961.

Mundell, R., 'Capital Mobility and Stabilization Policy under Fixed and Flexible Exchange Rates', *Canadian Journal of Economics and Political Science* 29 (Nov. 1963).

Nash, R., *Wilderness and the American Mind*, Yale University Press, New Haven, 1974.

Needham, J., *Science and Civilisation in China*, Cambridge University Press, Cambridge, 1954.

Newby, N., *Green and Pleasant Land: Social Change in Rural England*, Hutchinson, London, 1979.

Nordlinger, E., *On the Autonomy of the Democratic State*, Harvard University Press, Cambridge, 1983.

Noskov, Y. G., 'Environmental Devastation in the USSR during the Second World War', *Environmental Management in the USSR* (1985).

Nove, A., *The Economic History of the USSR*, Allen Lane, London, 1969.

—— *The Economics of a Feasible Socialism*, Allen and Unwin, London, 1983.

Oberschall, A., *Social Conflict and Social Movements*, Prentice Hall, Englewood-Cliffs, 1973.

O'Connor, J., *The Fiscal Crisis of the State*, St Martin's Press, New York, 1973.

Offe, C., *Contradictions of the Welfare State*, ed. J. Keane, Hutchinson, London, 1984.

—— *Disorganized Capitalism*, ed. J. Keane, Polity, Cambridge, 1985.

—— 'Challenging the Boundaries of the Political', *Social Research* 52 (1985).

Offe, C. and Heinze, R., *Beyond Employment: Time, Work and the Informal Economy*, trans. A. Braley, Polity, Cambridge, 1992.

Opschoor, J. and Vos, H., *The Application of Economic Instruments to Environmental Protection in OECD Member Countries*, OECD, Paris, 1988.
O'Riordan, T., *Environmentalism*, Pion, London, 1981.
—— 'The Cognitive and Political Dimension of Risk Analysis', *Journal of Environmental Psychology* 3 (1983).
Paehlke, R. C., *Environmentalism and the Future of Progressive Politics*, Yale University Press, New Haven, 1989.
Panos, *Greenwar: Environment and Conflict*, Panos Institute, London, 1991.
Parsons, H. (ed.), *Marx and Engels on Ecology*, Greenwood, Westport, 1977.
Parsons, T., *The Structure of Social Action*, McGraw Hill, New York, 1937.
Passmore, J., *Man's Responsibility for Nature*, Duckworth, London, 1974.
Pearce, D. et al., *Blueprint for a Green Economy*, Earthscan, London, 1990.
Pearce, D. and Turner, R., *Economics of Natural Resources and the Environment*, Harvester Press, Hemel Hempstead, 1990.
Pearce, F., *Watershed: the Water Crisis in Britain*, Junction Books, London, 1982.
Pepper, D., *The Roots of Modern Environmentalism*, Routledge, London, 1984.
Pigou, A., *Wealth and Welfare*, Macmillan, London, 1912.
Piore, M. and Sabel, C., *The Second Industrial Divide*, Basic Books, New York, 1984.
Plowden, S., *Transport Reform*, PSI, London, 1985.
Plowden, W., *The Motor Car and Politics 1896–1970*, Pelican, London, 1973.
Ponting, C., *A Green History of the World*, Sinclair-Stevenson, London, 1991.
Polanyi, K., *The Great Transformation*, rev. edn, Beacon Press, Boston, 1957.
Porrit, J. and Winner, D., *The Coming of the Greens*, Fontana, London, 1988.
Pryde, P. R., *Environmental Management in the Soviet Union*, Cambridge University Press, Cambridge, 1991.
Przeworski, A., *Capitalism and Social Democracy*, Cambridge University Press, Cambridge, 1985.
Rackham, O., *The History of the Countryside*, Dent, London, 1986.
Rappaport, R., *Pigs for the Ancestors: Ritual Ecology of a New Guinea People*, Yale University Press, New Haven, 1984.
Rasmussen, D., *Reading Habermas*, Blackwell, Oxford, 1990.
Rawls, J., *A Theory of Justice*, Oxford University Press, Oxford, 1973.
Redclift, M. and Benton, T., 'Sociology and the Environment: Discordant Discourse?', in M. Redclift and T. Benton (eds), *Social Theory and the Global Environment*, Routledge, London, 1994.
—— (eds), *Social Theory and the Global Environment*, Routledge, London, 1994.
Ricardo, D., *On the Principles of Political Economy and Taxation*, in *Works and Correspondence of David Ricardo*, vol. 1, ed. P. Saffra, Cambridge University Press, Cambridge, 1951.
Richards, J., 'Global Patterns of Land Conversion', *Environment* 26 (Nov. 1984).
Richardson, J. J. and Kimber, R. (eds), *Campaigning for the Environment*, Routledge, London, 1974.
Riley, J. C., 'The Dutch Economy after 1650: Decline or Growth?' *Journal of European Economic History* 13 (1984).
Robertson, J., *Future Wealth*, Temple Smith, London, 1985.
Robinson, M., *The Greening of British Political Parties*, Manchester University Press, Manchester, 1992.
Roderick, R., *Habermas and the Foundations of Critical Theory*, Macmillan, London, 1985.

Rose, C. and Pye-Smith, C., *Crisis and Conservation: Conflict in the British Countryside*, Penguin, London, 1984.

Ross, G., Hoffman, S. and Malzacher, S. (eds), *The Mitterrand Experiment*, Polity, Cambridge, 1987.

Rostow, W. W., *The Stages of Economic Growth*, Cambridge University Press, Cambridge, 1960.

Rowthorn, R. and Wells, J., *De-industrialisation and Foreign Trade*, Cambridge University Press, Cambridge, 1987.

Russel, C. (ed.), *Collective Decision Making*, Johns Hopkins University Press, Baltimore, 1979.

Ryle, M., *Ecology and Socialism*, Radius, London, 1988.

Sagoff, M., *The Economy of the Earth*, Cambridge University Press, Cambridge, 1988.

Salaman, R., *The History and Social Influence of the Potato*, Cambridge University Press, Cambridge, 1947.

Salamon, J. -J. 'What is Technology? The Issue of its Origins and Definitions', *History of Technology* 1 (1984).

Samuelson, P., 'The Pure Theory of Public Expenditures', *Review of Economics and Statistics* 36 (1954).

Sartre, J. -P., *The Critique of Dialectical Reason I: The Theory of Practical Ensembles*, trans. Alan Sheridan-Smith, NLB, London, 1976.

Saunders, P., *Social Theory and the Urban Question*, 2nd edn, Unwin Hyman, London, 1987.

—— 'Space, Urbanism and the Created Environment', in D. Held and J. B. Thompson (eds), *The Social Theory of Modern Societies*, Cambridge University Press, Cambridge, 1989.

Savas, E. V., *The Organisation and Efficiency of Solid Waste Collection*, D. C Heath, Lexington, 1977.

Schmidt, A., *The Concept of Nature in Marx*, trans. B. Fowkes, New Left Books, London, 1971.

Schorger, A. W., *The Passenger Pigeon: Its Natural History and Extinction*, University of Wisconsin Press, Madison, 1953.

Schumacher, E. F., *Small is Beautiful*, Abacus, London, 1974.

Scott, A., *Ideology and the New Social Movements*, Unwin Hyman, London, 1990.

Short, J. F., 'The Social Fabric of Risk: Towards the Social Transformation of Risk Analysis', *American Sociological Review* 49 (1984).

Silver, T., *A New Face on the Countryside: Indians, Colonists and Slaves in South Atlantic Forests*, Cambridge University Press, Cambridge, 1990.

Singleton, F. (ed.), *Environmental Misuse in the Soviet Union*, Praeger, New York, 1976.

Skocpol, T. (ed.), *Vision and Method in Historical Sociology*, Cambridge University Press, Cambridge, 1984.

Smelser, N., *Theories of Collective Behaviour*, Free Press, New York, 1962.

Solesbury, W., 'The Environmental Agenda', *Public Administration* 54 (1976).

Spencer, H., *On Social Evolution*, University of Chicago Press, Chicago, 1972.

Tarr, J., 'Historical Perspectives on Hazardous Wastes in the United States', *Waste Management and Research* 3 (1985).

TeBrake, W. R., 'Air Pollution and Fuel Crises in Pre-industrial London, 1250–1650', *Technology and Culture* 16 (1975).

TEST, *The Company Car Factor*, TEST, London, 1984.

Therborn, G., *Why Are Some People More Unemployed than Other People?* Verso, London, 1986.

Thomas, K., *Man and the Natural World: Changing Attitudes in England, 1500–1800*, Allen Lane, London, 1983.

Thompson, F. M. L., 'Nineteenth-Century Horse Sense', *Economic History Review*, 2nd ser., 29 (1976).

Thompson, J. B., *Critical Hermeneutics: a Study in the Thought of Paul Ricoeur and Jürgen Habermas*, Cambridge University Press, Cambridge, 1981.

—— *Studies in the Theory of Ideology*, Polity, Cambridge, 1984.

Toffler, A., *Future Shock*, Pan, London, 1970.

—— *The Third Wave*, Pan, London, 1980.

—— *Previews and Premises*, Pan, London, 1984.

Tönnies, F., *Community and Association*, trans. C. Loomis, Harper and Row, New York, 1957.

Tracy, J. D., (ed.), *The Political Economy of Merchant Empires: State Power and World Trade, 1350–1750*, Cambridge University Press, Cambridge, 1991.

Unger, R. W., 'Energy Sources for the Dutch Golden Age: Peat, Wind and Coal', *Research in Economic History* 9 (1984).

Vogel, D., *National Styles of Regulation*, Cornell University Press, Ithaca, 1986.

Volf'son, Z., *The Destruction of Nature in the Soviet Union*, Pluto, London, 1981.

Volgyes, I. (ed.), *Environmental Deterioration in the Soviet Union and Eastern Europe*, Praeger, New York, 1976.

von Tunzelmann, G. N., 'Trends in Real Wages, 1750–1850, Revisited', *Economic History Review*, 2nd ser., 32 (1979).

Walzer, M., *Spheres of Justice: a Defence of Pluralism and Equality*, Blackwell, Oxford, 1983.

Weale, A., *The New Politics of Pollution*, Manchester University Press, Manchester, 1992.

Weber, M., *Ancient Judaism*, Free Press, New York, 1952.

—— *The Religion of India*, Free Press, New York, 1958.

—— *The Religion of China*, Free Press, New York, 1964.

—— *Economy and Society*, vol. 1, University of California Press, Berkeley, 1968.

—— *The Agrarian Sociology of Ancient Civilizations*, New Left Books, London 1976.

Weiner, D. R., *Models of Nature: Conservation, Ecology and Cultural Revolution in Soviet Russia*, Indiana University Press, Bloomington, 1988.

Weston, J., *The FOE Experience*, Oxford Polytechnic, Oxford, 1986.

White, R., 'American Environmental History: the Development of a New Historical Field', *Pacific Historical Review* 54 (1985).

White, S. K., *The Recent Work of Jürgen Habermas: Reason, Justice and Modernity*, Cambridge University Press, Cambridge, 1988.

Williams, R., *The Country and the City*, Chatto and Windus, London, 1973.

—— *Towards 2000*, Chatto and Windus, London, 1983.

Willis, P., *Learning to Labour: How Working Class Kids Get Working Class Jobs*, Saxon House, Farnborough, 1977.

Wilson, F., 'Neo-corporatism and New Social Movements', in R. Dalton and M. Kuechler (eds), *Challenging the Political Order*, Polity, Cambridge, 1990.

Winch, P., *The Idea of a Social Science*, Routledge, London, 1958.

Wirth, L., 'Urbanism as a Way of Life', *American Journal of Sociology* 44 (1938).

Wistrich, E., *The Politics of Transport*, Longman, London, 1983.

Wittfogel, K., *Oriental Despotism: a Comparative Study of Total Power*, Yale University Press, New Haven, 1957.

Wohl, A. S., *The Eternal Slum: Housing and Social Policy in Victorian Britain*, Edward Arnold, London, 1977.

—— *Endangered Lives: Public Health in Victorian Britain*, Dent, London, 1983.

Worster, D., *Nature's Economy: a History of Ecological Ideas*, Cambridge University Press, Cambridge, 1977.

—— *Dust Bowl: the Southern Plains in the 1930s*, Oxford University Press, Oxford, 1979.

—— (ed.), *The Ends of the Earth*, Cambridge University Press, Cambridge, 1988.

Wrigley, E. A. 'The Supply of Raw Materials in the Industrial Revolution', *Economic History Review*, 2nd ser., 15 (1962).

—— 'The Process of Modernisation and the Industrial Revolution in England', *Journal of Interdisciplinary History* 3 (1972).

—— *Continuity, Chance and Change: the Character of the Industrial Revolution in England*, Cambridge University Press, Cambridge, 1988.

—— *Cities, Wealth and People*, Cambridge University Press, Cambridge 1990.

Wrigley, E. A. and Schofield, R., *The Population History of England, 1541–1871: a Reconstruction*, Cambridge University Press, Cambridge, 1981.

Zald, M. and McCarthy, J. (eds), *Social Movements in an Organizational Society: Collected Essays*, Transaction Books, Oxford 1987.

Index